Nancy Silverton's

Pastries from the La Brea Bakery

VILLARD V NEW YORK

Nancy Silverton's

Pastries from the La Brea Bakery

IN COLLABORATION WITH TERI GELBER

PHOTOGRAPHS BY STEVEN ROTHFELD

Library of Congress Cataloging-in-Publication Data

Silverton, Nancy.
Pastries from the La Brea Bakery / Nancy Silverton,
in collaboration with Teri Gelber;
photographs by Steven Rothfeld.
p. cm.
ISBN 0-375-50193-2
1. Desserts.   I. Gelber, Teri.   II. La Brea Bakery.   III. Title.
TX773 .S5214 2000
641.8'65—dc21
99-462216

Villard Books website address: www.villard.com

Printed in the United States of America on acid-free paper

2   4   6   8   9   7   5   3

FIRST EDITION

Book design by Barbara M. Bachman

ACKNOWLEDGMENTS

In a way, the beginnings of this book started in Campanile's tiny, overcrowded up-stairs pastry section, where the pastry staff and I first began experimenting with just a handful of breakfast items—from croissants to sticky buns to cinnamon rolls. Because of that, my thanks go to the following:

To Sumi Chang, who was so instrumental in creating our pastries that to this day we think of her as the mother of Campanile breakfasts—even when she left us to open the wonderful Europane in Pasadena.

To Gerry Moss, who carried out my vision of what our rustic-style pastries could be, came up with the idea that we should sell as many kinds of sweets as we do bread, and then with energy and passion filled the display cases at the La Brea Bakery store.

To Jose Martinez, our star baker, who for the past few years has baked all night to fill the store shelves, spent all day testing recipes, and could always be relied upon when it came to hiring and training the very best. (Jose, we still haven't figured out when you sleep.)

To our talented pastry chef, Kim Sklar, who ran the pastry department with such grace and precision that it allowed me the time and freedom to write this book.

To those who helped us create and perfect: Merilee Atkinson, Jon Davis, Eliza Lee, Michelle Gayer, Marcelino Loya, Annie Miler, Christine Moore, Ramon Ramirez, Margy Rochlin, Joan Ruggles, and Giovanni Sanchez.

To those who've spent so many hardworking years behind the La Brea Bakery store counter, but who never forget to smile: manager Lora Davis, and her team—Sandra Avelar, Dakota Bertrand, Mia Elkin, Theresa Limon. And to George Rose, our vested authority on all things "so very La Brea."

A special thanks to Jack Stumpf, Jessica Buonocore, and Paul Schrade, all of whom took recipes that might be otherwise impossible for a novice chef, vetted them, and made them user-friendly.

No baking book of mine would be complete without the expertise and recipe contributions of my friend Izzy Cohen.

To Christopher Gelber, who made me listen to his opinions, even when I didn't ask for them.

To my editor, Peter Gethers, and his assistant, Shauna Toh, who saw me through this third collaboration with support and encouragement.

To my production editor, Benjamin Dreyer, who has always forgiven the excessive amount of corrections I ask for (but is especially tolerant right after I've sent him chocolate chip cookies and chocolate cherry bread).

To my agent, Janis Donnaud, who knows the recipe for a great deal.

To Margy Rochlin, who has turned popping in for a visit into a lesson in the art of true companionship. We knew our Caramel Candy Kisses were perfect when she asked for "just one more."

To my husband, Mark Peel, and my children, Vanessa, Ben, and Oliver.

To the best (but slowest) photographer, Steven Rothfeld, who believes that a blueberry scone deserves to be as well lit as Grace Kelly—even if it takes two hours to set up the shot.

To my coauthor Teri Gelber (pronounced Gel-BURR), whom I've known for so many years, in so many capacities. I can't thank her enough for the endless hours she spent with me in front of the computer, getting my voice exactly right and translating my pastries into words.

CONTENTS

"To this day, my heart still pounds when
I walk into La Brea Bakery."

INTRODUCTION

Back in 1989, when the La Brea Bakery first opened, we sold only bread. Customers would walk in, look around, and say, "Bread, is that *it*?" Some would then leave with a loaf; others would advise me that my dark, flour-dusted creations were burnt and dirty; but most were too skeptical to even try one of the large, crusty, hand-shaped loaves. Bread was something most Americans bought in plastic bags at the supermarket. Real bakeries sold cakes and cookies. With my reputation as a pastry chef, I was expected to satisfy their sweet tooth, not to provide something most often used to sandwich ham and cheese. But the demanding life of a bread baker was so new to me, it needed all of my attention. I just didn't have time for pastries. Besides, our space was too small to accommodate anything more than a display rack and the essential bread-making equipment: a mixer, some worktables, and a hearth-style oven.

Over time, a hard sell became an addiction. The bakery became so successful, we were running out of bread earlier and earlier each day. To keep our customers satisfied, we'd have to bake more. To bake more, we needed extra space. To gain extra space, we were forced to move our production to a larger facility. Suddenly, our tiny, chaotic retail bakery was transformed into a vast and cavernous shell with unused equipment and a lonely rack of bread. The charm of a working bakery was lost. The activity and smells of baking bread were replaced by the fumes of a delivery truck that dropped off the daily bake to be sold in the storefront.

To bring life back, we would have to bake again. And why not bake what people wanted in the first place: sweets? Not just any sweets, but the kind of sweets that I wanted to bake, that I wanted to eat, and that I wanted to look at. I didn't want refrigerated cases shelved with fragile cakes, elaborately constructed of countless creamy layers, architectural and overly decorated. Those show-off desserts are seldom about texture and flavor, but about the costly tools and learned techniques it takes to make them. Furthermore, fancy pastries would hardly make sense alongside my hearty, country-style bread.

The pastries we make are deliciously simple and rustic and never too sweet. Woven into many of them are my favorite flavors: butter, cinnamon, nuts, and fruit. They're familiar, uncomplicated, and satisfying. One taste and you're instantly comforted. Inspired by a sweet memory from childhood, a European classic, or a time-honored bakeshop standard, they are flavors you never tire of. Like my bread, these are pastries you want to eat every day.

Except for a sprinkling of nuts, a dusting of powdered sugar, or a drizzling of glaze, no fastidious finishing work is necessary. Once the pastry is in the oven, the baker's job is done. As these doughs and batters cook, their intrinsic beauty naturally evolves. Rich colors and alluring textures take us by surprise. Flaky, soft, or crumbly, tender, moist, or crisp, these treats compel you to take another bite. As the sugars caramelize in the oven, they accent the crust with a lustered sheen. Heat and alchemy produce a palate of deep, earthy tones from burnished reds and browns to dull and shiny golds and yellows. Scorched fruit might peek through the top of a Blueberry-Almond Muffin (page 195), as it puffs and forms its whimsical, rounded cap. Unpredictable cracks emerge, randomly decorating the surface of Ginger Scones (page 177) and Rosemary Corncakes (page 186). Ripe little tomatoes sit happily on top of a bed of melted Parmesan in a White Lily Savory Tart (page 91). Yeasted croissants, Danish Diamonds (page 324), and Apple Turnovers (page 332) rise and swell, each one with a mind of its own. No matter, all are unique. Even when baked in a mold, no two turn out the same.

To this day, my heart still pounds when I walk into La Brea Bakery. I never know what to expect. Like the pastries themselves, each day is different from the last. As I look around at all of the handsome shapes of crescents, twists, and coils and the delightful assortment of cookies, scones, tarts, savories, and confections, I am excited and amazed. But it's that final glance, that close-up view, that reveals their truth. Simple, humble, and beautiful, this is the stuff I love.

NANCY SILVERTON'S

PASTRIES FROM THE LA BREA BAKERY

EQUIPMENT: "USE YOUR IMAGINATION AND
IMPROVISE WHEN NECESSARY."

EQUIPMENT

Most of the equipment you need for the recipes in this book you probably have in your kitchen cupboards. Use your imagination and improvise when necessary. Here is a list of tools and supplies that will make your baking life easier.

Baking Sheets: Heavy-duty, 11 × 17-inch high-quality baking sheets are best. Cheap, lightweight sheets will warp under high heat and cause you more trouble than they are worth. Look for baking sheets with ½-inch-high edges, sometimes called *jelly-roll pans.* You'll be able to make brownies or fruit wedges as well as bake a tray of cookies. Invest in at least two or, even better, four so you're always prepared.

Bench Scraper or Dough Scraper: You'll find this tool indispensable when you're working with the stickier doughs, like the yeasted ones. A scraper is made from a semiflexible or firm piece of sheet metal attached to a handle. It removes the dough from the work surface better than anything else and makes cleanup much easier.

Cake Rings: Also called *entrement rings*, these circular metal molds have 2-inch-high sides, no bottom, and must be set on a baking sheet. They range from a small 3-inch diameter for small cakes and tarts such as Ginger Cakes and Lemon Cups, or up to 9 inches for the Armenian Coffee Cake. Available at specialty stores (see "Sources," page 393).

Cutters: A set of graduated round cutters, either plain or fluted, is useful for cutting out round cookies and some individual small tarts. For larger individual tarts, the graduated set of vol-au-vent cutters is great to have. If you don't have the right size cutter, use a plate or the rim of a glass as a guide.

Electric Mixer: A good heavy-duty freestanding mixer such as a KitchenAid is my favorite. If you like to bake, you'll find this item earns its price quickly. As the batters and dough mix, your hands are free to do other things, allowing you to make better use of your time.

Flan Rings: For baking tarts, my favorite ring is the French bottomless variety with smooth 1-inch-high sides. However, fluted tart rings with a removable bottom will work too. Most of the larger size tarts in this book are baked in either a 10-inch ring or a 12-inch ring. For the Cheese Bars (page 229), you will need a 12 × 4-inch rectangular mold with 2-inch sides. Small 3-inch- to 5-inch-diameter flan rings are perfect for individual tarts. Available at specialty stores or catalogs (see "Sources," page 393).

Food Processor: Though not essential, a food processor is good for grinding nuts and efficiently combining the butter with the dry ingredients.

Grater: A box-style stainless-steel grater with a wide variety of holes will come in handy. The small holes are used for grating nutmeg, the larger holes for cheese, almond paste, or frozen streusel topping.

Knives: The two knives you'll end up using the most for these recipes are a 4- to 6-inch paring knife for smaller jobs and an 8- to 10-inch chef knife for chopping and larger jobs. Since you only really need two, invest in high-quality knives. My favorite brands are Wüsthof and Henckels.

Measuring Cups and Spoons: For accuracy, dry ingredients should always be measured in dry measuring cups that come in graduated sizes from $1/8$ cup to 2 cups. The scoop-and-level method—scooping into the flour or sugar and using a knife to level—is the most exacting method. For liquids, use a liquid measuring cup, usually made out of glass or plastic with the measure marks printed on the cup. After you pour in the liquid, be sure to read the measure mark at eye level. Use measuring spoons for measurements less than $1/4$ cup, using the scoop-and-level technique for dry ingredients.

Metal Pie Weights: These small, reusable metal discs add weight to unfilled tart shells or pie crusts while baking to prevent the dough from rising up. If you don't have them, dried beans work just as well.

Mixing Bowls: A good range of stainless-steel or ceramic mixing bowls will get a lot of mileage when baking. Choose a large, wide, 9-quart bowl and work your way down in size.

Molds: From muffin pans to tartlet tins to cast-iron skillets, a variety of molds are used throughout this book. Some recipes, such as Madeleines and Canellé, require their own specific mold, while others, such as Daisy Cake or Capezzana Tiny Olive Oil Cakes, welcome a multitude of decorative shaped molds. For more details, refer to the individual recipes. See "Sources," page 393.

Nut Grinder: A manual nut grinder such as the Mouli grater works best. A clean, dry electric coffee grinder will also do the job for both nuts and spices. A food processor also works, as long as you process the nuts with sugar to prevent the nuts from becoming pasty.

Parchment Paper: Most pastry chefs couldn't live without this. Used to line baking sheets and sometimes molds, it provides a clean, nonstick surface. It is most often sold in sheets or on rolls. Once you get used to baking with it, you'll never give it up.

Pastry Brush: A paintbrush from the hardware store will work just as well as the fancy gourmet-variety pastry brush. Use for brushing egg wash and washing sugar down the sides of the pan.

Pepper Mill: A good-quality pepper mill is a must for any recipe that calls for freshly ground pepper.

Rolling Pin: I prefer the handleless French wooden version: a long cylinder about 2 × 16 inches.

Ruler: Use for measuring the dimensions of dough as you roll it out.

Saucepans and Sauté Pans: A saucepan is deep, with high, straight sides. Have a 2- and 4-quart heavy-duty, stainless-steel saucepan to use for heating liquids. A sauté pan is shallow, with sloping sides. Add a 12-inch sauté pan to your collection.

Silpat: An excellent alternative to parchment paper, this floppy, reusable nonstick baking mat is not a gimmick. Silpat is a brand name, though many other companies now make their own version. You'll find them at Dean & DeLuca, Sur La Table, and Williams Sonoma; see "Sources," page 393.

Spatulas: A heatproof rubber spatula is needed for stirring hot mixtures, scraping bowls, and folding together ingredients.

Strainers, Sifters, Sieves: If I call for ingredients to be sifted, it's usually just to help combine them more thoroughly. I prefer the drum-style sieves or *tamis*, a round, flat strainer stretched in a wooden or metal frame that can be set directly over a bowl. If I ask for a fine-mesh strainer, then I prefer the conical strainer with very small holes that allow nothing but liquid to pass through.

Thermometers: For frying doughnuts and cooking sugar, a deep-fat frying or candy thermometer, ranging from 75 to 400 degrees, with a clip to attach to the side of the pan, is essential. An oven thermometer will determine the accuracy of your oven.

Whisks: If you're going to own only one whisk, the 12-inch stainless-steel sauce whisk is the most practical one.

Wooden Spoons: Though they are harder to find, I prefer the French flat spatula-style spoons for stirring and scraping.

Zester: This great little tool removes the zest or colored part of the peel from citrus fruit. Don't waste your money on a zester that doesn't have the blade riveted into the handle. After a few lemons, the blade will pop off.

A Guide to the Ingredients

Almond Extract: Choose pure almond extract and beware of brands that use artificial flavorings.

Almond Paste: Almond paste is made from ground almonds and sugar. Marzipan is an acceptable replacement, although it's a bit softer and sweeter. Almond paste is available in some supermarkets and most specialty food stores. See "Sources," page 393.

Butter: All of the recipes in this book call for unsalted butter. Imported Normandy butter, or domestic Plugra, found at specialty shops and cheese stores, or Land O Lakes, found at many supermarkets, have the best flavor. However, many small American dairies are finally producing delicious butters. I am most familiar with Egg Farm Dairy on the East Coast and Strauss Family Creamery on the West Coast. If you plan to keep butter longer than a few days, it's best to store it in the freezer so it doesn't pick up off odors from your refrigerator.

Chocolate: My favorite chocolate brands are California-made Scharffen Berger, French Valrhona, and Venezuelan Chocolates El Rey. My favorite type of chocolate is bittersweet. All of these are couverture quality, and contain a higher percentage of cocoa butter. They are carried in most specialty food stores or can be ordered through the mail (see "Sources," page 393). To melt chocolate: Bring a large pot of water to boil and turn it down to a gentle simmer. Chop the chocolate in 2-inch pieces. Place the pieces in a clean, dry stainless-steel bowl several inches larger than the pot so the steam doesn't rise and contaminate the chocolate, which will cause it to lump. Cover the bowl tightly with plastic wrap and set over the pot of simmering

"ORGANIC FARMERS' MARKETS GUARANTEE THE
FRESHEST EGGS, UNLESS YOU'RE LUCKY ENOUGH TO HAVE A
CHICKEN COOP IN YOUR BACKYARD."

water. Keep the flame very low and be sure the bowl isn't touching the water, or it will burn and ruin the chocolate.

Cinnamon: Once you've tasted freshly ground cinnamon sticks, you'll never settle for preground cinnamon from a supermarket jar. Specialty spice stores (see "Sources," page 393) do sell preground Saigon cinnamon, the most flavorful variety of them all. To grind a cinnamon quill, break into small pieces and grind by itself in a spice mill or in a clean coffee grinder, or grind with a little bit of sugar until finely powdered.

Cocoa Powder: I prefer dark, unsweetened cocoa powder. Not so long ago, this high-quality cocoa powder was made only by European companies and was "Dutch-processed" (chemically treated). Now the American chocolate maker Scharffen Berger produces an excellent natural unsweetened cocoa powder, a bit lighter in color than the European ones but excellent in flavor.

Crème Fraîche: Similar in flavor to sour cream, this tangy and rich cream is found at specialty supermarkets or can easily be made at home. To make your own: In a small stainless-steel bowl, combine 1 cup heavy cream with 3 tablespoons buttermilk. Cover and allow the mixture to sit in a warm place for about 24 hours, until thickened. Store in the refrigerator for up to 2 weeks.

Eggs: I use extra-large eggs. Organic farmers' markets will guarantee the freshest and best-tasting eggs, unless you're lucky enough to have a chicken coop in your backyard, like I do.

Flour: Most of the recipes in this book call for unbleached pastry flour—a low-protein flour to ensure tender crusts, cookies, and cakes. It is a little difficult to find, but it can be ordered by mail (see "Sources," page 393). Unbleached all-purpose flour, slightly higher in protein, is the best alternative. Flour should be stored in airtight containers in the refrigerator or freezer.

Kosher Salt: I prefer the larger granulation of kosher salt to cook with, as it is a bit coarser than ordinary table salts. If you use a finer-grain salt, use half the amount. Look for the kosher salt variety without any chemical additives, available in some supermarkets, specialty stores, and most mail-order catalogs.

Nutmeg: I'm a stickler for freshly ground nutmeg. If you don't have whole nutmeg at home to grate, I would skip adding this spice altogether. To grate your own, use the smallest hole on a grater or buy a special nutmeg grinder.

Nuts: Because of their high oil content, nuts can go rancid easily. Whenever you can, buy your nuts seasonally, fresh from a farmers' market, to ensure that you get this year's crop. Store raw nuts in the freezer in an airtight container and toast only as you need them.

Vanilla: There is nothing like the fragrance and flavor of a soft, plump vanilla bean. This long and slender pod is a miraculous work of nature, imparting the deepest, richest flavor ever. I prefer Tahitian vanilla beans, which are about five inches long, more moist and plump, and packed with little wet seeds. Beware of the skinny, shriveled-up beans found in the supermarket; they are often dried out and void of any flavor. Find a good mail-order source (see "Sources," page 393) or specialty market that has a fresh source. Store in the refrigerator, tightly wrapped in plastic wrap or in an airtight container.

Don't throw your old used bean pods away; instead, make vanilla sugar by rinsing off the beans and allowing them to dry at room temperature or in a low-temperature oven until brittle. When you have about a dozen, grind them into a powder in the food processor or spice grinder, along with a few cups of powdered sugar. Strain through a fine-mesh strainer to remove any crunchy vanilla bean pieces. Use this to flavor whipped cream, to replace a small amount of plain sugar in a recipe, or to dust the tops of cookies.

When you buy vanilla extract, be sure the label reads "pure vanilla," and beware of artificial flavorings. The best is Tahitian vanilla extract, available in specialty stores and catalogs.

1. *Quickcakes and Quickbreads*

....

Though different from each other in shape and flavor, the one thing quickbreads and quickcakes have in common is their simplicity. As their name implies, they're easy to prepare, quick to bake, and require very little attention, if any, once they're out of the oven. Frostings and elaborate decoration have no place here. Think about it: When making a *fancy* cake, it's the decorating that takes the most time. Once you've chilled the cake, sliced it into layers, made your frostings (sometimes more than one), frosted the layers (you're still not done), it's time to shave the chocolate curls, whip the cream, and pipe the rosettes. By now, you've promised yourself you'll never bake another cake for the rest of your life.

Don't swear off baking cakes just yet. These quickbreads and quickcakes take a humbler route to adornment. The molds they're baked in, along with a modest topping, make your job so easy. Quickbreads, like Cranberry-Almond (page 31) or Chocolate Swirl–Almond Poundcake (page 29), call for familiar loaf pans, while quickcakes come in a variety of shapes and sizes. Some are baked in a traditional Bundt pan, like the Crème Fraîche Coffee Cake (page 33), while others such as Sticky Toffee Pudding (page 46) and Capezzana Tiny Olive Oil Cakes (page 23) are made in unique, decorative molds. These robust loaves and festive cakes ask only for the simplest of final touches—a light dusting of powdered sugar, a sweet and shiny glaze, a heap of toasted nuts, or a sprinkling of streusel topping.

You'll find the more common molds, like Bundt pans, loaf pans, and tartlet tins, at kitchen shops or in houseware catalogs. For the more offbeat models, you'll have to go on some treasure hunts. There's nothing more beautiful than an old Madeleine mold, darkened and well seasoned after hundreds of batches, much prettier than its new, shiny counterpart. Take some time to clean out your grandmother's attic, or make a quick dash to Paris and wind your way through the 3ème Arrondisement searching out the world's finest kitchen stores. With all of that foraging, you'll want to take care of your molds. Wipe them out with a damp cloth and to be sure they don't rust, dry them out immediately in a warm oven.

Chances are, your grandmother didn't have the same molds mine did. Don't be afraid to make adjustments. Your baking time will differ slightly and your yield will vary according to the size and capacity of your molds. To figure out your mold's cup capacity, fill it to the rim with water and transfer the water into a measuring cup. If your mold is smaller than mine, refrigerate the leftover batter and use it later.

Never overly rich or complex, most of these quickbreads and cakes can be eaten any time of the day. Some go along with coffee in the morning, like Banana-Nut Bread (page 15) and Summer Camp Coffeecake (page 49), while the Daisy Cake (page 35), light and lemony, is more appealing after lunch. When it's that *fancy* dessert you're looking for, the Chocolate-Almond Cake (page 24) is fancy looking, but not fancy to make. Whatever the occasion, these pretty cakes will make it more special and leave you cool, unruffled, and with very little mess to clean up.

Banana-Nut Bread

ELEGANTLY SLICED BANANAS BAKED ON TOP MAKE A FOSSIL-LIKE IMPRESSION on this moist and flavorful loaf.

Special Items: 6-CUP-CAPACITY LOAF PAN, LIGHTLY COATED WITH MELTED BUTTER

⅔ cup (2½ ounces) walnuts
⅔ cup (2½ ounces) pecans
3 to 4 bananas, very ripe, mashed to equal 1¼ cups, plus 1 whole banana for garnish
2 extra-large eggs
1½ teaspoons pure vanilla extract
1 stick (4 ounces) unsalted butter, chilled and cut into 1-inch cubes
1¼ teaspoons baking soda
2½ teaspoons baking powder
¾ teaspoon kosher salt
1 teaspoon ground cinnamon
¾ teaspoon freshly grated nutmeg
Scant ¼ teaspoon ground cloves
1 tablespoon poppy seeds
½ cup granulated sugar, plus 1 teaspoon extra for sprinkling
¼ cup plus 2 tablespoons light brown sugar, lightly packed
1½ cups unbleached all-purpose flour

Adjust the oven rack to the middle position and preheat the oven to 325 degrees.

Spread the nuts on a baking sheet and toast in the oven until lightly browned, about 8 to 10 minutes. Shake the pan halfway through to ensure that the nuts toast evenly. Cool, chop coarsely, and set aside.

Turn the oven up to 350 degrees.

In a medium bowl, whisk the banana puree, eggs, and vanilla extract to combine.

In the bowl of an electric mixer fitted with the paddle attachment, cream the butter, baking soda, baking powder, salt, cinnamon, nutmeg, cloves, and poppy seeds on low, 2 to 3 minutes, until softened. Add the sugars and turn the mixer up to medium, mixing another 3 to 4 minutes until fluffy, scraping down the sides of the bowl as needed.

Add the flour and the banana mixture alternately in 3 batches, beginning with the flour and mixing until just combined.

Remove the bowl from the mixer and fold in the nuts.

Pour the batter into the prepared loaf pan to just below the rim.

Cut two ¼-inch-thick strips from the remaining banana, slicing down the entire length. Arrange the two C shapes on top of the loaf, staggered, with the two ends slightly interlocking with each other in the center. Sprinkle about one teaspoon of granulated sugar over the surface.

Bake for 50 to 60 minutes, until nicely browned and firm to the touch.

Yield: 1 loaf

Brownies

THE WORLD IS MADE UP OF TWO TYPES OF PEOPLE: CHEWY AND FUDGEY OR DRY and cakey. If you're of the former type, then you'll love these brownies. They're rich, super-moist, and super-chocolatey. I like to eat them cold, straight out of the refrigerator, with the door still open.

Special Item: 11 × 17-INCH JELLY-ROLL PAN, LIGHTLY COATED WITH
MELTED BUTTER

3 cups (12 ounces) walnut halves
3 sticks (12 ounces) unsalted butter
1 pound bittersweet chocolate
3½ cups granulated sugar
6 extra-large eggs
1 tablespoon pure vanilla extract
¾ teaspoon kosher salt
3¼ cups unbleached pastry flour or unbleached all-purpose flour
Unsweetened cocoa powder for dusting, optional

Adjust the oven rack to the middle position and preheat the oven to 325 degrees.

Spread the walnuts on a baking sheet and toast in the oven until lightly browned, about 10 to 12 minutes. Shake the pan halfway through to ensure that the nuts toast evenly.

In a stainless-steel mixing bowl set over a pot of gently simmering water, melt the butter and chocolate together.

Turn the oven up to 350 degrees.

In the bowl of an electric mixer fitted with the whisk attachment, beat the sugar, eggs, vanilla extract, and salt on medium-high until thick and mousselike, about 3 to 5 minutes. Add the flour in 3 batches, turning the mixer off before each addition and mixing on low until combined. Remove the bowl from the mixer and stir in the melted chocolate mixture and nuts.

Pour the batter into the prepared pan and spread to an even thickness.

Bake for 40 minutes, until firm to the touch.

Before serving, slice into 3 × 4-inch squares. If desired, sift a fine layer of cocoa powder over the surface, brushing off the excess cocoa for a velvety finish.

Yield: Fifteen 3 × 4-inch brownies

Brownies with Irish Whiskey and Currants

Just when you thought brownies couldn't be richer and more decadent —these are the X-rated adult version.

Special Item: 11 × 17-INCH JELLY-ROLL PAN, LIGHTLY COATED WITH
MELTED BUTTER

1 cup (5 ounces) hazelnuts
12 ounces bittersweet chocolate
2 sticks (8 ounces) unsalted butter
1¼ cups Irish whiskey
1½ cups currants or raisins
2 cups granulated sugar
4 extra-large eggs
½ teaspoon kosher salt
2¼ cups unbleached all-purpose flour or unbleached pastry flour
Unsweetened cocoa powder, optional

Adjust the oven rack to the middle position and preheat the oven to 325 degrees.

Spread the hazelnuts on a baking sheet and toast in the oven until lightly browned, about 10 to 15 minutes. Shake the pan halfway through to ensure that the nuts toast evenly. Allow to cool for a few minutes. Gather the nuts into a kitchen towel and rub together to remove the skins.

Turn the oven up to 350 degrees.

In a stainless-steel mixing bowl set over a pot of gently simmering water, melt the chocolate and butter together. Transfer to a large mixing bowl.

In a small saucepan over low heat, heat 1 cup of the whiskey with the currants or raisins, stirring constantly to prevent the liquid from burning on the sides of the pan. Cook until the liquid is sticky, bubbly, and reduced, about 3 to 5 minutes. Set aside.

In the bowl of an electric mixer fitted with the whisk attachment, beat the sugar, eggs, and salt on medium-high until thick and mousselike, about 3 to 5 minutes.

Add the flour in 3 batches, turning the mixer off before each addition and mixing on low until combined. Remove the bowl from the mixer and stir in the melted chocolate mixture. Stir in the currant mixture, hazelnuts, and remaining ¼ cup of whiskey.

Pour into the prepared pan and spread to an even thickness.

Bake for 20 to 25 minutes, until firm to the touch.

Cool and refrigerate. Before serving, slice into squares. If desired, sift a fine layer of cocoa powder over the surface, brushing off the excess cocoa for a velvety finish.

Yield: Fifteen 3 × 4-inch brownies

Canellés

THESE PRECIOUS MEDIEVAL CAKES CAUGHT MY EYE ON A RECENT VISIT TO one of my favorite Parisian bakeries, Maison Kaiser. Originally from the Bordeaux region, Canellés found their way to Paris and are finally finding their way to us in America. Their dark, crunchy exterior gives way to a delicate, moist center—very sweet and slightly decadent.

Canellés (pronounced kah-neh-lay) get their name from the small, cavernous, fluted molds they are always baked in. The first few times you use your molds, coat them well with vegetable oil to prevent the batter from sticking. Treat the molds like a cast-iron skillet: Don't ever wash them with soap. Simply wipe them out with a damp cloth and eventually, your seasoned Canellé mold will no longer require oiling.

The batter must sit overnight and be used within two days. Because of their dark color, it's almost impossible to tell when Canellés are cooked all the way through. Until you get your timing down, you may have to sacrifice one to check for doneness.

Special Item: 18 CANELLÉ MOLDS (SEE "SOURCES," PAGE 393), SEASONED OR LIGHTLY COATED WITH VEGETABLE OIL

4 cups whole milk
½ stick (2 ounces) unsalted butter, cut into 1-inch cubes
5 extra-large egg yolks
1 extra-large egg
2½ cups granulated sugar
2 cups unbleached pastry flour or unbleached all-purpose flour
2 teaspoons pure vanilla extract
1 teaspoon rum or brandy

Prepare the batter 1 day in advance: In a medium saucepan over high heat, bring 2½ cups of the milk and the butter to a full boil. Remove from heat and set aside to cool slightly.

In a large bowl, whisk together the egg yolks, egg, and sugar. Add the flour and mix to combine. Whisk in the remaining 1¾ cups of the milk, vanilla extract, and rum or brandy.

In a steady stream, pour the warm milk mixture into the egg mixture, whisking to combine.

Place a fine-mesh sieve over a bowl or plastic container and strain the batter. Cover and refrigerate for at least 24 hours and no longer than 48 hours.

Adjust the oven rack to the middle position and preheat the oven to 400 degrees. Place the prepared molds 1½ inches apart on a baking sheet.

Remove the bowl from the refrigerator and stir the batter to reincorporate. Fill each mold to the top.

Bake for about 2 hours, until they are very dark on the outside and the interior is cooked. Rotate the Canellés halfway through to ensure even baking.

Yield: 18 Canellés

Capezzana Tiny Olive Oil Cakes

I KNEW I'D BE DRINKING PLENTY OF GREAT WINE THAT SPRING WHEN ROLANDO Beramendi invited Mark and me to be guest chefs at Capezzana Winery in Tuscany. What I didn't know was that Capezzana also produces some of the world's best olive oils, which their kitchen staff put to good use. Every morning, served with our cappuccino, was a moist slice of this incredible olive oil cake. By the end of our stay, we were hooked.

I wouldn't dare alter the ingredients in this family recipe, but I did risk changing the traditional 8-inch round pan it's baked in. A thick wedge or slice is fine, but lots of little cakes yield more of that tasty, golden crust. If you have them, use tartlet molds in different shapes such as oval barquettes, fluted rounds, or flat financier molds for a decorative and delicious platter. And one last thing: the better the olive oil, the better the cake.

Special Item:　SEVERAL ¼-CUP-CAPACITY TARTLET MOLDS, LIGHTLY COATED WITH OLIVE OIL, OR TWO ROUND 9-INCH CAKE PANS

2 cups plus 2 tablespoons unbleached pastry flour
1½ cups granulated sugar
½ teaspoon baking soda
½ teaspoon baking powder
3 extra-large eggs
1½ cups whole milk
1½ cups extra-virgin olive oil
3 tablespoons grated orange zest (about 2 to 3 oranges)

Adjust the oven rack to the middle position and preheat the oven to 350 degrees.

Over a large mixing bowl, sift to combine the flour, sugar, baking soda, and baking powder. Make a large well in the center and pour in the eggs, milk, and olive oil. Whisk to combine the liquids, and slowly draw in the dry ingredients, whisking until incorporated. The mixture should be fairly smooth before you draw in more dry ingredients. If necessary, strain to dissolve any lumps of flour. Stir in the orange zest.

Pour the batter into the prepared molds to three-quarters full and place on 1–2 baking sheets, half an inch apart.

Bake for 25 to 30 minutes until nicely browned and firm to the touch.

Yield: Approximately 30 small cakes, depending on the size of the molds

Chocolate–Almond Cake

I'M NOT SURE WHO GAVE ME THIS RECIPE, OTHERWISE I WOULD BE GIVING "you" the credit. This low, dark, rich cake has been one of our standards here at the bakery. Because it's flourless, it's a staple of ours for Passover. If you bake it in a jelly-roll pan rather than a cake pan, you can cut the cake out into different shapes, such as hearts or circles, after it's baked.

Special Item: 9-INCH CAKE RING OR SPRINGFORM PAN OR II × 17-INCH JELLY-ROLL PAN, COATED WITH MELTED BUTTER

FOR THE CAKE:
1½ sticks (6 ounces) unsalted butter, chilled and cut into 1-inch cubes
¾ cup granulated sugar
1 cup (8 ounces) almond paste
½ cup plus 2 tablespoons unsweetened imported cocoa powder, sifted
4 extra-large eggs, lightly beaten

FOR DECORATING:
¼ cup (¾ ounce) unblanched sliced almonds

FOR THE GLAZE:
8 ounces bittersweet chocolate, chopped coarsely
1½ sticks (6 ounces) unsalted butter, chilled and cut into 1-inch cubes
2 tablespoons light corn syrup
2 tablespoons brandy or rum, optional

Adjust the oven rack to the middle position and preheat the oven to 350 degrees.

To prepare the cake: In the bowl of an electric mixer fitted with the paddle attachment, cream the butter on low, 2 to 3 minutes, until softened. Add the sugar and turn the mixer to medium, mixing 3 to 4 minutes until light and fluffy, scraping down the sides of the bowl as needed. Slowly add the almond paste, a few tablespoons at a time, mixing well between each addition.

Turn the mixer off and add the cocoa powder. Turn the mixer to low and mix until combined. Add the eggs a few teaspoons at a time and mix until incorporated. Transfer the mixture to the prepared cake ring, spread to an even thickness, and bake for 20 to 25 minutes, until slightly firm to the touch. Allow to cool completely.

Turn the oven down to 325 degrees.

Spread the sliced almonds on a baking sheet and toast in the oven until lightly toasted, about 5 to 7 minutes. Shake the pan halfway through to ensure that the nuts toast evenly.

To prepare the glaze: In a small stainless-steel bowl set over a pot of very gently simmering water, melt the chocolate with the butter and corn syrup. Stir in the brandy or rum, if desired.

To decorate the cake: When the glaze is warm but not hot, hold the cake flat on the palm of your hand. Pour or ladle the glaze over the surface, tilting and shaking the cake a bit, letting the glaze run down the sides to make a thin, even coating. Set the cake down on a flat surface. To avoid any drip marks, let the cake sit perfectly still for 10 to 15 minutes until the glaze begins to set. Transfer the cake back to the palm of your hand. Press the almond slices onto the side of the cake. Chill 20 to 30 minutes more to completely set. Store the leftover glaze in the refrigerator (it will keep for several weeks).

Yield: One 9-inch cake, 1 inch high

Chocolate Steamed Pudding

THIS IS CALLED A STEAMED PUDDING BECAUSE IT'S COOKED IN A MOLD AND steamed in a water bath—you have a choice of cooking it either on top of the stove or in the oven. This dessert is actually a cross between chocolate cake and chocolate pudding. Rich, chocolatey, and creamy, it's best served with a dollop of crème fraîche or whipped cream.

Special Items: ONE 8-CUP-CAPACITY PUDDING MOLD, LIGHTLY COATED WITH
MELTED BUTTER, CHILLED, AND DUSTED WITH COCOA POWDER
ONE LARGE POT, BIG ENOUGH TO HOLD THE MOLD AND DEEP
ENOUGH TO HOLD ENOUGH BOILING WATER TO COME HALFWAY
UP THE MOLD

FOR THE FUDGE SWIRL:

$\frac{1}{4}$ cup plus 1 tablespoon water

$\frac{1}{4}$ cup light corn syrup

2 tablespoons granulated sugar

$\frac{1}{4}$ cup plus 2 tablespoons unsweetened cocoa powder

1 teaspoon instant espresso powder

4 ounces bittersweet chocolate, melted according to the instructions on page 7

1 tablespoon plus 1 teaspoon cognac or brandy

FOR THE PUDDING:

$\frac{1}{4}$ cup water

$\frac{1}{4}$ cup buttermilk

$\frac{1}{4}$ cup imported unsweetened cocoa powder, plus extra for dusting

1 teaspoon instant espresso powder

3 ounces bittersweet chocolate, melted according to the instructions on page 7

$\frac{1}{4}$ cup sour cream

1 stick (4 ounces) unsalted butter, chilled and cut into 1-inch cubes

$1\frac{1}{4}$ teaspoons baking soda, dissolved in 2 tablespoons boiling water

$\frac{1}{4}$ cup plus 2 tablespoons light brown sugar, lightly packed

6 tablespoons (3 ounces) almond paste

4 extra-large egg yolks

1 cup soft prunes, pitted and sliced into thirds
1 cup plus 2 tablespoons unbleached pastry flour or unbleached all-purpose flour, sifted
4 extra-large egg whites
2 tablespoons granulated sugar

If you're going to use the oven method, adjust the oven rack to the lower position and preheat the oven to 350 degrees.

To prepare the fudge swirl: In a medium saucepan over medium heat, combine the water, corn syrup, sugar, cocoa powder, and espresso powder and bring to a boil, whisking constantly. Stir in the melted chocolate and the cognac or brandy and set aside to cool.

To make the pudding: In a small saucepan over medium heat, whisk together the water, buttermilk, cocoa powder, and espresso powder. Bring to a boil, whisking constantly. Remove from the heat and whisk in the melted chocolate and sour cream and set aside to cool.

In the bowl of an electric mixer fitted with the paddle attachment, cream the butter and baking soda on low, about 2 to 3 minutes, until softened. Add the brown sugar, turn the mixer up to medium, and mix for 3 to 4 minutes until light and fluffy, scraping down the sides of the bowl as needed. Add the almond paste a tablespoon at a time, mixing well between each addition. Add the egg yolks, one at a time, and mix on medium until incorporated. Add the chocolate mixture and prunes. Add the flour in 3 batches, turning the mixer off before each addition and mixing on low until just combined. Transfer the mixture to a large bowl and set aside.

Wash and thoroughly dry the bowl of the electric mixer. Using the whisk attachment, beat the egg whites on low until frothy. Increase the speed to medium and beat another 2 to 3 minutes, until soft peaks form. Increase the speed to high and gradually add the granulated sugar and beat until shiny and stiff. Quickly stir half of the egg whites into the pudding mixture until combined. Fold in the remaining whites. Pour all the fudge swirl onto the mixture, folding only once or twice to marble the batter, leaving large streaks of fudge.

Transfer the batter to the prepared mold. Latch the mold securely and set it into the pot of water, making sure the water comes halfway up the mold. Over medium-high heat bring the pot of water to a boil. If making it on a stovetop, continue to cook over medium heat, so the water maintains a gentle boil. If you're baking it, place the pot in the preheated oven. Cook for 90 minutes until firm to the touch. After 30 minutes, check the water level; it should never fall below halfway down the mold. Add more water if needed. Cool the pudding in the mold for 20 minutes before inverting and unmolding it.

Yield: 1 cake, 8 to 10 servings

Chocolate Swirl–Almond Poundcake

Just read the ingredients and you'll see how rich and almondy this cake is. Another bestseller at our store, this moist loaf will satisfy both your craving for poundcake and your craving for chocolate. If wrapped well, it will stay fresh much longer than the average loaf.

Special Item: 6-CUP-CAPACITY LOAF PAN, LIGHTLY COATED WITH MELTED BUTTER

2 sticks (8 ounces) unsalted butter, chilled and cut into 1-inch cubes
3/4 teaspoon baking powder
1/4 cup granulated sugar
1 cup (8 ounces) almond paste
5 extra-large eggs, lightly beaten
2 cups unbleached pastry flour or unbleached all-purpose flour
4 ounces bittersweet chocolate, melted according to the instructions on page 7

FOR THE STREUSEL TOPPING:
1/2 cup unbleached pastry flour or unbleached all-purpose flour
1/2 cup granulated sugar
1 stick (4 ounces) unsalted butter, cut into 1/2-inch cubes and frozen

Adjust the oven rack to the middle position and preheat the oven to 350 degrees.

In the bowl of an electric mixer fitted with the paddle attachment, cream the butter and baking powder on low, 2 to 3 minutes, until softened. Add the sugar and mix 3 to 4 minutes on medium, until light and fluffy, scraping down the sides of the bowl as needed. Add the almond paste a tablespoon at a time, mixing well between each addition.

Add the eggs, a few teaspoons at a time, mixing well between each addition. If the mixture begins to separate, add 1 tablespoon of the measured flour.

Add the flour in 3 batches, turning the mixer off before each addition and mixing on low until just combined.

Pour the batter into the prepared loaf pan. Pour the melted chocolate over the surface and using a fork or toothpick, swirl the chocolate into the batter a few times by making circular motions with the fork in the batter.

To prepare the topping: In a food processor fitted with a steel blade, or in an electric mixer fitted with a paddle attachment, combine the flour and sugar. Add the butter and pulse on and off or mix on low until it's the consistency of a coarse meal. Crumble the topping over the surface and bake for 45 to 55 minutes, until firm to the touch.

Yield: 1 loaf

Cranberry-Almond Tea Bread

Topped with a layer of crunchy glistening almonds, this simple little loaf is sweet and tart at the same time.

Special Item: 6-cup-capacity loaf pan, lightly coated with melted butter

1½ sticks plus 1 tablespoon (6½ ounces) unsalted butter, chilled and cut into 1-inch cubes
½ teaspoon baking soda
1 tablespoon plus ½ teaspoon finely chopped lemon zest (about 1 lemon)
½ cup plus 2 tablespoons granulated sugar
2 extra-large egg yolks
1 teaspoon pure almond extract
1 tablespoon lemon juice
1½ cups unbleached pastry flour or unbleached all-purpose flour
¼ cup plus 2 tablespoons plain yogurt
2 extra-large egg whites
½ heaping cup (2½ ounces) fresh or frozen cranberries

FOR THE TOPPING:
1 extra-large egg white
1 tablespoon plus 2 teaspoons granulated sugar
½ cup plus 2 tablespoons (2 ounces) sliced unblanched almonds

Adjust the oven rack to the middle position and preheat the oven to 350 degrees.

In the bowl of an electric mixer fitted with the paddle attachment, cream the butter, baking soda, and lemon zest on low, about 2 to 3 minutes, until softened. Add half of the sugar, turn the mixer to medium, and mix for 3 to 4 minutes until light and fluffy, scraping down the sides of the bowl as needed. Turn the mixer to low and add the egg yolks one at a time. Add the almond extract and lemon juice, and mix until just combined.

Add the flour and the yogurt alternately in 3 batches and mix on low until just combined. Remove the bowl from the mixer and transfer the batter to a large bowl.

Thoroughly wash and dry the bowl of the electric mixer. Using the whisk attachment, whip the egg whites on low until frothy, about 2 to 3 minutes. Turn the mixer up to medium and beat another 2 to 3 minutes until soft peaks form. Turn the mixer to high and gradually add in the remaining sugar and beat until shiny and stiff.

Remove the bowl from the mixer. Stir about half of the egg whites into the batter to loosen it. Fold in the remaining egg whites and fold in the cranberries.

Pour the batter into the prepared pan and smooth to even.

To make the topping: In a medium bowl, whisk the egg white until frothy. Stir in the sugar and almonds. Pour the topping onto the batter and spread evenly over the surface.

Bake for 45 minutes, until the topping is nicely browned and the cake is firm to the touch. Halfway through baking, check the loaf. If the cake has cracked through the topping, press it down with the palms of your hands to deflate and continue baking. You should have a solid, crispy nut surface.

Yield: 1 loaf

Crème Fraîche Coffee Cake

ALTHOUGH THIS RECIPE WAS PREVIOUSLY PUBLISHED IN ANOTHER BOOK OF mine, I would feel like I was gypping you if I didn't include it this time around. It's the ultimate morning coffee cake, screaming out for a hot cup of coffee or a big glass of ice-cold milk.

Special Item: 10-INCH, 14-CUP-CAPACITY BUNDT PAN, LIGHTLY COATED WITH MELTED BUTTER

FOR THE TOPPING:
1 cup (4 ounces) pecans
¼ cup plus 2 tablespoons light brown sugar, lightly packed
2 teaspoons ground cinnamon

FOR THE BATTER:
2 extra-large eggs
2 cups crème fraîche or sour cream
1 tablespoon pure vanilla extract
2 sticks (8 ounces) unsalted butter, chilled and cut into 1-inch cubes
1 tablespoon chopped lemon zest (about 1 lemon)
1 tablespoon baking powder
½ teaspoon kosher salt
2 cups granulated sugar
3 cups unbleached pastry flour or unbleached all-purpose flour

Adjust the oven rack to the middle position and preheat the oven to 325 degrees.

To prepare the topping: Spread the pecans on a baking sheet and toast in the oven until lightly browned, about 10 to 12 minutes. Shake the pan halfway through to ensure that the nuts toast evenly. Cool and chop coarsely. In a small bowl, combine the nuts with the brown sugar and cinnamon, and set aside.

Turn the oven up to 350 degrees.

In a small bowl, whisk together the eggs, crème fraîche or sour cream, and vanilla extract.

In the bowl of an electric mixer fitted with the paddle attachment, cream the butter, lemon zest, baking powder, and salt on low, about 2 to 3 minutes, until softened. Add the sugar and turn the mixer up to medium for 3 to 4 minutes, until light and fluffy, scraping down the sides of the bowl as needed. Turn the mixer to low, add the egg mixture, a few tablespoons at a time, and mix until incorporated.

Add the flour to the butter mixture in 3 batches, turning the mixer off before each addition and mixing on low until just combined.

Pour half of the batter into the prepared pan and spread to even. Sprinkle half of the topping over the surface and pour the remaining batter over it, spreading evenly. Sprinkle the surface with the remaining topping.

Bake for about 1 hour, until firm to the touch.

Yield: 10 to 12 pieces

Daisy Cake

Part of the fun of being in our pastry kitchen is the teamwork involved. Someone lays the groundwork for a new recipe and after many tries, we tailor it into something we can call our own. Merilee brought in her version of a lemon polenta cake, which in the end became this bright and tangy Daisy Cake. Grapefruits or oranges will also work, though they won't be as tart as lemons.

Special Item: 5-CUP-CAPACITY DAISY-SHAPED MOLD, BUNDT PAN, OR SPRINGFORM PAN, LIGHTLY COATED WITH MELTED BUTTER, CHILLED, AND DUSTED WITH SEMOLINA FLOUR

²/₃ cup (3 ounces) unblanched whole almonds
²/₃ cup plus 2 tablespoons granulated sugar
1¹/₂ lemons, cut into quarters, seeds removed
2 tablespoons light corn syrup
²/₃ cup plus 2 tablespoons powdered sugar
¹/₂ cup semolina flour
¹/₂ cup polenta or fine cornmeal
1¹/₃ sticks (5.3 ounces) unsalted butter, chilled and cut into 1-inch cubes
1¹/₂ teaspoons baking powder
3 tablespoons lemon zest, finely chopped (about 2 lemons)
2 extra-large eggs, lightly beaten

FOR GARNISHING THE DAISY MOLD:
8 to 10 unblanched whole almonds, optional

FOR SOAKING THE CAKE:
¹/₄ cup water
¹/₄ cup granulated sugar
¹/₂ cup lemon juice, about 3 to 4 lemons

Adjust the oven rack to the middle position and preheat the oven to 350 degrees. In the bowl of a food processor fitted with the steel blade, combine the nuts with

¼ cup of the granulated sugar and process until it's the consistency of a fine meal. Transfer to a small bowl.

In the food processor, fitted with the steel blade, combine the whole lemons, corn syrup, and powdered sugar, and process for a minute until coarsely ground. Set aside.

In a medium bowl, sift to combine the semolina flour and polenta.

In the bowl of an electric mixer fitted with the paddle attachment, cream the butter, baking powder, and lemon zest on low, 2 to 3 minutes, until softened. Add the remaining granulated sugar and mix on medium for 3 to 4 minutes, until light and fluffy, scraping down the sides of the bowl as needed.

Add the ground nuts to the butter mixture and mix on low to combine. Add the eggs, 1 tablespoon at a time, mixing well between each addition. If the mixture begins to separate, add 1 tablespoon of the measured flour. Add the lemon mixture and mix on low until incorporated. Turn the mixer off and add the flour mixture, mixing on low until just combined.

If you are using the daisy mold, place one whole almond in the middle of each groove in the prepared pan. Fill the mold almost to the top, smooth to even, and bake for about 1 hour, until slightly firm to the touch.

Allow to cool slightly, about 10 minutes.

To prepare the soaking liquid: In a small bowl, whisk to combine the water, sugar, and lemon juice. Brush the cake with half of the liquid. Allow to cool another 10 to 15 minutes and turn the cake out onto a platter. Brush the remaining juice over the top of the cake.

Yield: 8 slices

Ginger Cakes

T HERE ARE ALL TYPES OF GINGER CAKES OUT THERE. U NTRUE TO THEIR NAMES, most are dominated by the flavors of brown sugar and molasses. I like ginger cakes that taste like real ginger. These spicy autumn cakes are definitely gingery, moist, and satisfying.

Special Item: TEN 2-INCH-TALL, 3-INCH-DIAMETER CAKE RINGS (SEE "SOURCES," PAGE 393), LIGHTLY COATED WITH MELTED BUTTER AND CHILLED

FOR THE BREAD-CRUMB COATING:
½ small loaf sourdough bread
1½ teaspoons ground ginger
2 tablespoons plus 1 teaspoon granulated sugar

FOR THE BATTER:
2 sticks plus 2 tablespoons (9 ounces) unsalted butter
1 cup whole milk
3¼ cups unbleached pastry flour or unbleached all-purpose flour
1 tablespoon plus 2 teaspoons baking powder
1 tablespoon ground ginger
¾ teaspoon ground white pepper
4 extra-large eggs
2¼ cups plus 1 tablespoon dark brown sugar, lightly packed
2 tablespoons molasses
2 tablespoons freshly grated ginger, about one 3-inch piece of ginger

Adjust the oven rack to the lower position and preheat the oven to 325 degrees.

To prepare the bread-crumb coating: Cut or tear the bread into 2-inch pieces. Spread onto a baking sheet and toast until firm, but not colored. Allow to cool. In the bowl of a food processor fitted with the steel blade, grind the pieces of bread to a medium coarse meal. Measure out 1½ cups of the crumbs and save the rest for another use. In the food processor, combine the bread crumbs, ground ginger, and sugar and process until it's the consistency of a fine meal. Remove the rings from the refrigerator and dust the insides with the bread-crumb mixture, reserving the extra for sprinkling over the tops of the cakes. Place the rings on a parchment-lined baking sheet and set aside.

Turn the oven up to 350 degrees.

To prepare the batter: In a small saucepan, over medium-high heat, melt the butter with the milk and set aside to cool.

Sift to combine the flour, baking powder, ground ginger, and white pepper.

In the bowl of an electric mixer fitted with the whisk attachment, beat the eggs and brown sugar on medium until thickened, about 3 to 5 minutes. Turn the mixer to low and add the molasses and fresh ginger, mixing until combined. Add the dry ingredients alternately with the butter mixture, in 2 batches, mixing until combined. The batter will be fairly thin.

Pour the batter into the cake rings to two-thirds full. Sprinkle about 2 tablespoons of the crumb mixture over the tops of each.

Bake for 25 to 30 minutes, until not quite firm to the touch.

Yield: 10 small cakes

Madeleines

THIS CLASSIC FRENCH CAKE (THOUGH SOME WOULD ARGUE IT'S A COOKIE) IS recognized by its scalloped shell shape on one side and its protruding hump on the other side. You must have a Madeleine mold to call it a Madeleine; otherwise, it's just a cake. Steel molds will give you a better crust than the Teflon variety; however, like a cast-iron pan, they will rust if not properly cared for.

This chapter includes three varieties of this spongy, light cake: traditional, Chocolate (page 41), and Spiced (page 43). For a superior Madeleine, make the batter I day ahead. If you have any leftover cakes, dry them out, grind them in your food processor and freeze them to use for the Crumb Biscotti (page 120).

Special Items: 1 TO 2 MADELEINE MOLDS, HEAVILY COATED WITH MELTED BUTTER
PASTRY BAG FITTED WITH A #3 TIP, OPTIONAL

1½ sticks plus 2 tablespoons (7 ounces) unsalted butter
1 vanilla bean
3 tablespoons finely chopped lemon zest (about 2 or 3 lemons)
3 tablespoons (1 ounce) whole blanched almonds
1 cup plus 2 tablespoons granulated sugar
4 extra-large eggs
1 extra-large egg yolk
1½ cups plus 2 tablespoons unbleached pastry flour or unbleached all-purpose flour
1 tablespoon plus 2 teaspoons baking powder

In a medium saucepan, over medium-high heat, begin to melt the butter. Using a small paring knife, split the vanilla bean lengthwise and with the back of the knife, scrape out the pulp and the seeds and add the scrapings and the pod to the butter. When the butter begins to bubble, remove from the heat. Add the lemon zest and set aside. Remove the vanilla bean.

In the bowl of a food processor fitted with the steel blade, combine the nuts with 2 tablespoons of the sugar and process until it's the consistency of a fine meal. Set aside.

In the bowl of an electric mixer fitted with the whisk attachment, whip the whole eggs and egg yolk with the remaining sugar on medium-high, 5 to 8 minutes, until thick and mousselike.

Meanwhile, over a medium bowl, sift to combine the flour, baking powder, and ground nut mixture. If any nuts remain in the sifter, add them back to the flour mixture.

Remove the bowl from the mixer. In 3 additions, gently fold the flour mixture into the eggs, deflating the batter as little as possible.

Transfer approximately 2 cups of the batter to a medium mixing bowl. Whisk in the melted butter until thoroughly incorporated. Gently fold the two batters together to combine.

Chill at least 24 hours or up to 3 days.

Adjust the oven rack to the upper position and preheat the oven to 375 degrees.

Pipe or spoon the batter into the prepared molds, completely filling each section to the top.

Bake 12 to 18 minutes, until lightly browned and springy to the touch.

Allow to cool a few minutes before unmolding, and place on a platter scalloped side down.

Yield: 18 to 30 cakes, depending on the size of your molds

Chocolate Madeleines

IF YOU HAVE ANY LEFTOVER CAKES, DRY THEM OUT, GRIND THEM IN YOUR FOOD processor, and freeze them to use for the Bobka Muffins (page 197) and Russian Coffee Cake (page 284).

Special Items: 1 TO 2 MADELEINE MOLDS, HEAVILY COATED WITH MELTED BUTTER
PASTRY BAG FITTED WITH A #3 TIP, OPTIONAL

½ cup water
¼ cup unsweetened imported cocoa powder
3 ounces bittersweet chocolate, melted according to the instructions on page 7
2 teaspoons pure vanilla extract
¾ stick (3 ounces) unsalted butter, softened
¼ cup plus 3 tablespoons crème fraîche or sour cream
2 extra-large eggs
1 extra-large egg yolk
¾ cup granulated sugar
1 cup plus 5 tablespoons unbleached pastry flour or unbleached all-purpose flour
1½ teaspoons baking soda
1 teaspoon baking powder
½ teaspoon kosher salt

In a small saucepan over medium heat, whisk together the water and cocoa powder. Bring to a boil, whisking constantly. Remove from the heat and whisk in the chocolate, vanilla extract, and butter. Stir in the crème fraîche and set aside.

In the bowl of an electric mixer fitted with the whisk attachment, whip the whole eggs and egg yolk with the sugar on medium-high, 5 to 8 minutes, until thick and mousselike. Remove the bowl from the mixer and whisk in the chocolate mixture.

Over a medium mixing bowl, sift to combine the flour, baking soda, baking powder, and salt. In 3 additions, gently fold the flour mixture into the egg mixture, deflating the batter as little as possible.

Chill at least 24 hours or up to 3 days.

Adjust the oven rack to the upper position and preheat the oven to 375 degrees.

Pipe or spoon the batter into the prepared molds, completely filling each section to the top.

Bake 12 to 18 minutes, until springy to the touch.

Allow to cool a few minutes before unmolding. Place on a platter, scalloped side down.

Yield: 18 to 30 cakes, depending on the size of your molds

Spiced Madeleines

Special Items: 1 TO 2 MADELEINE MOLDS, HEAVILY COATED WITH MELTED BUTTER
PASTRY BAG FITTED WITH A #3 TIP, OPTIONAL

1½ sticks plus 2 tablespoons (7 ounces) unsalted butter, cut into 1-inch cubes
¾ teaspoon kosher salt
1 tablespoon ground cinnamon
1 tablespoon ground cardamom
½ teaspoon freshly grated nutmeg
Pinch of ground cloves
4 extra-large eggs
1 extra-large egg yolk
1 cup light brown sugar, lightly packed
¼ cup plus 2 tablespoons mild-flavored honey, such as clover
1½ cups plus 2 tablespoons unbleached pastry flour or unbleached all-purpose flour
1 tablespoon plus 2 teaspoons baking powder

In a small saucepan over medium heat, melt the butter with the salt, cinnamon, cardamom, nutmeg, and cloves. When the butter begins to bubble, remove from the heat.

In the bowl of an electric mixer fitted with the whisk attachment, whip the whole eggs, egg yolk, brown sugar, and honey on medium-high about 5 to 8 minutes, until thick and mousselike.

Meanwhile, over a medium bowl, sift to combine the flour and baking powder.

Remove the bowl from the mixer. In 3 additions, gently fold the flour mixture into the egg mixture, deflating the batter as little as possible.

Transfer approximately 2 cups of the batter to a medium mixing bowl. Whisk in the melted butter until thoroughly incorporated. Gently fold the two batters together to combine.

Chill at least 24 hours or up to 3 days.

Adjust the oven rack to the upper position and preheat the oven to 375 degrees.

Pipe or spoon the batter into the prepared molds, completely filling each section to the top.

Bake 12 to 18 minutes, until lightly browned and springy to the touch.

Allow to cool a few minutes before unmolding, and place on a platter, scalloped side down.

Yield: 18 to 30 cakes, depending on the size of your molds

Mini Maple Bundt Cakes

LIKE THE SYRUP, MAPLE SUGAR (SEE "SOURCES," PAGE 393) IS MADE FROM THE boiled sap of a maple tree. In a pinch, you can substitute brown sugar, though the cakes won't have that same mapley, earthy sweetness. And if you do use brown sugar or a different mold, you'll just have to change the name.

Special Item: 13 MINI BUNDT PANS OR DECORATIVE MOLDS (SEE "SOURCES," PAGE 393), 7-OUNCE CAPACITY, LIGHTLY COATED WITH MELTED BUTTER

FOR THE BATTER:
1 cup (4 ounces) walnuts
4 sticks (1 pound) unsalted butter, chilled and cut into 1-inch cubes
2 teaspoons baking soda
1 tablespoon baking powder
2 cups maple sugar or brown sugar
10 extra-large egg yolks
¾ cup crème fraîche or sour cream
3 cups unbleached pastry flour or unbleached all-purpose flour
10 extra-large egg whites

FOR THE GLAZE:
¼ cup pure maple syrup
1 cup powdered sugar
2 teaspoons instant coffee mixed with 1 teaspoon water

Adjust the oven rack to the middle position and preheat the oven to 325 degrees.

Spread the walnuts on a baking sheet and toast in the oven until lightly browned, about 10 to 12 minutes. Shake the pan halfway through to ensure that the nuts toast evenly. Cool, chop finely, and set aside.

Turn the oven up to 350 degrees.

In the bowl of an electric mixer fitted with the paddle attachment, cream the butter, baking soda, and baking powder for 2 to 3 minutes on low, until softened. Add the maple sugar and turn the mixer up to medium and mix for 3 to 4 minutes, until light and fluffy, scraping down the sides of the bowl as needed. Turn the mixer to low and add the egg yolks, one at a time. Turn the mixer up to medium and continue to mix for another minute until well combined. Add the crème fraîche and mix on low until just combined.

Add the flour in 3 batches, turning the mixer off before each addition and mixing on low until just combined. Transfer the batter to a large bowl and set aside.

Thoroughly wash and dry the bowl of the electric mixer. Using the whisk attachment, whip the egg whites on low until frothy. Turn the mixer up to medium and beat until soft peaks form, about 2 to 3 minutes. Increase the speed to high and beat another minute or two, until stiff but not dry.

Quickly stir half of the egg whites into the batter to combine. Fold in the remaining whites. Pour into the prepared molds to one-third full. Sprinkle 1 tablespoon of the chopped nuts over the batter and spoon more batter in to fill the molds to three-quarters full. Place the molds 1 inch apart on a baking sheet.

Bake for about 30 minutes, until firm to the touch. Allow the cakes to cool. Remove them from the molds and invert them onto a work surface.

To prepare the glaze: In a small bowl, combine the maple syrup, powdered sugar, and coffee.

Dip the fingers of one hand into the glaze. Holding your hand just above the cake, quickly move your hand back and forth to drizzle the glaze over the surface, allowing it to run down the sides. Continue with the remaining cakes.

Yield: 13 small cakes

Sticky Toffee Pudding

I KEPT COMING ACROSS THIS ODD-SOUNDING ENGLISH DESSERT. JUST THE NAME itself conjured up the exact type of dessert I would never eat, too sweet and sticky. I ventured to try a few recipes from various British magazines, but the results were awful. Intuitively, I knew there had to be a better recipe out there. Finally, when I was introduced to Tamara Milstein, an Australian cookbook writer, the first thing I asked her was, "Do you have a good recipe for sticky toffee pudding?"

Don't be confused by the name *pudding*, a term the English use for all desserts. Similar to carrot cake, the texture is super-moist and filled with supple chunks of dates. Self-rising flour has a prescribed amount of leavening added to it, and is available at many supermarkets.

Special Item: 14 SMALL BRIOCHE MOLDS, ½-CUP CAPACITY, OR OTHER DECORATIVE MOLDS (SEE "SOURCES," PAGE 393), OR ONE 10-INCH SPRINGFORM PAN, LIGHTLY COATED WITH MELTED BUTTER

FOR THE BATTER:
7 large, soft Medjool dates
1 teaspoon baking soda
1¼ cups water
½ stick (2 ounces) unsalted butter, chilled and cut into 1-inch cubes
1 cup dark brown sugar, lightly packed
2 extra-large eggs, lightly beaten
1¼ cups plus 1½ tablespoons self-rising flour
1 tablespoon pure vanilla extract

FOR THE TOFFEE SAUCE:
4 tablespoons plus 2 teaspoons (2.6 ounces) unsalted butter
1 vanilla bean
1 cup heavy cream
1 cup dark brown sugar, lightly packed

Adjust the oven rack to the middle position and preheat the oven to 350 degrees. Cut the dates in half, remove the pits, and slice them into thirds. Place them in a

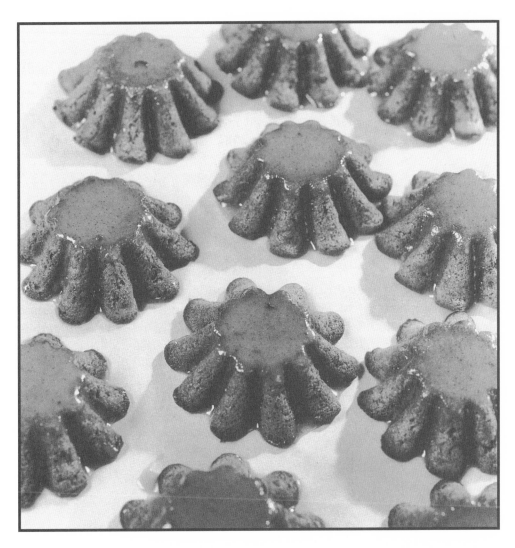

small bowl. In a small saucepan, combine the baking soda with the water and bring to a boil. Pour the liquid over the dates and allow them to cool.

In the bowl of an electric mixer fitted with the paddle attachment, cream the butter on low, 2 to 3 minutes, until softened. Add the brown sugar and mix on medium for 3 to 4 minutes, until light and fluffy, scraping down the sides of the bowl as needed.

Add the eggs a few teaspoons at a time, mixing on medium-low until incorporated. Turn the mixer to low and add the flour, mixing until combined.

Remove the bowl from the mixer and stir in the date mixture and vanilla extract. The mixture will be thin. Fill the prepared molds three-quarters full, stirring the batter between each spoonful to incorporate the dates. Place the molds 1 inch apart on a baking sheet.

Bake for about 30 to 35 minutes until spongy, slightly firm to the touch, and nicely browned. Allow the cakes to cool and invert them onto a flat surface.

To prepare the toffee sauce: In a small saucepan, over medium-low heat, begin to melt the butter. Using a small paring knife, split the vanilla bean lengthwise and with the back of the knife, scrape out the pulp and seeds, and add the scrapings and pod to the butter.

When the butter is melted, stir in the cream and brown sugar and bring to a boil. Turn the heat down to a low simmer. Stirring frequently, continue to simmer for about 5 minutes, until thickened and a bit sticky. Set aside to cool slightly. Remove the vanilla bean.

Spoon about 1 tablespoon of the warm toffee sauce over each cake, allowing it to run over the sides.

Yield: 12 small cakes

Summer Camp Coffee Cake

IF YOU EVER WENT TO SUMMER CAMP OR ATE AT YOUR JUNIOR HIGH SCHOOL cafeteria, you will definitely recognize this coffee cake when you see it. Probably made from a mix, those old-time cakes were baked in deep baking pans, cut into giant wedges, and always served warm. This homemade version will give you a whole new perspective. It's delicious!

Special Item: 13 × 9 × 2½-INCH BAKING DISH, LIGHTLY COATED WITH
                   MELTED BUTTER

FOR THE STREUSEL:
1½ cups (6 ounces) walnuts
¼ cup granulated sugar
¼ cup light brown sugar, lightly packed

FOR THE BATTER:
2 sticks (8 ounces) unsalted butter, chilled and cut into 1-inch cubes
1¾ teaspoons baking soda
2 teaspoons baking powder
2 teaspoons kosher salt
2½ cups granulated sugar
4 cups unbleached all-purpose flour
3 extra-large eggs, lightly beaten
2 cups sour cream

To prepare the streusel: Adjust the oven rack to the middle position and preheat the oven to 325 degrees. Spread the nuts on a baking sheet and toast in the oven until lightly browned, about 10 to 12 minutes. Shake the pan halfway through to ensure that the nuts toast evenly. Cool and chop finely. In a small bowl, combine the walnuts and sugars and set aside.

Turn the oven up to 350 degrees.

To prepare the batter: In the bowl of an electric mixer fitted with the paddle attachment, cream the butter, baking soda, baking powder, and salt on low, 2 to 3 minutes, until softened. Add the sugar and mix on medium for 3 to 4 minutes, until light and fluffy, scraping down the sides of the bowl as needed.

Turn the mixer to low and add the flour and the eggs alternately, in 3 batches. Mix until just combined. Stir in the sour cream.

Spoon half of the batter into the prepared pan and spread to even. Sprinkle half of the streusel over the batter. Pour the remaining batter over the streusel and sprinkle the surface with the remaining streusel.

Bake for 45 minutes, until firm to the touch and the topping is nicely browned and crunchy.

Yield: 10 to 12 servings

Thimble Cakes

THESE PERFECT ONE-BITE CAKES ARE MOIST AND RICH AND NUTTY. LIKE CAPEZ-zana Tiny Olive Oil Cakes (page 23), they're best baked in small molds for a crisp crust and tender cake.

Special Item: SEVERAL DECORATIVE MOLDS, ¼-CUP CAPACITY, LIGHTLY COATED
WITH MELTED BUTTER

1 stick (4 ounces) unsalted butter
1 vanilla bean
1 cup (5 ounces) unblanched almonds
1 cup granulated sugar
½ cup unbleached pastry flour or unbleached all-purpose flour
1¼ teaspoons kosher salt
6 extra-large egg whites

Adjust the oven rack to the middle position and preheat the oven to 350 degrees.

In a medium saucepan, over medium-high heat, begin to melt the butter. Using a small paring knife, split the vanilla bean lengthwise and with the back of the knife, scrape out the pulp and the seeds and add the scrapings and the pod to the butter. Swirl the pan to ensure the butter cooks evenly and doesn't burn. It will bubble somewhat vigorously as it browns. Continue cooking another 3 to 5 minutes until the bubbles subside and the liquid is dark brown with a nutty, toasty aroma. Remove the vanilla bean. Pour the butter and dark flecks into a medium bowl, whisking to help cool the butter.

In the bowl of a food processor fitted with the steel blade, combine the almonds with half of the sugar and process until it's the consistency of a fine meal. Add the flour and salt, and pulse to combine.

In the bowl of an electric mixer fitted with the whisk attachment, whip the egg whites on low until frothy. Turn the mixer up to medium-high and beat another 2 to 3 minutes, until soft peaks form. Turn the mixer to high and gradually add the remaining sugar and beat until shiny and stiff, about 2 to 3 more minutes.

Remove the bowl from the mixer. Gently fold the flour mixture into the egg whites in 3 additions, deflating the batter as little as possible.

Transfer about one-third of the batter into the browned butter and whisk until thoroughly incorporated. Gently fold the two batters together to combine. Pour the batter into the prepared molds, filling to just below the tops. Place the molds ¾ inch apart on a baking sheet.

Bake for about 20 minutes, until slightly firm to the touch and nicely browned.

Yield: 16 small cakes

Y2K Fig Cake

WHEN THE PRODUCERS FROM *GOOD FOOD*, A LOCAL PUBLIC RADIO SHOW, ASKED me to submit a dessert recipe for the Y2K, this wonderful no-need-to-bake Spanish fig cake came to mind. With no electricity and no ovens, this simple sweet cake would be the perfect finish to that unpredictable New Year's candlelight meal.

In this compact, delicious cake, a layer of whole almonds is sandwiched between layers of sliced black figs and white figs, all held together by honey and flavored with anise and a hint of fresh rosemary. Be sure to use only very soft dried figs; if they're too dry the layers won't adhere to each other. I use a 4-inch flan ring to layer the figs and nuts, but almost any mold will work. Try a pie pan, or a tuna fish can with the top and bottom cut out, or even a cereal bowl. Depending on the size of your mold, you'll have to calculate the exact amount of ingredients you'll need. In preparation for the big night, I cheated a little and pretoasted the almonds and seeds. Of course, by the time you're reading this, the Y2K scare is long over and hopefully your kitchen is back to normal working order. Make lots of these fig cakes and keep them unrefrigerated indefinitely for the Y3K.

About ⅓ cup (1½ ounces) whole unblanched almonds
1 teaspoon anise seeds
2 tablespoons sesame seeds
16 (4 to 5 ounces) dried black mission figs, very soft, with stems removed
8 to 10 (4 to 5 ounces) dried, large white kadota figs, very soft with stems removed
2 tablespoons honey
1 teaspoon finely chopped fresh rosemary

Adjust the oven rack to the middle position and preheat the oven to 325 degrees.

Spread the almonds on a baking sheet and toast in the oven until lightly browned, about 12 to 15 minutes. Shake the pan halfway through to ensure that the nuts toast evenly.

In a small sauté pan, over medium-low heat, toast the anise and sesame seeds, stirring occasionally until the anise becomes aromatic and the seeds turn slightly brown, about 2 to 3 minutes. Allow to cool and coarsely chop.

Line the mold with plastic wrap, leaving enough plastic hanging over the edges to cover the cake once it's in the mold.

Slice the figs vertically into thirds or halves (depending on the size of the fig), about ¼ inch thick. Set the figs aside, keeping the 2 colors separate. Press a solid layer of the black mission fig slices on the bottom of the ring, seed side down. Sprinkle the figs with about one-third of the anise and one-third of the sesame seeds, and drizzle about 1½ teaspoons of honey over. Sprinkle the rosemary over the honey. Cover with a layer of the white fig slices, sprinkle with half of the remaining anise seeds, and drizzle with 1½ teaspoons of the honey. Press a layer of almonds over the figs and drizzle another 1½ teaspoons of the honey over the nuts. Press on the final layer of white fig slices, sprinkle the remaining anise and sesame seeds, and drizzle with the remaining honey. For the top, layer with the remaining black figs, seed side up. Cover with the overhanging plastic wrap. Place a very heavy object on top, like a heavy cast-iron skillet filled with canned food. Allow to stand for about 2 hours, until the cake is compressed.

Yield: One 4-inch cake

2. *Savories*

Whenever I'm in Europe, I scout the neighborhood bakeries, peering into windows and poking my head through doors, searching for inspiration and that comforting indulgence of something homey, something baked. In America, bakeries are usually crowded with platters of cookies, trays of cakes, and rows of sweet rolls—not a salty snack in sight. When I go to a bakery, it's not always my sweet tooth I'm trying to satisfy. Thankfully, in Europe, amidst the shelves filled with creamy éclairs and fruit tarts, there are always a few savory morsels to admire and devour. Though the choices may not be as abundant as their sugary companions, it's clear that the same care and attention went into their preparation. In keeping with that tradition, at La Brea Bakery you'll find plenty of savories to tempt you among the many shelves of breads and sweets.

If you like to bake and you like to eat, this is the chapter for you. Cheeses, cured meats, vegetables, eggs, and herbs are the stuff savories are made of. Here's your opportunity to combine your baking wizardry with some very basic cooking skills. You'll caramelize onions, oven-dry tomatoes, grate some Parmesan cheese, and cream a few ears of corn. Whether shaped into a cracker, baked in a brioche, or layered in puff pastry, these savory pastries, buttery, rich, and irresistible, are the way to my heart.

Served straight from the oven or eaten later at room temperature, savories make the perfect quick snack, picnic food, or pass-around finger foods. With the addition of a small green salad, a healthy and filling meal is in the making.

Asparagus–Egg Pie with Potato Crust

An infinite number of possibilities and combinations will work in this tasty, quichelike savory. Just because I prefer asparagus, that's no reason for you to stop there. Crisp bacon, salmon with fresh dill, roasted vegetables, artichoke hearts, or whole raw spinach leaves are some of my other favorites. As long as you have the correct ratio of custard to ingredients, it's foolproof!

Use the extra garlic oil to marinate meats and vegetables or to dress a salad.

Special Item: 9-INCH ROUND BAKING DISH, LIGHTLY COATED WITH
MELTED BUTTER

FOR THE CRUST:
2 to 3 russet potatoes (1 pound)
¼ teaspoon kosher salt
Freshly ground black pepper, to taste

FOR THE CUSTARD:
¾ cup whole milk
¾ cup heavy cream
¼ teaspoon cayenne pepper
1 teaspoon kosher salt
3 extra-large eggs
2 extra-large egg yolks
3 tablespoons crème fraîche or sour cream
¾ cup (3 ounces) grated Parmesan Reggiano cheese
1 cup (4 ounces) grated Gruyère or Comte cheese
2 tablespoons finely chopped fresh thyme

FOR THE PIE:
18 small to medium whole garlic cloves, peeled
¾ cup extra-virgin olive oil
1 teaspoon lemon zest (about ½ lemon)
16 fresh asparagus stalks, trimmed of the tough ends
¼ teaspoon kosher salt

Freshly ground black pepper, to taste
1 tablespoon (½ ounce) unsalted butter, softened

Adjust the oven rack to the middle position and preheat the oven to 400 degrees.

Place the potatoes directly on the oven rack and bake until cooked all the way through, about 45 minutes to an hour. Allow to cool. Peel the potatoes and mash them with a fork.

To prepare the crust: Using your fingers, press the mashed potatoes into the bottom and sides of the prepared pan. Sprinkle with ¼ teaspoon of the salt and the pepper, and bake for about 15 minutes, until dry.

To prepare the custard: In a medium saucepan over medium-high heat, bring the milk, cream, cayenne, and 1 teaspoon of the salt to a boil. Remove from the heat and allow to cool for about 10 minutes.

In a small bowl, whisk together the whole eggs and egg yolks.

Add the crème fraîche, Parmesan, and Gruyère to the milk mixture, whisking to incorporate. Slowly whisk in the eggs and sprinkle in the thyme. Set aside.

In a small saucepan over medium heat, combine the garlic cloves, olive oil, and lemon zest, and bring to a simmer. Reduce the heat and continue to cook just below a simmer, until the garlic is tender all the way through when pierced with a knife, about 20 minutes. (If the oil begins to boil, remove the pan from the heat for 1 to 2 minutes to cool, reduce the heat, and then return the pan to the heat until the garlic is tender.) Strain the garlic, set aside, and reserve 2 tablespoons of the oil for the asparagus, setting the rest aside for another use.

Place the asparagus in a roasting pan, toss with the garlic oil, and sprinkle with the ¼ teaspoon salt and pepper. Roast for about 10 minutes, until cooked but still slightly firm.

Cool and slice 12 of the asparagus stalks into 1-inch pieces.

Evenly distribute the garlic cloves and asparagus in the crust, reserving the tips. Pour the custard over and dot with butter. Arrange the tips in a starburst pattern on top.

Place the dish on a baking sheet, and bake for 50 to 60 minutes until set.

Yield: 8 to 10 servings

Buttermilk Crackers

Homemade crackers are so easy to make, I can't give you a good enough excuse not to make them. For a perfectly shaped cracker, cut the dough with a cutter into individual-sized squares or rounds. Or bake them in sheets and when cool, break them into uneven shards. For an eye-catching assortment, sprinkle some with seeds and others with coarse sea salt.

Special Items: 2½-INCH ROUND CUTTER, OPTIONAL
PIZZA WHEEL, OPTIONAL

3½ cups unbleached pastry flour or unbleached all-purpose flour
2 tablespoons granulated sugar
¾ teaspoon baking powder
½ teaspoon kosher salt
1 stick plus 2 tablespoons (5 ounces) butter, chilled and cut into 1-inch cubes
1¼ cups buttermilk

FOR SPRINKLING:
Fennel, anise, cumin, poppy, sesame, dill, mustard, flax, or caraway seeds, optional
Kosher salt
Freshly ground black pepper

In the bowl of a food processor fitted with the steel blade, combine the flour, sugar, baking powder, and salt, and pulse a few times to incorporate. Add the butter and pulse on and off until it's the consistency of a fine meal.

Transfer the mixture to a large bowl and make a well in the center. Pour in the buttermilk and using one hand, draw in the dry ingredients, mixing until just combined. The mixture will be sticky.

Wash and dry your hands and dust them with flour. Turn the dough out onto a lightly floured work surface and knead a few times to gather into a ball. Wrap in plastic and chill until firm, at least 3 hours or overnight.

Cut the dough into quarters and return three pieces to the refrigerator. Dust the surface of the dough with flour, and on a heavily floured surface, roll the dough out to $\frac{1}{16}$-inch thickness. You should be able to see the color of the countertop through the dough.

Dust the surface of the dough with flour and roll it around a rolling pin to transfer it. Place the rolling pin over a parchment-lined baking sheet to unroll. Using the tines of a fork, dock the surface of the dough several times to prevent it from rising. Chill until firm, about half an hour. Repeat with the remaining pieces of dough, rolling out only as much dough as you have baking sheets.

Adjust the oven racks to the upper and lower positions and preheat the oven to 350 degrees.

Use a cutter to cut the dough into individual shapes or leave in one big sheet or score the sheet into $3\frac{1}{2}$-inch squares or triangles. Chill for about 10 to 15 minutes. Brush or spray lightly with water and sprinkle on your choice of seeds and salt and pepper.

Bake two baking sheets of crackers at a time, for 25 to 30 minutes, until lightly browned and crispy. Halfway through baking, rotate the baking sheets to ensure the crackers evenly bake.

Allow to cool. Break sheets into uneven shards or, if scored, break along the score marks.

Yield: 1½ pounds crackers

Cheese Coins

Most often known as cheese crackers, cheese wafers, or cheese thins, these are my version of that classic savory snack. For a more pungent flavor, I use a ripe English Stilton to replace the Cheddar. For a variety of shapes, form the dough into rectangular logs or round logs. Coat them with an assortment of seeds and spices to add color and texture. Store the logs in the freezer, ready to slice and bake whenever you like.

3 sticks plus 1 tablespoon (12½ ounces) unsalted butter, chilled and cut into 1-inch cubes
1 tablespoon kosher salt
Pinch of dried chili flakes
4½ cups unbleached pastry flour or unbleached all-purpose flour
1 cup crème fraîche or sour cream
1 cup (4 ounces) grated Parmesan Reggiano cheese
1 cup (4 ounces) grated white Cheddar cheese or Stilton
¾ cup (3 ounces) grated Pecorino Romano or Gruyère cheese

FOR THE COATING:
1 extra-large egg white, lightly beaten
¼ cup polenta or finely ground cornmeal, optional
¼ cup coarsely ground black pepper, optional
¼ cup paprika, optional
¼ cup seeds such as fennel, sesame, or caraway, optional

In the bowl of an electric mixer fitted with the paddle attachment, cream the butter, salt, and chili flakes on low, 2 to 3 minutes, until softened. Turn the mixer up to medium and continue to mix another 2 minutes, scraping down the sides of the bowl as needed. Turn the mixer off, add the flour, and mix on low until it's the consistency of a coarse meal.

Add the crème fraîche and grated cheeses, mixing until the dough just comes together.

Turn the dough out onto a lightly floured work surface and knead a few times to gather it together. Divide the dough into three pieces and flatten it into rectangles, about 1 inch thick. Wrap in plastic and chill until firm enough to shape, about an hour.

Working with one piece of dough at a time, drop each side of the rectangle against the work surface to help compress the dough and eliminate air pockets. For rectangular crackers: Shape the dough into a rectangular bar, 1½ inches wide and 8 inches long, packing and compressing the sides. For round crackers: Working from the center out, roll the dough into tight circular logs, about 1½ inches in diameter and 8 inches long. Wrap each log in plastic and chill in the freezer for about 2 hours, until very firm.

Adjust the oven rack to the middle position and preheat the oven to 350 degrees.

Keeping each type of coating separate, spread them on a work surface. Brush the logs with egg white and roll each log in a different coating to cover. Place the logs on a cutting board and using a very sharp knife, cut into ⅛-inch-thick slices. Place them ½ inch apart on a parchment-lined baking sheet. If you don't want to slice and bake all of the dough, wrap the logs in plastic and store in the freezer.

Bake for 10 to 15 minutes, until very lightly browned and crisp.

Yield: 6 to 7 dozen coins

Cheese Croissants

CHEESE CROISSANTS ARE A CINCH IF YOU HAVE YOUR DOUGH MADE AHEAD OF time. Never heavy or greasy, this savory is stuffed with a lemony ricotta filling and sprinkled with poppy seeds. It's light, delicious, and irresistible.

FOR THE FILLING:
1½ cups (12 ounces) ricotta cheese
¼ cup plus 2 tablespoons crème fraîche or sour cream
2 tablespoons finely chopped lemon zest (about 2 lemons)
¼ cup granulated sugar

1 recipe Croissant dough (see page 294), chilled for at least 3 hours
1 extra-large egg, lightly beaten

FOR THE TOPPING:
1 tablespoon plus ½ teaspoon poppy seeds

To prepare the filling: In a medium bowl, stir together the ricotta, crème fraîche or sour cream, lemon zest, and sugar, and set aside.

Divide the dough into quarters and work with one quarter at a time, returning the rest to the refrigerator. On a lightly floured work surface, roll the dough out to a long rectangle slightly larger than 17 × 4½ inches, ¼ inch thick, pulling out the edges and corners to maintain the rectangle. Trim the edges even and cut three equal pieces, 5–6 inches each.

Working with 1 piece of dough at a time, place the longer side parallel to the edge of the counter and spoon 2 tablespoons of filling into the center. Shape the filling into a 4-inch rope and brush the top and bottom edges of the dough with the beaten egg.

Bring the top and bottom edges up to meet in the middle above the filling. Pinch the 2 edges together to seal, being careful that the filling doesn't come out. Invert it seam side down on a parchment-lined baking sheet. Flatten slightly with the palm of your hand. Continue with the remaining rectangles, placing them about 2 inches apart on the baking sheet.

Using a razor blade or sharp knife, score five ½-inch-deep diagonal lines across the top of each croissant and set aside in a warm place to proof until slightly puffy and spongy to the touch, about 2 hours. Continue with the remaining dough.

Adjust the oven racks to the upper and lower positions and preheat the oven to 425 degrees.

Brush the surface of each croissant with the remainder of the beaten egg and sprinkle with ¼ teaspoon of poppy seeds. Steam the oven according to the directions on page 295.

Bake for 35 minutes, until lightly browned, rotating the baking sheets halfway through to ensure even baking.

Yield: 12 croissants

Country Feta Pies

THE SALTY FETA CHEESE BRIGHTENS UP THESE RUSTIC LITTLE PIES. BAKED IN individual crusts, these tasty savories are just right for a quick-grab breakfast or lunch on the run.

Special Items: 3¹/₂-INCH ROUND CUTTER
TWO ¹/₂-CUP-CAPACITY MUFFIN TINS, LIGHTLY COATED WITH
MELTED BUTTER
PARCHMENT PAPER OR COFFEE FILTERS, CUT INTO 18 TO 20
3¹/₂-INCH CIRCLES TO FIT THE INSIDE OF THE MUFFIN CUPS
METAL PIE WEIGHTS OR DRIED BEANS (SEE "SOURCES," PAGE 393)

FOR THE DOUGH:
4 cups unbleached pastry flour or unbleached all-purpose flour
2 teaspoons kosher salt
4 sticks (1 pound) unsalted butter, chilled and cut into 1-inch cubes
2 extra-large eggs
4 extra-large egg yolks
1 tablespoon unsalted butter, melted, for brushing

FOR THE FILLING:
1 onion, coarsely chopped to equal 1¹/₂ cups
2 tablespoons extra-virgin olive oil
1¹/₂ cups heavy cream
6 extra-large eggs
Kosher salt, to taste
Freshly ground black pepper, to taste
¹/₂ cup (4 ounces) feta cheese, preferably Valbreso or Bulgarian, crumbled

In the bowl of a food processor fitted with a steel blade or in the bowl of an electric mixer fitted with the paddle attachment, combine the flour and salt and pulse, or mix on low, to combine. Add the butter and process or mix on low until it's the consistency of a fine meal.

In a small bowl, whisk together the whole eggs and egg yolks. Add to the flour mixture and pulse a few times, or mix on low, until the dough barely comes together.

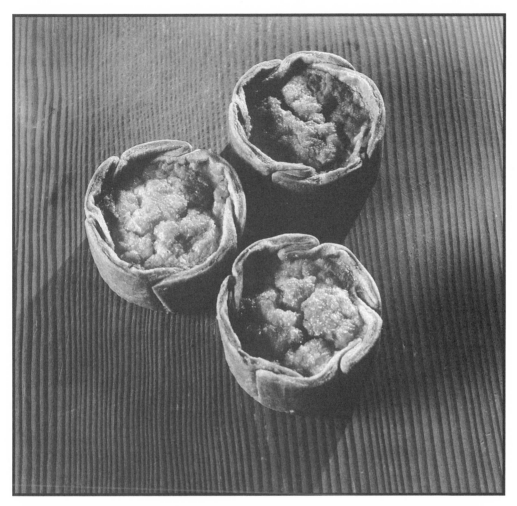

COUNTRY FETA PIES: "JUST RIGHT FOR A QUICK-GRAB
BREAKFAST OR LUNCH ON THE RUN."

Turn the dough out onto a lightly floured work surface. Dip the heel of your hand in flour and, working with small sections at a time, smear the dough away from you to blend it together. When the dough has been all smeared out, scrape and gather it together using a metal spatula. Knead a few times to gather into a ball and flatten into a 2-inch-thick disk. Wrap in plastic to chill until firm, at least 2 hours.

Divide the dough in half and return half to the refrigerator. On a lightly floured surface, roll the dough out to a circle, ¼ inch thick. Cutting as closely together as possible, cut out 18 to 20 circles and place them in the prepared muffin tins. You may need to gather the scraps to reroll and cut out. Using your fingers, gently press the circles of dough into the muffin cups, pleating the dough when necessary, to ensure that they fit snugly. Chill for about half an hour, until firm. Continue with the remaining dough.

Adjust the oven racks to the upper and lower positions and preheat the oven to 350 degrees.

Lightly brush the dough with melted butter and line each section of dough with the cut-out circles of parchment paper. Fill the lining up to the top rim of the dough with metal pie weights or dried beans and bake for about 25 minutes, until lightly browned.

Meanwhile, in a small sauté pan over medium-low heat, sauté the onion in the oil until softened, but not colored, about 3 to 4 minutes. Set aside to cool.

In a medium mixing bowl, whisk together the cream, eggs, salt, and pepper.

Remove the paper and weights or beans from the pie shells. Fill each shell with $\frac{1}{4}$ cup of the cream mixture, to just below the top edge of the tin. Spoon a heaping tablespoon of the onion and crumble 1 tablespoon of feta cheese into each.

Bake for 20 minutes, until the crust is browned and the custard is set, rotating the cups halfway through to ensure even baking.

Yield: 18 to 20 individual pies

Creamed Cornbread

CREAMING FRESH CORN, BY GRATING IT AND COOKING IT WITH BUTTER, ADDS extra moisture and incredible flavor to this American classic. Bake it and serve directly from the cast-iron skillet for big hearty hunks of cornbread. For a daintier cornbread, bake it in individual servings by using small molds or mini poundcake tins. Place a small sage leaf on the bottom of the mold before filling it with batter. This prevents the leaf from drying out in the oven and preserves the color and the texture of the sage for an elegant finish when served leaf side up.

Special Item: 12-INCH CAST-IRON SKILLET OR SEVERAL ¼- TO ½-CUP
INDIVIDUAL MOLDS, LIGHTLY COATED WITH MELTED BUTTER

3 ears of corn, shucked and cut in half
2 sticks (8 ounces) unsalted butter, plus 2 tablespoons for brushing on top
4 large fresh sage leaves, plus several smaller leaves if you are using individual molds
1 tablespoon plus 1 teaspoon kosher salt, to taste
1½ cups coarsely ground yellow cornmeal
4 cups plus 4 tablespoons unbleached pastry flour or unbleached all-purpose flour
1 teaspoon baking soda
4 teaspoons baking powder
¼ cup plus 2 tablespoons granulated sugar
4 extra-large eggs
1¾ cups buttermilk

Adjust the oven rack to the middle position and preheat the oven to 450 degrees.

Using the largest round hole on a grater, grate the corn into a medium bowl to remove as much of the creamy kernels as possible without grating the cob. Turn the cob upside-down to grate in the opposite direction, removing the rest of the kernels. Stir the liquid and kernels together, measure 1 cup, and set aside.

In a medium saucepan over low heat, melt 2 sticks of the butter; do not allow it to boil. Add the measured corn, 4 large sage leaves, and salt and cook until creamy and thickened, about 5 to 7 minutes, stirring constantly to prevent sticking. Allow to cool, then remove and discard the sage leaves.

In a large bowl, sift together the cornmeal, flour, baking soda, baking powder, and sugar. Make a well in the center and pour in the eggs, buttermilk, and corn mixture. Whisk the liquids together and slowly begin to draw in the dry ingredients, whisking until combined.

Pour the batter into the prepared skillet. For the small breads, place a sage leaf in each of the molds, pour in the batter two-thirds full, place on a baking sheet ½ inch apart, and bake for 45 minutes until springy to the touch and nicely browned (the individual loaves will bake more quickly).

Meanwhile, melt the remaining 2 tablespoons of butter. Fifteen minutes (or 5 minutes if you're making individual loaves) before the cornbread is ready, brush the surface with the melted butter and return it to the oven to finish baking.

Yield: 12 to 15 wedges or several small breads

Farmhouse Tortes

THESE MINIATURE SAVORY TORTES ARE QUICK AND EASY. THERE'S NOTHING to it; just combine all of the ingredients together and fill your cake rings. As they cool, they collapse into unique rich and cheesy discs. If you don't have cake rings, use muffin tins; however, they won't puff up as much as I like.

Special Item: TEN 3 × 3-INCH METAL CAKE RINGS, LIGHTLY COATED WITH MELTED BUTTER, OR 1/2-CUP-CAPACITY MUFFIN TINS

6 cups (3 pounds) fresh ricotta cheese
2 cups (8 ounces) grated Parmesan Reggiano cheese
4 extra-large eggs
1 teaspoon kosher salt
15 fresh sage leaves, finely chopped
Freshly ground black pepper, to taste

Adjust the oven rack to the middle position and preheat the oven to 375 degrees.

In a large bowl, combine the ricotta cheese, 1⅓ cups of the Parmesan, the eggs, salt, sage, and pepper.

Place the rings on a parchment-lined baking sheet. Spoon the mixture into the cake rings, filling the cups to just below the rim. Sprinkle about a tablespoon of Parmesan on top of each. Bake for about 25 to 30 minutes, until firm and lightly browned.

Yield: 10 tortes

FARMHOUSE TORTES: "NOTHING TO IT; JUST COMBINE ALL
OF THE INGREDIENTS AND FILL YOUR CAKE RINGS."

Nut Medley

IN MY VERSION OF "MIXED NUTS" THE NUTS ARE SEASONED SEPARATELY TO retain the distinct flavors of the spices and seeds. Store them in separate containers to keep their flavors distinguishable and toss together before you eat them.

FOR THE SPICY PUMPKIN SEEDS:
2 teaspoons light vegetable oil
1 cup (4 ounces) hulled pumpkin seeds
½ teaspoon kosher salt
1½ to 1¾ teaspoons fresh ground dried chilis or chili flakes

In a 10-inch sauté pan over medium-low heat, stir together the oil and the pumpkin seeds. Cook the nuts until they start popping and a few just begin to brown, being careful not to overcook them. Add the salt and chilis, and continue to cook, stirring occasionally, until the nuts are puffed and most of them are lightly browned. Pour onto a baking sheet to cool.

FOR THE SALTED CASHEWS:
1 cup (4 ounces) whole cashews
2 teaspoons light vegetable oil
1 tablespoon kosher salt

Adjust the oven rack to the middle position and preheat the oven to 325 degrees. In a small mixing bowl, toss together the nuts, oil, and salt.
Spread in an even layer on a parchment-lined baking sheet and toast until lightly browned, about 10 to 15 minutes, stirring the nuts occasionally.

FOR THE FENNEL ALMONDS:
1 cup (4 ounces) whole unblanched almonds
2 teaspoons light vegetable oil
1 tablespoon freshly ground fennel seeds
1 teaspoon kosher salt

Adjust the oven rack to the middle position and preheat the oven to 325 degrees.

In a small bowl, toss together the almonds, oil, fennel seeds, and salt. Spread in an even layer onto a parchment-lined baking sheet and toast until lightly browned, stirring the nuts occasionally, about 15 to 20 minutes.

FOR THE CUMIN PECANS:
1 extra-large egg white
1/2 teaspoon kosher salt
2 teaspoons ground cumin
1 1/2 cups (6 ounces) pecan halves

Adjust the oven rack to the middle position and preheat the oven to 325 degrees.

In a large mixing bowl, whisk the egg white until white and frothy. Whisk in the salt and cumin and add the pecans. Toss the nuts to coat them and place them on a parchment-lined baking sheet to toast for 10 to 12 minutes.

Yield: 4 1/2 cups mixed nuts

Oat Biscuits

Somewhere between a cookie and a cracker, these English-style biscuits are super-oaty and slightly sweet. Eat them with a hearty cheese, such as Stilton or an aged farmhouse Cheddar.

Special Item: 3-INCH ROUND FLUTED CUTTER

1 cup plus 2 tablespoons unbleached pastry flour or unbleached all-purpose flour
½ cup stone-ground whole-wheat flour, plus extra for dusting
3 cups rolled oats
1½ teaspoons baking soda
1½ teaspoons kosher salt
2 tablespoons light brown sugar, lightly packed
2 sticks (8 ounces) unsalted butter, chilled frozen and cut into 1-inch cubes
½ cup plus 2 tablespoons buttermilk

In the bowl of a food processor fitted with the steel blade or in the bowl of an electric mixer fitted with the paddle attachment, combine the flours, oats, baking soda, salt, and brown sugar, and pulse, or mix on low, to incorporate. Add the butter and pulse a few times or mix on low until it's the consistency of a fine meal.

Transfer to a large bowl and make a well in the center. Pour in the buttermilk and using one hand, draw in the dry ingredients, mixing until just combined.

Wash and dry your hands. Turn the dough out onto a lightly floured work surface and knead a few times to gather into a ball. Wrap in plastic and chill until firm, about 2 hours.

On a lightly floured surface, roll the dough out to ⅛-inch thickness, flouring the surface of the dough as necessary. Cutting as closely together as possible, cut out the biscuits. Gather the scraps and cut out the remaining dough. Place them on two parchment-lined baking sheets, ½ inch apart. Chill for 10 to 15 minutes, until firm.

Adjust the oven rack to the middle position and preheat the oven to 350 degrees.

Bake for 15 to 18 minutes, until lightly browned.

Yield: 50 biscuits

Onion Tart

THE COMBINATION OF ONIONS AND PUFF PASTRY IS ABOUT AS CLASSIC AND AS French as it gets. I added ricotta cheese for a slightly richer, even better onion tart.

¼ recipe (about 1 pound) Puff Pastry (see page 330)
1 or 2 yellow onions, diced into 1-inch pieces to equal 1½ cups
1 tablespoon extra-virgin olive oil
3 tablespoons ricotta cheese
1 tablespoon crème fraîche or sour cream
Kosher salt, to taste
Freshly ground black pepper, to taste
2 teaspoons chopped fresh thyme
¼ cup (1 ounce) grated Parmesan Reggiano cheese

On a lightly floured work surface, roll the Puff Pastry out to a 14-inch circle, ¼ inch thick, lightly flouring the surface as necessary and rotating the dough to maintain a circular shape. Transfer to a parchment-lined baking sheet and chill until firm, about 30 minutes to an hour.

Make a scalloped edge by pushing the thumb of one hand against the thumb and index finger of the other hand. Continue around the entire edge of the circle. You should have a small, scalloped rim, about ¼ inch high. Chill in the freezer about 15 to 30 minutes, until firm.

Adjust the oven rack to the middle position and preheat the oven to 375 degrees.

In a medium bowl, toss the onions with the olive oil to coat, and spread on a baking sheet. Roast in the oven to soften without coloring, about 25 minutes. Allow to cool.

In a medium bowl, combine the ricotta, crème fraîche, salt, pepper, and ½ teaspoon of the chopped thyme.

Spread the ricotta mixture evenly over the surface of the tart shell. Evenly distribute the onions, and sprinkle on the Parmesan and remaining thyme.

Bake for 35 to 40 minutes, until the crust is nicely browned.

Yield: 8 to 10 servings

Parma Braids

DON'T BE DECEIVED BY WHAT MIGHT LOOK LIKE A COMPLICATED TECHNIQUE. It takes more time to describe how to assemble Parma Braids than to actually assemble them. Slightly salty and very buttery, these croissant dough braids are one of my favorite savories. It's hard to resist the temptation to grab one as I walk by the full basket in the morning.

½ recipe (about 2 pounds) Croissant dough (see page 294), chilled for at least 3 hours
8 ounces prosciutto, thinly sliced into 24 pieces
Freshly ground black pepper, to taste
½ cup (2 ounces) grated Parmesan Reggiano cheese

FOR THE TOPPING:
1 extra-large egg yolk, lightly beaten with a few drops of water
¼ cup sesame seeds

Divide the dough in half and return one half to the refrigerator. On a lightly floured work surface, roll the dough into a rectangle, 16½ × 7 inches, ¼ inch thick, flouring the surface of the dough as necessary and lifting the dough to square off the edges and corners to help maintain a rectangular shape and an even thickness. Trim the edges straight and brush off any excess flour.

Working with the longer side parallel to the edge of the counter, cut the rectangle horizontally into two strips, each 16½ × 3½ inches. Cut each strip into three pieces, each 5½ × 3½ inches.

Working with one piece at a time, place the longer side parallel to the edge of the work surface and gently score two horizontal lines across the center, 1 inch apart. Make 10 cuts through the dough spaced ½ inch apart along the long edge, stopping ¼ inch away from the scored line. Repeat the cuts along the opposite side. Separate the strips slightly, so that they no longer touch.

Place two pieces of the prosciutto the same length as the rectangle on top of each other and roll them up tightly. Place the rolled prosciutto inside of the two horizontal lines in the center of the dough and sprinkle a pinch of pepper and about 2 rounded teaspoons of the Parmesan.

"It takes more to time to describe how to assemble
Parma Braids than to actually assemble them."

Working quickly, place the shorter side parallel to the edge of the work surface.
Make a crisscross pattern by taking the top right strip and crossing it over the middle
to the edge of the prosciutto along the second strip from the top on the opposite
side. You may need to stretch the dough slightly to reach. Press down gently to ensure
that the two pieces stick together. Cross the top left strip over the middle to the edge
of the prosciutto along the second strip from the top on the opposite side, pressing

down to seal. Continue crisscrossing in this manner with the remaining strips, as you would lace a shoe. When you get to the last two pieces, tuck them underneath the bottom of the braid and gently press together. You'll end up with a braid about 5 inches long and 1¾ inches wide. Place on a parchment-lined baking sheet and continue with the other rectangles. Set the braids aside in a warm place and allow to rise until spongy to the touch, about an hour. Repeat the process with the remaining dough.

Adjust the oven rack to the middle position and preheat the oven to 425 degrees.

Brush the surface with the egg yolk and sprinkle a teaspoon of sesame seeds over each braid.

Steam the oven according to the directions on page 295 and bake for 25 to 30 minutes, until lightly browned and crisp.

Yield: 12 braids

Pasta Torte

THE ITALIANS DISCOVERED THE NATURAL AFFINITY OF BACON, EGGS, AND PASTA hundreds of years ago in that rich and tasty dish, pasta carbonara. Here, those comforting flavors come together again, baked in a potato crust for one of the tastiest pies I've ever had.

Special Item: 9- TO 10-INCH ROUND BAKING DISH, LIGHTLY COATED WITH MELTED BUTTER

FOR THE CRUST:
3 russet potatoes (1½ pounds)
¼ teaspoon kosher salt
Freshly ground black pepper, to taste

FOR THE CUSTARD:
¾ cup whole milk
¾ cup heavy cream
⅛ teaspoon cayenne pepper
¾ teaspoon kosher salt
3 extra-large eggs
2 extra-large egg yolks
3 tablespoons crème fraîche or sour cream
1 cup (4 ounces) grated Parmesan Reggiano cheese
¼ cup chives, minced

FOR THE TORTE:
8 ounces cooked (al dente) angel-hair pasta or capellini
4 to 6 slices of cooked bacon, chewy, not too crisp, pulled into small pieces
8 to 10 whole fresh basil leaves

Adjust the oven rack to the middle position and preheat the oven to 400 degrees. Place the potatoes directly on the oven rack and bake until cooked all the way through, about 45 minutes to an hour. Allow to cool. Peel the potatoes and mash them with a fork.

To prepare the crust: Using your fingers, press the mashed potatoes into the bottom and sides of the prepared pan. Sprinkle with $\frac{1}{4}$ teaspoon of the salt and the fresh pepper and bake for about 15 minutes, until dry.

Meanwhile, to make the custard: In a medium saucepan over medium-high heat, bring the milk, cream, cayenne, and the remaining salt to a boil. Remove from the heat and allow to cool for about 15 minutes.

In a small bowl, whisk together the whole eggs and egg yolks.

Add the crème fraîche and Parmesan to the milk mixture, whisking to incorporate. Slowly whisk in the eggs, and sprinkle in the chives.

Evenly distribute the cooked pasta over the potato crust. Sprinkle in the bacon and pour in the custard. Arrange the basil leaves on the surface.

Bake for 40 to 50 minutes, until the top is nicely browned and the custard is set.

Yield: 8 to 10 servings

Prosciutto Pie

THE COMBINATION OF PROSCIUTTO AND PARMESAN IS ONE OF MY FAVORITES. This rich and intense puff pastry pie is the savory to serve when you're entertaining—a small piece goes a long way.

About ⅓ recipe (1½ pounds) Puff Pastry (see page 330), chilled
1 extra-large egg
¼ cup crème fraîche or sour cream
Freshly ground black pepper, to taste
¼ cup unbleached pastry flour or unbleached all-purpose flour
2 tablespoons plus 1 teaspoon whole milk
½ cup (2 ounces) grated Parmesan Reggiano cheese
4 ounces prosciutto, thinly sliced
1 extra-large egg, lightly beaten, for brushing

Divide the Puff Pastry in half and return one half to the refrigerator. On a lightly floured work surface, roll the Puff Pastry out to ¼-inch thickness, flouring the surface as necessary and rotating the dough to maintain a circular shape. Cut out a circle slightly larger than 12 inches in diameter and place on a baking sheet to chill 30 minutes to an hour, until firm. Repeat with the other half of the dough.

In a medium bowl, whisk together the egg, crème fraîche, and pepper. Sift the flour into the mixture and whisk to combine.

In a small saucepan, over medium-low heat, scald the milk and Parmesan until the cheese melts, stirring constantly. It will be thick at first, but continue heating until melted and thin.

Slowly add the hot milk mixture to the egg mixture, whisking as you pour. Allow to cool.

Remove the 2 circles of dough from the refrigerator, trim each to 12 inches in diameter, and return 1 circle to the refrigerator. Spread half of the filling in an even layer over the surface of the dough, leaving a 1-inch border around the edge. Place half of the slices of prosciutto over the cheese mixture. Spread the remaining filling over the layer of prosciutto and place the remaining prosciutto over it. Brush a 1-inch border of beaten egg around the edge.

Remove the other circle of dough from the refrigerator and place it on top of the prosciutto, pressing gently around the edges to seal. Pierce the center of the dough with the tip of a knife and rotate the knife to enlarge the opening to $\frac{1}{4}$ inch. Score a decorative pattern of lines stemming outward from the opening, and brush the entire surface with egg.

Chill until firm, about 30 minutes to an hour.

Adjust the oven rack to the middle position and preheat the oven to 375 degrees.

Bake for 30 to 40 minutes, until well browned.

Yield: 10 to 12 slices

Savory Brioche Pockets

SIMILAR TO KNISHES, THESE IRRESISTIBLE POCKETS ARE STUFFED WITH POTATO, spinach, and goat cheese. More delicate than their Russian-Jewish predecessors, these are encased in a rich, yeasty, buttery brioche dough that practically melts in your mouth and demands you take another bite.

Special Items: 4½-INCH ROUND CUTTER
3¾-INCH ROUND CUTTER

FOR THE FILLING:
3 to 4 (2 pounds) russet potatoes
½ cup crème fraîche or sour cream
⅔ cup (6 ounces) fresh goat cheese, crumbled
1½ teaspoons kosher salt
1 large garlic clove, thinly sliced
½ small yellow onion, thinly sliced
3 tablespoons extra-virgin olive oil
8 cups loosely packed fresh spinach, washed and stems removed
½ teaspoon fresh lemon juice

1 recipe Brioche Dough, made 1 day ahead (see page 287), chilled

FOR GARNISHING:
2 to 3 extra-large egg yolks, lightly beaten with a few drops of water
Poppy seeds for sprinkling, optional
24 to 30 fresh whole sage leaves, optional

Adjust the oven rack to the middle position and preheat the oven to 400 degrees. Place the potatoes directly on the oven rack and bake until cooked all the way through, about 45 minutes to an hour. Allow to cool, and peel the potatoes.

In a medium bowl, break up about 1½ cups of the potatoes into 1-inch pieces. Add the crème fraîche, goat cheese, and 1 teaspoon of the salt and mix together, keeping the mixture chunky. Set aside.

Note: Depending on the size of your pan, you can divide the spinach and other ingredients more or less equally into 2 or 3 batches, to fit in your skillet.

In a skillet over medium-low heat, cook the garlic and onion in the olive oil until softened, but not colored, about 3 to 4 minutes. Turn the heat to high and add the spinach, remaining salt, and the lemon juice. Cook quickly, stirring until the spinach wilts. Remove from the heat and place the spinach in a strainer and press out the excess liquid. Cool completely.

Divide the Brioche Dough in half and return one half to the refrigerator. On a lightly floured work surface, roll the dough out ⅛ inch thick, flouring the surface as necessary. Using a floured 4½-inch round cutter, cut out the circles, cutting as closely together as possible. Place them on a parchment-lined baking sheet to chill 15 to 30 minutes, until slightly firm. Repeat the process with the remaining dough.

Adjust the oven racks to the upper and lower positions and preheat to 350 degrees.

Remove the first half of the circles from the refrigerator. Place 1 tablespoon of the spinach mixture in the middle of each circle and top with 2 tablespoons of the potato mixture to form a mound. Brush around the filling with the beaten egg yolk.

Remove the second half of the circles from the refrigerator. Place a circle of dough over the mound of filling and gently press with your fingertips around the edges of the filling. Using the dull side of the smaller cutter, press down gently around the outer edge of the mound of filling, pressing to seal the two layers together, but not cutting through the dough. To create a decorative border, pick up both layers of dough and fold a ½-inch section of the edge up toward the filling. Continue in the same manner, folding and pleating around the entire perimeter of the pocket. Press down gently to seal the pleats. (*Note:* At this point the pockets can be wrapped and frozen.) Place on 2 parchment-lined baking sheets, spaced at least 2 inches apart.

Brush the pockets with the beaten egg and sprinkle a pinch of poppy seeds over the surface. If desired, place 2 whole sage leaves, stems together and slightly overlapping, in the center. Set the pockets aside in a warm place to rise, uncovered at room temperature, until slightly puffy and spongy to the touch, about 20 to 30 minutes.

Bake for 15 to 20 minutes, until lightly browned, rotating the baking sheets halfway through to ensure even baking.

Yield: 12 to 15 pockets

Savory Rustic Tarts

This delicious pizzalike tart can be baked as one large tart and sliced into wedges, or made into small individual tarts. At the bakery, we sell several variations. Our most popular are ricotta with tomato or red peppers and plain tomato rustic tarts. For the Ricotta Tomato Tart you must oven-dry the tomatoes to eliminate excess moisture, resulting in a sweet slice of concentrated flavor. I use Roma tomatoes for their firm membrane, which stays intact while drying. For the Ricotta Red Pepper Tart, you can roast your own peppers or choose a high-quality jarred red pepper. My favorite jarred peppers are Pequillo peppers from Spain, which you'll find at upscale markets and specialty stores. If you're not in the mood for cheese, a plain tomato tart is tasty, but use only the tiny Sweet 100 tomatoes or currant tomatoes. Cherry tomatoes are too big and too watery.

Special Items: METAL COOLING RACK OR WIRE RACK THAT FITS INSIDE BAKING
SHEET, FOR DRYING THE TOMATOES, OPTIONAL
5½-INCH CUTTER

FOR THE DOUGH:

2 cups unbleached pastry flour or unbleached all-purpose flour
2 teaspoons kosher salt
2 sticks (8 ounces) unsalted butter, chilled and cut into 1-inch cubes
2 tablespoons heavy cream
3 tablespoons cold water

FOR THE FILLING:

8 to 10 (2 pounds) vine-ripened Roma tomatoes, cut into about thirty ¼-inch-thick slices, or an
*   8-ounce jar of roasted Pequillo peppers, torn into thirds, or 3 cups Sweet 100s or currant*
*   tomatoes*
2 cups (1 pound) fresh ricotta cheese
½ cup minced chives
2 teaspoons kosher salt
Freshly ground black pepper, to taste
¼ cup extra-virgin olive oil, plus extra for brushing on the tomatoes and oven racks (if you're
*   making the plain tomato tart, without the filling, you'll need about ½ cup of oil in all)*

2 extra-large egg yolks, lightly beaten with a splash of water
20 small sprigs fresh thyme
½ cup anise, cumin seeds, fennel seeds, sesame seeds, or poppy seeds, optional

To prepare the dough: In the bowl of a food processor fitted with a steel blade or in the bowl of an electric mixer fitted with the paddle attachment, combine the flour and salt and pulse or mix on low to incorporate. Add the butter and process or mix on low until it's the consistency of a fine meal.

In a small bowl, whisk together the cream and water. Add to the butter mixture and pulse a few times or mix on low until the dough barely comes together.

Turn the dough out onto a lightly floured work surface. Dip the heel of your hand in flour and, working with small sections at a time, smear the dough away from you to blend it together. When the dough has been all smeared out, using a metal scraper or spatula, scrape and gather it together and knead a few times to gather into a ball. Flatten into a disc, wrap in plastic and chill until firm, at least 2 hours or overnight.

For the ricotta and tomato tart:

Adjust the oven rack to the middle position and preheat the oven to 400 degrees.

Brush a wire rack with oil and set it on top of a baking sheet. Place the tomato slices on the rack, brush them with olive oil, and dry in the oven until the tomatoes begin to lighten in color, the skin begins to wrinkle, but the membrane is still soft. After about 20 minutes, rotate the baking sheets to ensure even cooking. Turn the oven down to 325 and dry for another 30 to 50 minutes until the membrane dries out. Remove from the oven and allow to cool.

In a medium bowl, combine the ricotta, chives, salt, black pepper, and ¼ cup of the oil. Chill until ready to use.

On a lightly floured work surface, roll the dough out 1/16 inch thick, flouring the surface of the dough as necessary. Cutting as closely together as possible, cut out 8 to 10 circles. It may be necessary to gather the scraps together and reroll the dough to cut out all the circles. Place on a parchment-lined baking sheet and chill 15 minutes, until firm.

Remove the circles of dough from the refrigerator. Working with one at a time (it may be necessary to chill some of the circles so the dough doesn't become too soft), spread 3 tablespoons of the ricotta filling to within 1¼ inches of the edge of each circle. Cover the cheese with 3 slices of the tomato or pepper. For the cheeseless tomato tart, place a heaping $\frac{1}{4}$ cup of Sweet 100 tomatoes in the center.

Fold a $\frac{3}{4}$-inch section of the edge of the dough up toward the filling and press down to seal. Rotate the circle slightly and fold another small section of the edge of the dough up toward the filling, allowing the dough to pleat as you fold. Continue working your way around the tart to make 6 folds. Gently cup your hand over the entire tart and press down the pleats to ensure that they seal well and will not unfold while baking. Repeat with the remaining circles and place them on two parchment-lined baking sheets, spaced 2 inches apart. Chill until firm, about 30 minutes.

Adjust the oven racks to the upper and lower positions and preheat the oven to 375 degrees.

Brush the dough with the egg yolk. Poke 2 to 3 sprigs of the thyme into the center of each tart, and sprinkle with the seeds if you're using them. If making the plain tomato version, drizzle the tomatoes with about 2 teaspoons of the olive oil, sprinkle with salt, and poke 2 to 3 sprigs of the thyme into the center. Bake for 10 minutes and turn the oven down to 350 degrees for about 25 minutes until the crust is lightly browned, rotating the baking sheets halfway through to ensure even baking.

Yield: 10 tarts

Spicy Country Crackers

BREAK THESE TASTY CRACKERS INTO LARGE SHARDS AND PILE THEM ON TOP OF one another in the middle of the table. Just watch the hands start grabbing and the pile quickly disappear.

FOR THE DOUGH:

3 cups unbleached pastry flour or unbleached all-purpose flour
1 teaspoon kosher salt
1 cup plus 2 tablespoons cold water

FOR THE TOPPING:

¼ cup extra-virgin olive oil
2 teaspoons crushed dried chilis
Kosher salt, to taste
Freshly ground black pepper, to taste
¼ cup chopped fresh thyme
½ cup (2 ounces) grated Parmesan Reggiano cheese

In the bowl of an electric mixer fitted with the paddle attachment, combine the flour, salt, and water, and mix on low until just incorporated. Turn the dough out onto a lightly floured work surface and knead a few times to gather into a ball. Flatten into a disc, wrap in plastic, and allow to rest in the refrigerator for 30 minutes.

Meanwhile, to make the topping: Heat the olive oil until warm and remove from the heat. Add the chilis and allow to steep at least half an hour.

Adjust the oven racks to the upper and lower positions and preheat the oven to 350 degrees.

Divide the dough in half and return one half to the refrigerator. On a lightly floured surface, roll the dough (in two or more pieces) out to ¹⁄₁₆-inch thickness. You should be able to see the color of the countertop through the dough.

Dust the surface of the dough with flour and roll it up around a rolling pin to transfer it. Place the rolling pin over the parchment-lined baking sheets to unroll. Brush the dough lightly with the chili oil and sprinkle with salt, pepper, thyme, and cheese. Repeat with the remaining dough, rolling out only as much dough as you have baking sheets.

Bake for 15 minutes, until lightly browned and crispy. Halfway through, rotate the baking sheets to ensure the crackers bake evenly.

Allow to cool and break into several uneven pieces.

Yield: 1 pound or fourteen 5 × 6-inch pieces

White Lily Savory Tart

Covered in caramelized onions, olives, and fresh thyme and scattered with tomatoes and cheese, or made in the style of a classic pissaladière with olives, anchovies, and onions, this tart is pure Provence. Joan in the pastry kitchen convinced me that the White Lily flour (see "Sources," page 393) milled in her husband's home state of Tennessee makes the most tender and flaky crust. I'm usually not a fan of bleached flour, but in this case she's right—this flour, made from soft wheat, yields the lightest crust ever.

Special Items: 12-INCH FLUTED RING WITH A REMOVABLE BOTTOM, OR A 12-INCH FLAN RING

BAKING STONE, OPTIONAL

FOR THE DOUGH:

2 cups White Lily flour

1½ teaspoons kosher salt

1½ sticks (6 ounces) unsalted butter, chilled and cut into 1-inch cubes

4 to 5 tablespoons whole milk, cold

FOR THE FILLING:

2 tablespoons extra-virgin olive oil

2 large yellow onions, cut in half through the root and sliced into ⅛-inch-thick slices

Kosher salt, to taste

Freshly ground pepper, to taste

2 to 4 tablespoons dry sherry, optional

1½ cups grated strong cheese, such as Aged Dry Jack or Gouda

25 to 30 red or yellow cherry tomatoes, tossed in a teaspoon of olive oil

25 to 30 pitted black olives—Saracene, Kalamata, or Niçoise

8 to 10 whole thyme sprigs

To prepare the dough: In the bowl of a food processor fitted with the steel blade or in the bowl of an electric mixer fitted with the paddle attachment, combine the flour and salt and pulse or mix on low to incorporate. Add the butter and pulse a few times or mix on low, until it's the consistency of a fine meal. Add the milk and pulse or mix on low until the dough barely comes together.

Turn the dough out onto a lightly floured work surface. Dip the heel of your hand in flour and, working with small sections, smear the dough away from you to blend it together. When the dough has been all smeared out, using a metal scraper or spatula, scrape and gather it together and knead a few times to gather into a ball. Flatten into a disc, and wrap in plastic to chill until firm, about 1 to 2 hours or overnight.

In a large saucepan, over low heat, combine the olive oil, onions, salt, and pepper. Add half of the sherry and cook slowly for about 45 minutes to an hour until caramelized, stirring occasionally. Stir in another tablespoon of sherry, to taste, and set aside to cool.

On a lightly floured surface, roll the dough out to a circle, ⅛ inch thick, flouring the surface of the dough as necessary. Line the tart ring according to the directions on page 215. Chill until firm, about 30 minutes.

Remove the oven rack from the oven and place the baking stone directly on the floor of the oven. If you don't have a baking stone, you'll still need to remove the rack and place the tart on a baking sheet directly on the floor of the oven. Preheat the oven to 375 degrees at least one hour before baking to warm up the baking stone.

Evenly distribute the onions over the dough. Sprinkle with the cheese and scatter the tomatoes. Cover the tart loosely with foil, taking care that the foil doesn't touch the tomatoes.

Bake for 1½ hours. About 30 minutes before the tart is done, remove it from the oven and lift off the foil. Evenly distribute the olives and thyme sprigs on top, and return the tart to the oven to finish baking.

FOR THE PISSALADIÈRE:
Onions, see above
3 anchovies, packed in salt and rinsed in cool water, broken into ¼-inch pieces
Olives, see above
Thyme sprigs, see above

Follow the directions above for caramelizing the onions and spread evenly over the dough. Bake according the directions above, and scatter the anchovies, olives, and thyme over the tart during the last 30 minutes of baking.

Yield: One 12-inch tart

3. *Cobblers, Crisps,*
and Crumbles

....

Our cobblers, crisps, and crumbles never stick around very long at La Brea Bakery. We sell them by the pound, directly out of the dish or skillet they're baked in, their juices piping hot and still bubbling. The first customer who spies that hot fruit dessert often ends up buying the entire portion, leaving the next person in line irate and wishing she had arrived sooner. Let's face it, it's hard to find someone who doesn't like the combination of cooked fruit topped with buttery biscuits or crunchy streusel.

There are almost as many names for these American fruit desserts as there are fruits. We argued and tried to reason on our side of the counter, but every cookbook told us something different. Finally, *Cook's Illustrated* magazine came to the rescue. From the popular crisps, cobblers, and crumbles to the more offbeat grunts, buckles, and pandowdies, it's their topping that defines them.

A crisp is only a crisp when topped with butter, sugar, flour, and often nuts. A crumble also has that streusel topping, but with oats instead of nuts. And cobblers are always topped with dough, whether it's firm enough to roll, as in the Strawberry-Rhubarb (page 107); soft enough to drop, as in the Peach (page 103); or thin enough to pour, as in Everyone's Mother's Berry Cobbler (page 99). Always baked in a low, shallow dish or skillet, crisps, cobblers, and crumbles naturally achieve that proper ratio of topping to fruit.

There's only one way to ruin a cobbler or crisp: bad fruit. Ripe, sweet, and flavorful fruit always guarantees a great result. Cobblers aren't magical; they can't revive overripe and moldy fruit or make underripe and out-of-season fruit sweet and juicy before its time. Visit your local farmers' markets, look for what's in season, and find the best fruit available. In fall, use cranberries for a crisp and in winter, use apples for a crumble. Peaches and berries are best for summertime, and strawberries and rhubarb for spring. My sugar quantities lean toward the less sweet side, so taste the fruit before it goes in the oven. If it's not sweet enough, sprinkle in a little more sugar.

Ideally, a perfect crisp or cobbler has lots of thickened sauce with a glossy sheen. Because the water content varies from one tree or bush to the next, it's hard to predict just how juicy the fruit will be. The riper the fruit, the more juice it gives off. Cornstarch thickens the natural fruit juices into a syrupy, shiny sauce. I've tried my best to give the correct measurements for cornstarch, although nature will be nature, so you might need to experiment. In the end, if the cobbler is a little bit runny, it will still be delicious. In the end, if it seems dry, there's nothing a little cream can't remedy.

These are my favorite combinations of fruit, but you don't need my permission to change them. All of the fruits are interchangeable with the different toppings, except for Everyone's Mother's Berry Cobbler. I encourage you to experiment—turn a cobbler into a crisp or a crumble into a cobbler. Make the Apple

Crumble (page 97) into a crisp by using the streusel from the Pear Crisp (page 105). Turn the Pear Crisp into a cobbler by covering it with biscuits. When you put the topping over the fruit, whether it's streusel or biscuit, be sure to leave some fruit poking through for color. For even more color, you can always add some berries.

Much less intimidating to make, but just as delicious as a pie, these are the perfect desserts for the not-so-confident baker. There are no pie shells to line or fancy latticework to fret over. Their crustless form and saucy nature make serving predictably easy. For an informal and casual presentation, serve them family style, directly out of the baking dish. Spoon each serving into an oversize soup bowl and pour a few tablespoons of heavy cream around the edge. For fancier fare, bake them in individual oven-proof bowls, one for each guest. No matter how they're served, these humbler pies are always delicious, homey, and comforting.

Apple Crumble

By combining the apples with browned butter and a vanilla bean, we give this classic American dessert new depth and flavor. If you overmix the butter in the streusel and it clumps, freeze the streusel until firm and grate it—on the largest hole of the grater—directly over the fruit.

Special Item: 6-CUP-CAPACITY BAKING DISH

FOR THE FILLING:
7 to 8 (3 pounds) large, tart green apples such as Granny Smith, peeled, cored, and cut into
    ³/₄-inch cubes, to equal about 6 cups
¹/₃ cup granulated sugar
2 tablespoons light brown sugar, lightly packed
3 tablespoons (1¹/₂ ounces) unsalted butter
1 vanilla bean
2 tablespoons cornstarch
2 tablespoons apple juice or water

FOR THE STREUSEL TOPPING:
¹/₂ cup plus 2 tablespoons unbleached pastry flour or unbleached all-purpose flour
¹/₂ cup plus 2 tablespoons granulated sugar
¹/₄ teaspoon ground cinnamon
1 stick plus 2 tablespoons (5 ounces) unsalted butter, cut into 1-inch cubes and frozen
¹/₂ cup plus 2 tablespoons rolled oats

In a large bowl, toss together the apples and sugars. Set aside for an hour until the apples start to break down and just begin to release their juice.

To prepare the topping: In the bowl of a food processor fitted with the steel blade, or in the bowl of an electric mixer fitted with the paddle attachment, combine the flour, sugar, and cinnamon and pulse or mix on low to incorporate. Add the butter and pulse on and off or mix on low until it's the consistency of a coarse meal.

Transfer to a bowl and, using your hands, toss in the oats. Chill until ready to use.

To prepare the filling: In a medium saucepan over high heat, begin to melt the butter. Using a small paring knife, split the vanilla bean lengthwise. With the back of the knife, scrape out the pulp and the seeds and add the scrapings and the pod to the butter. Swirl the pan to ensure the butter cooks evenly and doesn't burn. It will bubble somewhat vigorously as it browns. Continue cooking 3 to 5 more minutes until the bubbles subside and the liquid is dark brown with a nutty, toasty aroma. Remove the vanilla bean. Pour the butter and brown flecks over the apples, tossing to combine.

Adjust the oven rack to the upper position and preheat the oven to 425 degrees.

In a small bowl, combine the cornstarch with the apple juice or water, mixing well to remove the lumps. Place a strainer over the bowl of apples and strain the cornstarch liquid onto the apples. Toss together and transfer to the baking dish.

Crumble the topping over the apples, squeezing it together in your fist to create a coarse, uneven, lumpy texture.

Place the dish on a baking sheet and bake for 35 minutes, until the juices are bubbling. Turn the oven down to 375 degrees and bake for another 50 to 55 minutes, until the top is nicely browned and the juices are caramelized.

Yield: 8 to 10 servings

Everyone's Mother's Berry Cobbler

THE FIRST TIME I EVER HAD A BATTER COBBLER WAS WHEN A FELLOW LOS Angeles pastry chef, my friend Lorraine, made one based on her mother's recipe. Years later *Cook's Illustrated* magazine ran a similar version based on a recipe by Natalie Dupree. This recipe is so fast and simple, it takes longer to preheat the oven than to actually make the cobbler.

Not really a cake, not really a biscuit, this soft and buttery cobbler is golden brown and crisp around the edges, pitted with tender, cooked fruit. The amount of sugar you add depends on the sweetness of your berries, so taste them first. Serve hot, in the middle of the table, and hand everyone a spoon.

Special Item: 6- TO 8-CUP-CAPACITY OVAL GRATIN DISH, 12 × 8 INCHES, OR A
10-INCH SKILLET

½ stick (2 ounces) unsalted butter
1 vanilla bean
1 cup unbleached pastry flour or unbleached all-purpose flour
¾ cup granulated sugar, plus 1 to 2 tablespoons extra for sprinkling
2 teaspoons baking powder
1 cup buttermilk
2 teaspoons pure vanilla extract
¾ pound (1½ to 2 cups) blueberries, blackberries, boysenberries, sliced strawberries, or a
  combination of all

Adjust the oven rack to the middle position and preheat the oven to 350 degrees.

In a medium saucepan over medium-high heat, begin to melt the butter. Using a small paring knife, split the vanilla bean lengthwise and with the back of the knife, scrape out the pulp and the seeds and add the scrapings and the pod to the butter. Swirl the pan to ensure the butter cooks evenly and doesn't burn. It will bubble somewhat vigorously as it browns. Continue cooking another 3 to 5 minutes until the bubbles subside and the liquid is dark brown with a nutty, toasty aroma. Remove the vanilla bean. Pour the butter and brown flecks into the baking dish and set aside.

In a large bowl, sift to combine the flour, sugar, and baking powder. Make a well in the center and pour in the buttermilk and vanilla extract, whisking the liquids to combine. Slowly draw in the dry ingredients, and mix until incorporated.

Over a large bowl, strain the batter through a fine-mesh sieve. Pour the batter into the baking dish.

Evenly distribute the fruit over the batter and sprinkle 1 to 2 tablespoons of sugar over the top.

Bake for 45 to 50 minutes, until the juices are bubbling and the top is evenly browned.

Yield: 6 servings

Nectarine-Ginger Crisp

Special Item: 8- TO 9-CUP-CAPACITY BAKING DISH

FOR THE FILLING:

7 nectarines (3 pounds), pitted, cut into eighths and cut in half diagonally to equal 8 cups

3 tablespoons granulated sugar

2 tablespoons cornstarch

1 heaping cup fresh raspberries, blackberries, or blueberries

2 tablespoons candied ginger, finely chopped

2 tablespoons pure vanilla extract

¼ cup crème fraîche

FOR THE STREUSEL TOPPING:

1¼ cups unbleached pastry flour or unbleached all-purpose flour

¼ cup granulated sugar

¾ teaspoon kosher salt

¾ teaspoon baking powder

½ stick plus 1 tablespoon (2½ ounces) unsalted butter, cut into 1-inch cubes and frozen

1 extra-large egg, beaten

Adjust the oven rack to the upper position and preheat the oven to 400 degrees.

In a large bowl, toss together the nectarines and sugar and set aside for 30 minutes, until the fruit has released its juices.

To prepare the topping: In the bowl of a food processor fitted with the steel blade or in the bowl of an electric mixer fitted with the paddle attachment, combine the flour, sugar, salt, and baking powder and pulse or mix on low to incorporate. Add the butter and pulse on and off, or mix on low, until it's the consistency of a coarse meal.

Transfer the mixture to a large bowl. Add the egg and toss together with your hands until combined. Chill until ready to use.

To prepare the filling: Over a small bowl, strain and reserve the juices from the nectarines. Transfer the nectarines to a baking dish. Add the cornstarch to the nectarine juice, whisking well to remove the lumps, and stir in the vanilla extract and crème fraîche. Hold a fine-mesh sieve above the fruit and strain the cornstarch liquid into the fruit, tossing to combine. Evenly distribute the berries and ginger throughout. Crumble the topping over the fruit, squeezing it in your fist to create a coarse, uneven texture.

Bake for 45 minutes to 1 hour, until the fruit is bubbling and the topping is golden brown and crisp.

Yield: 6 to 8 servings

Peach Cobbler with Cream Biscuits

To cook the peaches properly it is important not to overcrowd them in the pan. Depending on the size of your pan, you can divide the peaches and other ingredients more or less equally into 2 or 3 batches.

Special Item: 8- to 9-cup-capacity or 12 × 8-inch baking dish

FOR THE COMPOTE:

¼ cup water

¾ cup granulated sugar, plus an extra tablespoon for sprinkling over the fruit

1 vanilla bean

7 to 8 (3½ pounds) peaches, pitted, cut into eighths, and cut in half diagonally, to equal about 9 cups

6 to 8 gratings of fresh whole nutmeg

½ cup brandy

¼ cup cornstarch

1 heaping cup fresh whole boysenberries, blackberries, raspberries, or blueberries

FOR THE BISCUITS:

1⅔ cups unbleached pastry flour or unbleached all-purpose flour

¾ teaspoon kosher salt

2¼ teaspoons baking powder

3 tablespoons granulated sugar

1¼ cups heavy cream, plus 1 tablespoon for brushing

FOR GARNISHING:

¼ cup sliced almonds

1 to 2 tablespoons granulated sugar

Powdered sugar

Adjust the oven rack to the middle position and preheat the oven to 425 degrees.

To prepare the compote: In a large heavy-duty skillet, stir together the water and sugar. Using a small paring knife, split the vanilla bean lengthwise. With the back of the knife, scrape out the pulp and the seeds, and add the scrapings and the pod to the sugar mixture. Over medium-high heat, bring the mixture to a boil without stirring. Using a pastry brush dipped in water, brush down the sides of the pan to remove any undissolved sugar granules. When the sugar begins to color, after about 3 to 4 minutes, tilt and swirl the pan to cook evenly. When the mixture reaches an even medium caramel color, remove from the heat.

Add the peaches and a few gratings of the nutmeg, tossing to coat. The mixture may spatter and the sugar may seize and harden. Remove from the heat, add the brandy, and return it to the heat. Tilt the pan slightly toward the flame to ignite the brandy, letting it burn until the flames die down and most of the sugar melts, about a minute.

Place a large strainer over a bowl and pour in the fruit, straining the liquid into the bowl. Remove the vanilla bean and transfer the peaches to the baking dish.

In a small saucepan, stir together the reserved liquid and cornstarch. Over medium heat, bring the mixture to a boil, whisking constantly. Pour the thickened juice over the peaches and scatter the berries evenly throughout.

To make the biscuits: In a large bowl, sift to combine the flour, salt, baking powder, and sugar. Make a well in the center and pour on the cream. Using one hand, draw in the dry ingredients, mixing until just combined.

Wash and dry your hands and dust them with flour. Pick up 3 to 4 tablespoons of the dough, gently stretch it to ½-inch thickness, and place it on top of the peaches. Continue with the rest of the dough, making an uneven scattering of stretched biscuit over the fruit, leaving some of the peaches poking through.

Brush the dough with the tablespoon of cream and grate a few gratings of nutmeg over. Arrange the sliced almonds in a single layer on the dough and sprinkle with granulated sugar.

Bake for about 45 minutes to an hour, until the biscuits are lightly browned and the liquid is bubbling. Cool for 5 minutes and sift a fine layer of powdered sugar over the top.

Yield: 6 to 8 servings

Pear Crisp in a Skillet

ALL OF US HAVE OUR DEEP DARK SECRETS, THOSE SKELETONS IN THE CLOSET we don't want anyone to discover. I have mine too. When I want a poached pear, I use canned organic pears. There's nothing to be ashamed of, they're just ripe Bartlett pears in a sugar syrup. Unlike other fruits, pears are more unpredictable and temperamental; it's hard to find them at the perfect stage of ripeness for poaching. Because pears ripen unevenly from the inside out, it's hard to tell how ripe they really are. Most often, they're hard and mealy on the outer section and mushy and overripe toward the center. For those of you who can't bear to open a can, skip this recipe and make the Pretty Pear Cookies (see page 148) instead, with plenty of thinly sliced fresh pears piled on top.

Special Item: 10- OR 12-INCH SKILLET

FOR THE STREUSEL TOPPING:
Heaping ¹⁄₂ cup (2 ounces) pecans
1 tablespoon plus 1 teaspoon light brown sugar, lightly packed
1 tablespoon plus 1 teaspoon granulated sugar
¹⁄₂ teaspoon kosher salt
¹⁄₂ teaspoon baking powder
¹⁄₂ teaspoon ground cinnamon
³⁄₄ cup unbleached pastry flour or unbleached all-purpose flour
3¹⁄₂ tablespoons (1³⁄₄ ounces) unsalted butter, cut into 1-inch cubes and frozen
¹⁄₂ extra-large egg, beaten, to equal 2 tablespoons

FOR THE FILLING:
16 canned pear halves in heavy syrup, drained with syrup reserved, sliced in half horizontally, and
*   cut into uneven 1-inch chunks to equal 4 heaping cups*
1¹⁄₂ cups reserved pear syrup
1 teaspoon cornstarch
1 tablespoon granulated sugar
1 tablespoon light brown sugar, lightly packed
¹⁄₂ stick (2 ounces) unsalted butter
1 vanilla bean

2 cinnamon sticks
5 star anise
¼ cup dried cranberries, optional

Adjust the oven rack to the middle position and preheat the oven to 400 degrees.

To prepare the topping: In the bowl of a food processor fitted with the steel blade, grind the pecans and sugars to a fine meal. Add the salt, baking powder, cinnamon, and flour, and process to combine. Add the butter and pulse on and off until it's the consistency of a coarse meal.

Transfer to a bowl. Add the measured egg and toss together to incorporate. Chill until ready to use.

To prepare the filling: In a small bowl, whisk together the pear syrup, cornstarch, and sugars.

In a medium saucepan over medium-high heat, begin to melt the butter. Using a small paring knife, split the vanilla bean lengthwise and with the back of the knife, scrape out the pulp and the seeds and add the scrapings and the pod to the butter. Add the cinnamon sticks and star anise. Swirl the pan to ensure the butter cooks evenly and doesn't burn. It will bubble somewhat vigorously as it browns. Continue cooking 3 to 5 more minutes until the bubbles subside and the butter is dark brown with a nutty, toasty aroma. Remove the vanilla bean.

Add the pears to the butter mixture, tossing to coat. Strain the syrup onto the pears and cook over high heat for about 10 minutes, until slightly thickened, making sure the pears stay intact and are not mushy. Stir in the cranberries, if desired. If the stovetop heat is weak and not rigorous enough to reduce the liquid quickly, strain the liquid so the fruit doesn't overcook. Set the fruit aside and return the liquid to the skillet to reduce until thickened. Turn off the heat and return the fruit to the skillet.

Crumble the topping over the fruit, squeezing it together in your fist to create a coarse, uneven texture. Leave a 1½-inch border of fruit around the perimeter.

Bake for about 20 minutes, until the juices are bubbling and the topping is nicely browned.

Yield: 6 to 8 servings

Strawberry–Rhubarb Cobbler with Brown Butter Biscuit

In THIS OLD-FASHIONED COBBLER, BROWN BUTTER BISCUITS PAVE THE WAY TO the sweet strawberries and tart rhubarb compote inside. Done in the style of James Beard's shortcakes with cooked egg yolks, these biscuits stand up best to the juiciness of the strawberries. While a softer biscuit would become soggy, mine, though buttery and tender, remains crisp and firm.

Special Items: 6-CUP-CAPACITY OR 8 × 4 × 2-INCH OVAL BAKING DISH
2¹⁄₂-INCH ROUND CUTTER

FOR THE BISCUITS:
¹⁄₄ cup plus 1 tablespoon unsalted butter
1 vanilla bean
1¹⁄₄ cups unbleached all-purpose flour
2 tablespoons granulated sugar, plus extra for sprinkling
¹⁄₄ cup white cornmeal, plus extra for dusting the tops of the biscuits
2 teaspoons baking powder
¹⁄₄ teaspoon kosher salt
2 extra-large eggs, hard-boiled
¹⁄₂ cup heavy cream, plus 2 tablespoons extra for brushing the tops of the biscuits

FOR THE COMPOTE:
1 pound rhubarb, dark red and firm
2 tablespoons water
¹⁄₄ cup granulated sugar
1 vanilla bean
1 cinnamon stick
3 to 4 gratings nutmeg
2 black peppercorns, crushed
¹⁄₄ cup dry white wine
1 pound strawberries, cut into ¹⁄₄-inch slices to equal 2¹⁄₂ cups

To prepare the biscuits: In a medium saucepan over medium-high heat, begin to melt the butter. Using a small paring knife, split the vanilla bean lengthwise. With the back of the knife, scrape out the pulp and the seeds and add the scrapings and the pod to the butter. Swirl the pan to ensure the butter cooks evenly and doesn't burn. It will bubble somewhat vigorously as it browns. Continue cooking 3 to 5 more minutes until the bubbles subside and the liquid is dark brown with a nutty, toasty aroma. Transfer to a bowl, remove the vanilla bean, and chill the butter and dark flecks until firm, about 1 hour.

To prepare the compote: Cut the stalks of rhubarb into 3-inch lengths and cut each piece into thirds or fourths, about the size of a pencil. Set aside.

In a large, heavy-duty deep skillet, stir together the water and sugar. Using a small paring knife, split the vanilla bean lengthwise. With the back of the knife, scrape out the pulp and the seeds and add the scrapings and the pod to the sugar mixture. Add the cinnamon stick, nutmeg, and peppercorns. Over medium-high heat, bring the mixture to a boil without stirring. Using a pastry brush dipped in water, brush down the sides of the pan to remove any undissolved sugar granules. When the sugar begins to color, after 3 to 4 minutes, begin to tilt and swirl the pan to cook evenly. When the mixture reaches an even medium caramel color, remove from the heat.

Add the rhubarb, tossing to coat. The mixture may spatter and the sugar may seize and harden. Remove from the heat, pour in the wine and continue to cook over high heat until the rhubarb is tender and just begins to break down, about 10 to 15 minutes. The fruit should remain intact and still have texture. Remove from the heat, stir in the strawberries, and transfer the fruit to the baking dish to cool. Remove the vanilla bean and cinnamon stick.

In the bowl of a food processor fitted with the steel blade or in the bowl of an electric mixer fitted with the paddle attachment, combine the flour, sugar, cornmeal, baking powder, and salt. Pulse or mix on low to incorporate. Separate and discard the whites of the eggs. Push the egg yolks through a fine-mesh sieve, scraping the yolks off the bottom of the sieve and into the flour mixture. Pulse on and off a few times or mix on low to combine. Cut up the chilled browned butter into $\frac{1}{2}$-inch cubes. Add to the egg mixture, and pulse on and off a few times or mix on low until it's the consistency of a fine meal.

Adjust the oven rack to the middle position and preheat the oven to 375 degrees.

Transfer the mixture to a bowl, make a well in the center, and pour in the cream. Using one hand, gently draw in the dry ingredients, mixing until just combined.

Wash and dry your hands and dust them with flour. Turn the dough out onto a lightly floured surface and gently knead a few times to gather it into a ball. Roll or pat the dough to ½-inch thickness. Cutting as closely together as possible, cut out 6 biscuits. Place them on top of the fruit in a ring shape, with the edges just touching, keeping the biscuits at least 1 inch away from the edge of the baking dish. Brush the tops of the biscuits with cream and sprinkle with a pinch of cornmeal and sugar.

Turn the oven down to 350 degrees and bake for about 25 minutes, until the biscuits are nicely browned and the fruit is bubbly.

Yield: 6 servings

4. Cookies

....

If I weren't around desserts all day, who knows, maybe I would be able to sit down to a big hunk of three-layer cake. But because I am around sweets so much of the time, big, sweet, and saucy desserts aren't very appealing. For me, cookies are the perfect dessert.

I'm always astounded when I ask someone what's for dessert and she embarrassingly mutters, "Just cookies." I never understood cookies' "less than" reputation. My cookies have the same set of standards and require the same attention to flavor, texture, and appearance as fancier desserts. The rustic Sbrisolona (page 156), scented with Old World flavors like orange flower water and almonds, has a sandy, crumbly texture, perfectly suited to big nutty chunks rather than pristine-shaped cookies. The Moravian Ginger Snap (page 140), crisp and slender, packs just the right amount of spice in every bite. The Pretty Pear Cookie (page 148), with its delicate, buttery crust, is covered with almond cream and elegantly stacked with paper-thin slices of pears—it's actually a cookie disguised as a tart.

Part of the fun of making these cookies is the variety of techniques used. If you were to make all of the cookies in this chapter, you'd find there isn't only one way to make a cookie. Some doughs are rolled and cut out, like the Linzers (page 136) or Graham Crackers (page 124). "Slice-and-bakes" are formed into bricks or logs and frozen, as in the Almond Slice-and-Bakes (page 115) or Swedish Ginger Wafers (page 162). Dunkers (page 122) and Walnut Toasts (page 164) are shaped into a loaf, baked, cooled, then sliced and baked again like a biscotti. Others, such as Orange-Almond Buttons (page 144) and S Cookies (page 155), are piped out of a pastry bag and baked immediately. For Rugelach (page 151), the cream cheese dough gets folded and turned, mocking a puff pastry for the flakiest, lightest, and tastiest Rugelach ever.

Because most cookies are so small and tend to get stale more quickly, I prefer to bake them as close to serving time as possible. From the simplest Shortbread to the more time-consuming Iced Raisin Squares (page 128), most of the doughs can be prepared in advance and baked as you need them. If you do have stale cookies (except for meringues and filled cookies), save them in the freezer to recycle into the crumbs you'll need for Crumb Biscotti.

The equipment for baking cookies is basic. Your best investment will be in heavy-duty baking sheets (see "Sources," page

393). The cheaper versions always warp and cause endless baking frustration. Parchment paper or Silpats (see "Sources") are necessary to prevent sticking and to provide a clean baking surface. Different ovens heat differently, so watch your baking time; it may differ slightly from mine. Rotating your baking sheets midway through baking is a good habit; especially if you're using both oven racks, you'll definitely need to switch them halfway through.

Just because cookies are small doesn't mean they're not sophisticated. They may not have two sauces, four fillings, and a mint sprig, but they are pretty to look at, full of flavor and, when served as an assortment, will accommodate everyone's tastes and moods. When made with love and attention, they're a first-rate dessert in my book.

Almond Slice-and-Bakes

THESE THIN, DELICATE BUTTER COOKIES ARE SIMPLE AND QUICK TO MAKE. Shape the dough into bricks, store in the freezer and you'll always have ready-to-bake cookies at a moment's notice.

Make sure the almonds for garnishing are freshly toasted. If you're baking small amounts of cookies at a time, toast only what you need. Hint: ½ cup of almonds is enough to garnish a dozen cookies.

4 cups (12 ounces) sliced unblanched almonds
4 cups (1¼ pounds) whole unblanched almonds (This amount will garnish the entire recipe of
  cookies. Toast as needed.)
1 tablespoon plus 2 teaspoons pure almond extract
2 teaspoons pure vanilla extract
3 extra-large eggs
4 sticks (1 pound) unsalted butter, chilled and cut into 1-inch cubes
1 teaspoon kosher salt
1 teaspoon baking soda
½ teaspoon freshly grated nutmeg
1 cup granulated sugar
1 cup light brown sugar, lightly packed
4 cups unbleached pastry flour or unbleached all-purpose flour

Adjust the oven rack to the middle position and preheat the oven to 325 degrees. Spread the sliced almonds on a baking sheet and toast in the oven until lightly browned, about 5 to 7 minutes. On another baking sheet, toast the desired amount of whole almonds 8 to 12 minutes, until lightly toasted. Shake the pan halfway through to ensure that the nuts toast evenly. Coarsely chop the whole almonds and set aside.

In a small bowl, whisk together the almond extract, vanilla extract, and eggs.

In the bowl of an electric mixer fitted with the paddle attachment, cream the butter, salt, baking soda, and nutmeg on low, 2 to 3 minutes, until softened. Add the sugars and turn the mixer up to medium, mixing another 3 to 4 minutes until light and fluffy, scraping down the sides of the bowl as needed.

"PART OF THE FUN OF MAKING COOKIES IS
THE VARIETY OF TECHNIQUES USED."

Add the egg mixture, 1 tablespoonful at a time, mixing well before each addition. If the mixture begins to separate, add a few tablespoons of the measured flour.

Add the flour in 3 batches, mixing on low and turning the mixer off before each addition. Mix until the dough barely comes together. Remove the bowl from the mixer and gently stir in the sliced almonds.

Turn the dough out onto a lightly floured work surface, divide it into 2 pieces, and flatten into 2 rough rectangles. Wrap in plastic and chill for 20 to 30 minutes, until firm.

Drop each side of the rectangles against the work surface to help compress the dough, eliminating any air pockets. Shape each one into a rectangular bar about 8 × 3½ inches and 1 inch high. Wrap in plastic and place the bars in the freezer until frozen, at least 2 hours or overnight.

Adjust the oven rack to the middle position and preheat the oven to 350 degrees.

Remove one bar of the dough from the freezer. Place it on a cutting board and, using a very sharp knife, cut slices slightly under ¼ inch thick and place them ½ inch apart on a parchment-lined baking sheet. Lightly brush each cookie with water and sprinkle the top with about 1 tablespoon of the chopped almonds, allowing some of the nuts to topple off the edges and some of the dough to peek through.

Bake for about 12 minutes, until lightly browned and crispy.

Repeat with the remaining dough or store in the freezer, wrapped tightly in plastic wrap.

Yield: 8 dozen cookies

Almond Sunflowers

THESE BUTTERY SHORTBREADS, NAMED FOR THEIR SIZE AND ALMOND SLICE petals, are so big that one will satisfy you. Since these cookies are all about the butter, shop for the best. An imported Normandy butter is my first choice, available at upscale markets or cheese shops.

Special Item: 5-INCH ROUND CUTTER

   2 sticks (8 ounces) unsalted butter, chilled and cut into 1-inch cubes
   ¼ teaspoon kosher salt
   ¼ cup granulated sugar
   ¼ cup light brown sugar, lightly packed
   2 cups unbleached pastry flour or unbleached all-purpose flour
   ¼ cup cornstarch
   3 extra-large egg yolks
   2 tablespoons pure vanilla extract

   FOR GARNISHING:
   25 unblanched sliced almonds (whole slices, not broken in pieces)

In the bowl of an electric mixer fitted with the paddle attachment, cream the butter and salt on low for 2 to 3 minutes, until softened. Add the sugars and mix on medium another 3 to 4 minutes, until light and fluffy, scraping down the sides of the bowl as needed.

In a medium bowl, sift to combine the flour and cornstarch.

In a small bowl, whisk the egg yolks and pour into a measuring cup. Pour half of the egg yolks back into the small bowl and whisk in the vanilla extract. Set aside the remaining yolks to brush on the cookies.

Turn the mixer to medium and add the egg mixture a teaspoon at a time, mixing well between each addition.

Add the flour mixture in 3 batches, mixing on low and turning the mixer off before each addition. Mix until the dough barely comes together.

Turn the dough out onto a lightly floured work surface and knead a few times to gather into a ball. Flatten into a disc, cover in plastic wrap, and chill until firm, at least 2 hours or overnight.

On a lightly floured surface, roll the dough out to slightly thicker than ¼ inch, flouring the surface of the dough as necessary. Cutting as closely together as possible, cut out the circles. Place the cookies 1 inch apart on two parchment-lined baking sheets. Gather the scraps and cut out the remaining dough.

Adjust the oven rack to the upper and lower positions and preheat the oven to 350 degrees.

In a small bowl, whisk the remaining egg yolk with a few drops of water and brush the surface of each cookie. Place the almond slices, touching, around the outer edge of the cookie, with the pointed tips facing outward. Press down on them lightly to ensure that they stick.

Bake for about 20 to 30 minutes, until lightly browned and firm to the touch. Halfway through baking, rotate the baking sheets to ensure the cookies bake evenly.

Yield: 9 large cookies

Crumb Biscotti

IF *BISCOTTI* MEANS "TWICE BAKED," THEN WHAT WOULD YOU CALL A COOKIE that's baked three times? This biscotti has already-baked cookie crumbs in the batter—that's once baked; it's baked into a loaf—that's twice; and then it's sliced into cookies and baked one last time. Developed as a way to use up leftover cookies at the bakery, it has become our new favorite. Any crumbs will work, from leftover cake trimmings to store-bought cookies to homemade Graham Crackers (page 124). At home, save your old cookies and cake scraps in the freezer, dry them out on a baking sheet in the oven, and get rid of your guilt by literally using up every last crumb.

1¼ cups unbleached pastry flour or unbleached all-purpose flour

1¼ cups dry cookie or chocolate cake crumbs, plus a few tablespoons for sprinkling

½ cup plus 2 tablespoons granulated sugar

½ teaspoon baking powder

½ teaspoon baking soda

½ teaspoon ground cinnamon

½ teaspoon ground ginger

1 extra-large egg

1 extra-large egg yolk

3 tablespoons (1½ ounces) unsalted butter, melted and cooled

1 extra-large egg white, slightly beaten, for brushing the tops of the biscotti

Adjust the oven rack to the middle position and preheat the oven to 350 degrees.

In the bowl of an electric mixer fitted with the paddle attachment, combine the flour, crumbs, sugar, baking powder, baking soda, cinnamon, and ginger, and mix on low to combine.

In a small bowl, whisk the whole egg and egg yolk together. Slowly whisk in the melted butter.

Turn the mixer to low and slowly pour in the butter mixture, mixing until just combined.

Turn the dough out onto a lightly floured work surface. Using your hands, flatten it into a rectangle and fold the dough over onto itself, packing it into a completely solid brick. Keep patting the dough and dropping it against the surface to compress it and eliminate all the air holes. Using both hands, roll the brick back and forth to round the edges. Continue rolling the dough until you have a log about 15 inches long.

Transfer the log to a parchment-lined baking sheet. Flatten it slightly to form a loaf, brush the top with the egg white, and sprinkle with the crumbs to cover.

Bake the loaf until firm to the touch, about 35 minutes.

Allow to cool completely.

Preheat the oven to 200 degrees.

Using a serrated knife, slice the loaf into cookies, about $1/4$ inch thick. Arrange the biscotti on a parchment-lined baking sheet.

Bake until firm and dry, about 20 to 30 minutes.

Yield: 36 biscotti

Dunkers

LIKE BISCOTTI, THESE COOKIES ARE BAKED IN ONE LARGE LOAF, SLICED, AND baked again. Buttery and crisp, they remind me of a slice of toasted poundcake, flavored with a touch of fennel. I prefer the shape of the Venison mold (see "Sources," page 393), a rounded loaf pan with a ribbed bottom. If you don't have one, any loaf-style pan will do. And as their name implies, these dense and flavorful cookies are best when dunked in coffee, tea, or milk.

Special Item: 12-INCH-LONG RIBBED VENISON MOLD OR 4-CUP-CAPACITY
LOAF PAN, LIGHTLY COATED WITH MELTED BUTTER

1 tablespoon fennel seeds
2 sticks (8 ounces) unsalted butter, chilled and cut into 1-inch cubes
1/4 teaspoon kosher salt
1 teaspoon baking powder
2 teaspoons finely chopped lemon zest (about 1 lemon)
1 cup granulated sugar
2 tablespoons heavy cream
2 extra-large eggs
2 teaspoons pure almond extract
3 cups unbleached pastry flour or unbleached all-purpose flour

Adjust the oven rack to the middle position and preheat the oven to 350 degrees.

In a small sauté pan over medium-low heat, toast the fennel seeds, stirring occasionally until they become aromatic and slightly browned, about 2 to 3 minutes. Allow to cool. In a spice grinder or clean coffee grinder, grind the seeds to a fine powder.

In the bowl of an electric mixer fitted with the paddle attachment, cream the butter, ground fennel, salt, baking powder, and lemon zest on low, 2 to 3 minutes, until softened. Add the sugar and mix on medium for 3 to 4 minutes, until light and fluffy, scraping down the sides of the bowl as needed.

In a small bowl, whisk together the cream, eggs, and almond extract. Turn the mixer to medium and add the egg mixture a few teaspoons at a time, mixing well between each addition.

Add the flour in 3 batches, turning the mixer off before each addition and mixing on low until just combined.

Transfer the dough to the prepared mold and spread to even. Bake for about 30 to 40 minutes. After about 15 to 20 minutes, check the loaf to see if it has inflated and cracked. If so, remove it from the oven. Using a towel, firmly press on the dough to deflate it, patting it with your hands to seal the cracks back together. Return the dough to the oven for the remaining baking time, until firm and lightly browned.

Allow to cool completely, and remove from the mold.

Turn the oven down to 200 degrees.

Using a serrated knife, slice the loaf into cookies, about ¾ inch thick, and arrange on a parchment-lined baking sheet.

Bake until very firm and lightly browned, about 30 minutes to an hour.

Yield: 15 cookies

Graham Crackers

GRAHAM CRACKERS ARE THE ULTIMATE CHILDHOOD COMFORT FOOD. First invented by an American minister who also preached fanatically on diet and health in the 1830s, graham crackers have a honey whole-wheat flavor and healthy reputation that have endured the test of time. Mothers feel guilt-free handing over a graham cracker when their kids ask for something sweet.

After making many versions of graham crackers, I found they tasted much better when you don't use whole-wheat flour. But if you can't ignore your guilty conscience, go ahead and substitute half the amount of flour with whole wheat. Whether dipped in milk, used as the crust for Cheese Bars (page 229), or sandwiched with homemade Marshmallows (page 382) and dark chocolate, these graham crackers come as close to the real thing as I've ever tasted.

2½ cups plus 2 tablespoons unbleached pastry flour or unbleached all-purpose flour
1 cup dark brown sugar, lightly packed
1 teaspoon baking soda
¾ teaspoon kosher salt
7 tablespoons (3½ ounces) unsalted butter, cut into 1-inch cubes and frozen
⅓ cup mild-flavored honey, such as clover
5 tablespoons whole milk
2 tablespoons pure vanilla extract

FOR THE TOPPING:
3 tablespoons granulated sugar
1 teaspoon ground cinnamon

In the bowl of a food processor fitted with the steel blade or in the bowl of an electric mixer fitted with the paddle attachment, combine the flour, brown sugar, baking soda, and salt. Pulse or mix on low to incorporate. Add the butter and pulse on and off, or mix on low, until the mixture is the consistency of a coarse meal.

In a small bowl, whisk together the honey, milk, and vanilla extract. Add to the flour mixture and pulse on and off a few times or mix on low until the dough barely comes together. It will be very soft and sticky.

Turn the dough out onto a lightly floured work surface and pat the dough into a rectangle about 1 inch thick. Wrap in plastic and chill until firm, about 2 hours or overnight.

To prepare the topping: In a small bowl, combine the sugar and cinnamon, and set aside.

Divide the dough in half and return one half to the refrigerator. Sift an even layer of flour onto the work surface and roll the dough into a long rectangle about $\frac{1}{8}$ inch thick. The dough will be sticky, so flour as necessary. Trim the edges of the rectangle to 4 inches wide. Working with the shorter side of the rectangle parallel to the work surface, cut the strip every $4\frac{1}{2}$ inches to make 4 crackers. Gather the scraps together and set aside. Place the crackers on one or two parchment-lined baking sheets and sprinkle with the topping. Chill until firm, about 30 to 45 minutes. Repeat with the second batch of dough.

Adjust the oven rack to the upper and lower positions and preheat the oven to 350 degrees.

Gather the scraps together into a ball, chill until firm, and reroll. Dust the surface with more flour and roll out the dough to get about two or three more crackers.

Mark a vertical line down the middle of each cracker, being careful not to cut through the dough. Using a toothpick or a skewer, prick the dough to form two dotted rows about $\frac{1}{2}$ inch from each side of the middle dividing line.

Bake for 25 minutes, until browned and slightly firm to the touch, rotating the baking sheets halfway through to ensure even baking.

Yield: 10 large crackers

Guatemalan Cookies

Every country has its plain, simple biscuit—Scotland has short-bread, Germany has rusks, and Italy has biscotti. When one of the night bakers made these biscuity Day of the Dead cookies for the retail store, I was instantly enamored. Shaped into primitive-style people and decorated with seeds, these adorable Latin American cookies are so beautiful to look at, you may just want to hang them on the wall. Make them into spiral shapes and you won't have any regrets when you eat them.

1 stick (4 ounces) unsalted butter, chilled and cut into 1-inch pieces
½ teaspoon kosher salt
1 teaspoon baking powder
1 teaspoon orange zest, finely chopped (about ½ orange)
1½ cups plus 1 tablespoon granulated sugar
1 tablespoon pure vanilla extract
3 extra-large egg yolks
4½ cups plus 2 tablespoons unbleached pastry flour or unbleached all-purpose flour

FOR DECORATING:
1 extra-large egg, slightly beaten
1 teaspoon poppy seeds, optional
1 teaspoon fennel seeds, optional
1 teaspoon sesame seeds, optional

In the bowl of an electric mixer fitted with the paddle attachment, cream the butter, salt, baking powder, and orange zest for 2 to 3 minutes on low, until softened. Add the sugar and mix on medium, 3 to 4 minutes, until light and fluffy, scraping down the sides of the bowl as needed.

In a small bowl, whisk together the vanilla extract and egg yolks. Add the egg yolk mixture a few teaspoons at a time, and mix until just combined.

Add the flour in 3 batches, turning the mixer off before each addition and mixing on low until just combined.

Turn the dough out onto a lightly floured work surface and pat it into a rectangle, about 1 inch thick. Wrap in plastic and chill until firm, at least 2 hours or overnight.

Adjust the oven rack to the upper and lower positions and preheat the oven to 350 degrees.

Divide the dough in half and return one half to the refrigerator.

To shape the primitive-style people: Roll out two ropes about 6 inches long, a little thicker than a pencil. Place one on top of the other to form an X, pressing down with your fingers where the two ropes intersect. Place on 1–2 parchment-lined baking sheets. Roll a 1-inch ball to form the stomach and gently press it into the middle of the X. Roll a slightly smaller ball for the head and press onto the dough just above the stomach. Lower the top ropes down so they look like arms. Adjust the legs. For the females, roll out 1½-inch-long very thin ropes and twist them together to form hair. Attach to the head by pressing down slightly. For men, roll out a ½-inch-long skinny coil to use as the mustache. Brush with egg wash and sprinkle poppy seeds to form bangs, or short hair for men. Use the fennel seeds as eyes. Continue with the remaining dough.

To shape the spiral cookies: Pick up about 2 tablespoons of the dough and roll it out into a 4-inch-long snake, about the width of a pencil. Working on 1–2 parchment-lined baking sheets, coil the end in and continue coiling the rope into a spiral shape. When you get to the end of the rope press it into the dough to ensure that it sticks.

Brush each shape with egg and sprinkle a few cookies with fennel seeds, a few with sesame seeds, and a few with poppy seeds.

Bake for about 20 minutes until firm, rotating the baking sheets halfway through to ensure even baking.

Yield: 12 to 24 cookies, depending on the shapes and sizes

Iced Raisin Squares

When I was growing up, the only cookies my mother would buy were the wholesome ones like Fig Newtons or raisin bars, those long, flat cookies whose ends fit together like a jigsaw puzzle and that came layered in a long, cellophane package. As a child, I resented her health-conscious choices, but now I can finally appreciate the pure, delicious simplicity of this cookie.

For that authentic look, use a fluted pastry wheel to achieve those charming zigzag edges. And once they're baked, break them along the scored zigzag marks to separate.

Special Items: FLUTED PASTRY WHEEL, OPTIONAL

FOR THE DOUGH:
1¼ cups unbleached pastry flour or unbleached all-purpose flour
½ teaspoon kosher salt
⅛ teaspoon ground cloves
1 teaspoon ground cinnamon
3 tablespoons granulated sugar
2 tablespoons light brown sugar, lightly packed
½ cup (4 ounces) almond paste
5 extra-large eggs, hard-boiled
2 tablespoons pure vanilla extract
1 stick (4 ounces) unsalted butter, chilled and cut into 1-inch cubes

FOR THE FILLING:
1¼ cups (7–8 ounces) raisins or currants
¾ cup water
1 extra-large egg yolk, beaten with a splash of water, for brushing the dough

FOR THE GLAZE:
3 tablespoons powdered sugar
1 tablespoon heavy cream

To prepare the dough: In the bowl of a food processor fitted with a steel blade or in the bowl of an electric mixer fitted with the paddle attachment, combine the flour,

salt, cloves, cinnamon, and sugars, and pulse or mix on low to incorporate. Crumble in the almond paste and process or mix on low to combine.

Separate and discard the whites of the eggs. Push the egg yolks through a fine-mesh sieve. Add to the flour mixture, and pulse or mix on low to combine. Add the vanilla extract and butter and pulse on and off, or mix on low, until it barely comes together.

Turn the dough out onto a lightly floured work surface and knead a few times to gather together. Divide the dough into four pieces and form each quarter into a rectangular bar about 1 inch thick. Wrap in plastic and chill until firm, about 1 to 2 hours.

Meanwhile, to prepare the filling: In a small saucepan, over medium-high heat, combine the raisins and water. Bring to a boil, shaking the pan to prevent the raisins from sticking. Cook until the liquid is completely reduced, about 5 minutes. Allow to cool a few minutes.

Finely chop the raisins and return them to the saucepan, and cook over medium-high heat, stirring constantly for about 1 to 2 minutes, until dry. Set aside and allow to cool.

Working with one piece of dough at a time and keeping the rest chilled, roll the dough out on a floured surface, into an 8 × 5-inch rectangle, ⅛ inch thick. The dough will be sticky, so flour as necessary, or roll it between two sheets of parchment or wax paper. Carefully transfer the dough to a parchment-lined baking sheet to chill 30 to 45 minutes until very firm. Continue with the remaining dough, placing the rectangular strips side by side on two baking sheets. (If you have only one baking sheet, stack the strips on top of each other, separated by parchment or wax paper to chill.)

To assemble the cookies: Working directly on the baking sheet, trim the edges of all four strips to 8 inches long and 4½ inches wide. Evenly distribute the raisins over the surface of the two strips of dough, to ½ inch from the edge. There will be some small gaps between the raisins. Brush the edges with the beaten egg yolk. Place the remaining two strips of dough over the raisins, aligning the edges with the bottom layer of dough. Lightly dust the surface of each with flour and, using a rolling pin, gently roll over the entire surface of the strips a few times until you can just see the color of the raisins peeking through the dough. Chill 10 to 15 minutes until firm.

Adjust the oven rack to the middle position and preheat the oven to 350 degrees.

Using a fluted pastry wheel, trim the edges of both strips to decorate and seal. Continuing with the fluted wheel, score a vertical line down the center of each strip, being careful not to break through the dough. At 2-inch intervals, score the dough horizontally to form eight rectangular cookies on each strip. Brush the entire surface with egg and, using a toothpick, dot each square 4 to 5 times to make 2 rows.

Bake for 20 to 25 minutes, until firm to the touch and lightly browned.

To make the glaze: In a small bowl, combine the sugar and cream.

Allow the bars to cool and brush the surface with glaze. If the glaze is too thin, add a touch more powdered sugar to thicken.

To break into individual cookies: Place the bar on the counter, with the shorter side closest to the edge. Align the first horizontal scored mark with the counter edge and break it off, using the edge of the counter as a guide to break against. You may first need to make a very short incision with a knife at the mark's edge to start the breaks. Slide the cookie down to the next mark and break off, continuing with the rest in the same manner. Break the bars in half at the vertical scored mark.

Yield: 16 cookies

Italian Nut Cookies

LIKE MACAROONS, THESE FLOURLESS COOKIES HAVE AN EGG-WHITE AND AL-
mond base, making them very moist and chewy. Their flavor reminds me of Italian
Amaretti cookies, but mine are nuttier and less bitter.

To decorate with powdered sugar, you'll need a bottle cap or small lid that fits
over the almond halves so just the cookie gets sugared, not the almonds.

2½ cups (10 ounces) whole unblanched almonds
1 cup granulated sugar
1 teaspoon baking powder
¼ cup citrus marmalade (orange, lemon, or grapefruit)
2 tablespoons pure almond extract
2 extra-large egg whites
Powdered sugar for dusting, optional

Adjust the oven rack to the middle position and preheat the oven to 325 degrees.

Separate out 36 almonds and, using a paring knife, slice the almonds in half
lengthwise, severing each from the pointed tip to the rounded bottom. If there are
any broken pieces or crumbs, set them aside. Place the almond halves split side up on
a baking sheet and toast in the oven for about 8 to 10 minutes, until lightly toasted.

In a food processor fitted with the steel blade, grind the remaining nuts and any
broken pieces of nuts with half of the sugar and baking powder until it's the consistency of a fine meal. Add the remaining sugar, marmalade, almond extract, and egg
whites, and pulse on and off until just combined. Chill until firm, about 1 hour.

Turn the oven up to 350 degrees.

Pick up a walnut-size portion of dough and squeeze it in the palm of your hand
to eliminate cracks and air pockets. Roll it between your palms to form a ½-inch ball
and continue with the remaining dough. Place the balls at least 1 inch apart on 2
parchment-lined baking sheets. Place 2 almond halves, skin side up, in the center of
each cookie, overlapping the wider ends to make a V shape. Press down to ensure that
they stick.

Bake for about 15 to 20 minutes, until firm, rotating the baking sheets halfway through to ensure even baking.

Allow to cool. Cover the almonds with a round bottle cap and dust the cookie with powdered sugar, if desired.

Yield: 36 cookies

Jewish–Chinese Almond Cookies

THIS IS THE COOKIE I LOOK FOR IN JEWISH DELIS, ENORMOUS AND ROUND and usually decorated with a big chocolate drop in the middle. When I first described these cookies to Izzy Cohen, longtime friend and Jewish baker, he confidently replied, "Yeah, yeah, the Chinese cookies." Picturing those stale, greasy Chinese restaurant cookies, I doubted him, argued with him, and finally bet him a million dollars that he had the wrong cookie. As you can see, I lost the bet. Just to spite him, I made them smaller, added oats, and skipped the chocolate.

The cookie's old-fashioned flavor and crunchy open texture is a result of baker's ammonia (see "Sources," page 393), a leavening agent similar to baking powder. Don't be put off by its foul ammonia odor; it disappears when baked. If you don't have baker's ammonia, substitute baking powder. The flavor will be slightly different and the cookie won't be quite as crisp.

1 extra-large egg
3 tablespoons pure almond extract
2 sticks (8 ounces) unsalted butter, chilled and cut into 1-inch cubes
1½ teaspoons kosher salt
2 teaspoons baker's ammonia (or 2 teaspoons baking powder)
½ teaspoon baking soda
1¼ cups plus 3 tablespoons granulated sugar
1½ cups rolled oats
3¼ cups plus 2 tablespoons unbleached pastry flour or unbleached all-purpose flour
½ cup plus 1 tablespoon (3 ounces) or 65–70 whole unblanched almonds

In a small bowl, whisk together the egg and almond extract.

In the bowl of an electric mixer fitted with the paddle attachment, cream the butter, salt, baker's ammonia, and baking soda on low, 2 to 3 minutes, until softened. Add the sugar and mix for 3 to 4 more minutes, until light and fluffy, scraping down the sides of the bowl as needed. Add the oats and mix on low until combined. Turn the mixer up to medium and add the egg mixture a little at a time, mixing well between each addition.

Add the flour in 3 batches, turning the mixer off before each addition and mixing on low until just combined.

Turn the dough out onto a lightly floured work surface and knead a few times to gather into a ball. Wrap in plastic and chill about 1 hour, until firm.

Adjust the oven rack to the upper and lower positions and preheat the oven to 350 degrees.

Pick up a walnut-size portion of dough and squeeze it into the palm of your hand to eliminate cracks and air pockets. Roll it between your palms to form a $\frac{1}{2}$-inch ball and continue with the remaining dough. Place the balls at least 2 inches apart on 2 parchment-lined baking sheets.

Firmly press a whole almond into the center of each ball of dough, pushing down to ensure that it sticks.

Bake for 20 to 25 minutes, until very lightly browned, rotating the baking sheets halfway through to ensure even baking.

Yield: 65 to 70 cookies

Linzer Cookies

I NEVER TIRE OF THE TASTE OF THAT CLASSIC LINZER COMBINATION, A SPICY nutty crust with sweet raspberry jam. These cut-out, sandwich-style cookies are best suited to simple shapes such as hearts, circles, squares, and diamonds.

Special Items: 2½-INCH ROUND OR HEART-, SQUARE- OR DIAMOND- OR STAR-SHAPED CUTTER OR PUNCH CUTTERS (SEE "SOURCES," PAGE 393)

I-INCH ROUND OR I-INCH HEART CUTTER, FOR CUTTING OUT THE CENTER OF THE COOKIES

¼ cup (1½ ounces) hazelnuts
½ cup (2½ ounces) whole unblanched almonds
½ cup plus 2 tablespoons granulated sugar
1 tablespoon ground cinnamon
2 cups plus 4 tablespoons unbleached pastry flour or unbleached all-purpose flour
4 extra-large eggs, hard-boiled
2 sticks (8 ounces) unsalted butter, chilled and cut into 1-inch cubes
1 teaspoon lemon zest, finely chopped (about ½ lemon)
1 teaspoon pure almond extract
Powdered sugar, for dusting
1 cup raspberry jam

Adjust the oven rack to the middle position and preheat the oven to 325 degrees. Spread the hazelnuts and almonds on a baking sheet and toast in the oven until lightly browned, about 10 to 12 minutes. Shake the pan halfway through baking to ensure that the nuts toast evenly. Allow the nuts to cool. Gather the hazelnuts into a kitchen towel and rub them together to remove the skins.

In the bowl of a food processor fitted with the steel blade, combine the hazelnuts and almonds with ¼ cup of the sugar and the cinnamon, and process until it's the consistency of a fine meal. Add the flour and pulse a few times to combine.

Separate and discard the whites of the eggs. Push the egg yolks through a fine-mesh sieve, scraping the yolks off the bottom of the sieve and into the flour mixture. Pulse on and off a few times to combine.

In the bowl of an electric mixer fitted with the paddle attachment, cream the butter and lemon zest on low, 2 to 3 minutes, until softened. Add the remaining sugar and mix on medium, 3 to 4 minutes, until light and fluffy, scraping down the sides of the bowl as needed. Add the almond extract and mix to combine. Turn the mixer off, add the nut mixture, and mix on low until just incorporated.

Turn the dough out onto a lightly floured work surface and flatten into a rectangle, about 1 inch thick. Wrap in plastic and chill until firm, 1 to 2 hours or overnight.

Divide the dough in half and return one half to the refrigerator. On a lightly floured surface, roll the dough out to ⅛-inch thickness, flouring the surface of the dough as necessary. Using the shaped cutter, cutting as closely together as possible, cut out the cookies. Place them 1 inch apart on 1–2 parchment-lined baking sheets to chill until firm, 30 to 45 minutes. Set the scraps aside.

Roll and cut out the remaining dough in the same manner. Gather all the scraps together, chill, roll, and cut to make the tops. Using the small cutter, cut out the centers of half of the cookies and chill until firm, 30 to 45 minutes.

Adjust the oven racks to the upper and lower positions and preheat the oven to 350 degrees.

Bake for 15 to 20 minutes, until firm to the touch and lightly browned, rotating the baking sheets halfway through to ensure even baking. The cookies with the holes may bake more quickly than the others.

Allow to cool and dust the perforated cookies with powdered sugar.

Flip over the cookies without holes, placing the darker side of the cookie underneath. Spoon about 1½ to 2 teaspoons of the raspberry jam into the center. Place the perforated cookies, powdered sugar side up, on top of the jam, matching up the edges and pressing gently to spread the jam.

Yield: 4 dozen 2-inch cookies, depending on the size of your cutters

Meringues

I AM A MERINGUE LOVER. THEY'RE SO PRETTY TO LOOK AT WHEN PILED ON top of a platter or stacked in the window of a French bakery. Though they're not for everybody, meringues are a great solution for the wheat-free sweet tooth and flour- or leaven-free holidays such as Passover. The nuts and chocolate balance out the sugary sweetness and add some crunch to the airy texture.

I like to serve both flavors of these meringues together. To do this, simply follow the recipe (using 4 egg whites) up to the point where you beat the egg whites, powdered sugar, and vanilla until cooled. Then, split the batter into two bowls and fold in half of the amount of almonds and cocoa powder into one bowl and half the amount of walnuts and chocolate into the other for 20 almond meringues and 20 walnut meringues. At the bakery, we make them the size of Ping-Pong balls, but you can make them whatever size you want. Watch that you don't overbake these; they're much better just slightly underdone and chewy.

Special Item: #3 SCOOP (2-TABLESPOON CAPACITY), OPTIONAL

FOR THE CHOCOLATE-ALMOND MERINGUES:

1½ cups (6 ounces) slivered blanched almonds
1 vanilla bean
4 extra-large egg whites
2 cups powdered sugar
1 tablespoon unsweetened cocoa powder

FOR THE CHOCOLATE-WALNUT MERINGUES:

1½ cups (6 ounces) walnut halves
1 vanilla bean
4 extra-large egg whites
2 cups powdered sugar
8 ounces coarsely chopped bittersweet chocolate

Adjust the oven rack to the middle position and preheat the oven to 325 degrees. Spread the nuts on a baking sheet and toast in the oven until lightly browned, about 10 to 15 minutes. Shake the pan halfway through to ensure that the nuts toast evenly.

Turn the oven down to 200 degrees.

Place the bowl of an electric mixer or a stainless-steel bowl over a pot of gently simmering water, making sure the bottom of the bowl isn't touching the water. Using a small paring knife, split the vanilla bean lengthwise and, with the back of the knife, scrape out the pulp and the seeds and add the scrapings to the bowl. Pour in the egg whites and powdered sugar, and whisk until opaque-white and slightly thickened and mousselike, about 5 to 7 minutes. The mixture should be just thick enough to coat the back of a spoon. Remove from the heat.

In the bowl of an electric mixer fitted with the whisk attachment, beat the mixture on high until stiff peaks form. Turn the mixer down to medium-low and beat about 5 more minutes until cooled and very stiff, smooth, and glossy.

Remove from the mixer and fold in the almonds and cocoa powder or the walnut halves and chocolate (or if you're making both types—see recipe introduction).

Scoop or spoon the meringues onto a parchment-lined baking sheet, using another spoon to scrape it off the scoop and flicking your wrist to encourage irregular spiky peaks to form on top of each meringue. They should each be about the size of a Ping-Pong ball. It may be necessary to dip the scoop or spoon into cool water (shaking off the excess) to help the meringues slide off more easily.

Bake for 45 minutes to an hour, until the meringues lift off the paper, the outsides are firm to the touch, and the center is still soft.

Yield: 40 meringues

Moravian Ginger Snaps

THIS COOKIE IS NOT FOR THE WIMPY OR SENSITIVE TONGUE. THE GINGER snaps I love are full of fresh ginger and plenty of spice. If you're not as macho as me, go ahead and decrease the amount of fresh ginger.

Special Item: 3-INCH ROUND CUTTER

> *1 stick (4 ounces) unsalted butter, chilled and cut into 1-inch cubes*
> *½ teaspoon baking soda*
> *¼ teaspoon kosher salt*
> *3 tablespoons ground ginger*
> *2 tablespoons fresh grated ginger (approximately one 2-inch piece)*
> *1 teaspoon ground cinnamon*
> *¼ teaspoon freshly grated nutmeg*
> *¼ teaspoon ground cloves*
> *¾ cup granulated sugar*
> *2 tablespoons light brown sugar, lightly packed*
> *2 tablespoons molasses*
> *1 extra-large egg white*
> *1 cup plus 4 tablespoons unbleached pastry flour or unbleached all-purpose flour*

In the bowl of an electric mixer fitted with the paddle attachment, cream the butter, baking soda, salt, ground ginger, fresh ginger, cinnamon, nutmeg, and cloves on low, 2 to 3 minutes, until softened. Add the sugars and mix on medium for 3 to 4 minutes until light and fluffy, scraping down the sides of the bowl as needed. Add the molasses and mix another half minute. Add the egg white and mix on low until combined.

Add the flour in 3 batches, turning the mixer off before each addition and mixing on low until just combined, scraping down the sides of the bowl as needed.

Turn the dough out onto a lightly floured work surface and flatten into a 1-inch-thick disc. Wrap in plastic and chill until firm, at least 4 to 6 hours or overnight.

Divide the dough in half and return one half to the refrigerator. On a floured surface, roll the dough out to ⅛-inch thickness. The dough will be sticky, so flour as necessary. Cutting as closely together as possible, cut out the cookies. Place them on

1–2 parchment-lined baking sheets and chill until firm, about 20 minutes. Set the scraps aside.

Adjust the oven racks to the upper and lower positions and preheat the oven to 350 degrees.

Roll and cut out the remaining dough in the same manner. Gather all of the scraps together, chill, roll, and cut.

Bake for 15 to 20 minutes, until nicely browned and crispy, rotating the baking sheets halfway through to ensure even baking.

Yield: Approximately 36 cookies

Nun's Breasts

Evocative-sounding and evocative-looking, these Sicilian treats won't allow you to repress anything, especially your appetite. Invented by a convent of nuns in Erice, Nun's Breasts, in my version, are crunchy cornmeal pastries filled with vanilla cream and dusted with powdered sugar. Discreetly ordered by our shyer customers, these delicious cookies fly out the door with a chuckle.

Special Items: 2½-INCH FLUTED CUTTER
2¾-INCH FLUTED CUTTER
1¾-INCH ROUND CUTTER (TO MARK INNER CIRCLE)
PASTRY BAG FITTED WITH A #3 PASTRY TIP, OPTIONAL

1¼ cups semolina flour
2¼ cups unbleached pastry flour or unbleached all-purpose flour, plus about 3 tablespoons extra for dusting
½ cup plus 3 tablespoons finely ground cornmeal
1½ teaspoons kosher salt
1¼ cups powdered sugar
1¾ sticks (7 ounces) unsalted butter, chilled and cut into small pieces
4 extra-large egg yolks, plus 1 additional extra-large yolk beaten with a few drops of water for brushing the dough
½ cup heavy cream
1 tablespoon pure vanilla extract
½ recipe Pastry Cream (see Kinder Pies, page 245), chilled

FOR DECORATING:
¼ cup powdered sugar

To prepare the dough: In the bowl of a food processor fitted with the steel blade or in the bowl of an electric mixer fitted with the paddle attachment, combine the flours, cornmeal, salt, and powdered sugar and pulse or mix on low to incorporate. Add the butter and pulse or mix on low until it's the consistency of a fine meal.

Transfer the mixture to a large bowl. Make a large well in the center and pour in the egg yolks, cream, and vanilla extract, and whisk together the liquids to combine. Using one hand, draw in the dry ingredients, mixing until combined.

Wash and dry your hands and dust them with flour. Turn the dough out onto a floured work surface. Knead the dough a few times, generously dusting it with flour. Continue kneading until it's no longer sticky and has the texture of modeling clay. Flatten the dough into a 1-inch-thick disc, wrap in plastic, and chill until firm, 2 hours or overnight.

Divide the dough in half and return one half to the refrigerator. On a lightly floured surface, roll the dough out to $\frac{1}{8}$-inch thickness, flouring the surface of the dough as necessary. Using the $2\frac{1}{2}$-inch fluted cutter, cutting as close together as possible, cut out 40 circles and place them 1 inch apart on 2 parchment-lined baking sheets.

On a floured surface, roll the remaining dough out to $\frac{1}{8}$-inch thickness. Using the $2\frac{3}{4}$-inch fluted cutter, cut out 40 circles.

If using a pastry bag, fill half full with Pastry Cream. Pipe or spoon a 1-inch-diameter circle (about 1 tablespoon) of cream into the center of each of the smaller circles of dough and brush the edges with the remaining egg yolk. Center the larger circle of dough over the mound of cream and gently press with your fingertips around the edges of the cream. Using the dull side of the plain round cutter, press down gently around the outer edge of the mound of cream filling, pressing to seal the two layers together (as you would for a ravioli), but not cutting through the dough. Chill until firm, about 30 minutes.

Adjust the oven rack to the middle position and preheat the oven to 350 degrees.

Bake for 30 minutes, until lightly browned, rotating the baking sheets halfway through to ensure even baking.

Cool and sift a fine layer of powdered sugar over the tops.

Yield: 40 cookies

Orange-Almond Buttons

LIKE A MERINGUE, THIS NUTTY ORANGE COOKIE IS LIGHT AND CRISPY. THE almonds on top add a little extra crunch, making these delicate buttons dangerously addictive. While you're eating them, you might recognize a familiar flavor. Does Trix breakfast cereal mean anything to you?

Special Item: PASTRY BAG FITTED WITH A #3 PASTRY TIP, OPTIONAL

> *Heaping ½ cup (2½ ounces) blanched or unblanched almonds*
> *½ cup granulated sugar*
> *3 tablespoons unbleached pastry flour or unbleached all-purpose flour*
> *1 tablespoon finely chopped orange zest (about 1 orange)*
> *2 extra-large egg whites*

> FOR DECORATING:
> *½ cup (about 2 ounces) sliced, blanched almonds*
> *powdered sugar*

Adjust the oven rack to the middle position and preheat the oven to 350 degrees.

In the bowl of a food processor fitted with the steel blade, combine the nuts with 2 tablespoons of the granulated sugar and process until it's the consistency of a fine meal. Add ¼ cup of the granulated sugar, the flour, and orange zest, and pulse on and off until just combined.

In the bowl of an electric mixer fitted with the whisk attachment, whip the egg whites on low, until frothy. Turn the mixer up to medium-high and beat until soft peaks form, another 2 to 3 minutes. Turn the mixer to high, gradually add the remaining 2 tablespoons of the sugar, and beat until stiff peaks form, about 2 to 3 more minutes.

Remove the bowl from the mixer. In 3 batches, gently fold in the nut mixture to incorporate.

If using a pastry bag, fill it half full. Working quickly, pipe or spoon the batter into circles, about 1 inch in diameter and spaced about 1 inch apart on a parchment-lined baking sheet. Scatter about 3 to 5 sliced almonds over each circle, allowing the nuts to topple off the edge slightly while still clinging to the batter. Sift a fine layer of powdered sugar over the cookies and bake about 20 minutes, until the nuts are lightly browned, and the cookies are slightly firm to the touch.

Yield: 36 cookies

Plum Pecorino Cookies

THIS IS THE COOKIE I EAT WHEN I CAN'T CHOOSE BETWEEN A SAVORY HUNK of cheese and a sweet pastry for dessert. Sweet red-fleshed plums covered with shavings of tangy Pecorino cheese prove once again that the classic pairing of fruit and cheese is eternally satisfying.

Special Items: 4³/₄-INCH ROUND FLUTED CUTTER
                              4-INCH ROUND CUTTER

2 recipes anise dough (see Red Plum Tart, page 270)
8 to 10 (2¹/₄ pounds) unpeeled, red-fleshed plums such as Santa Rosa or
*   Elephant Heart, ripe but firm*
1 recipe Almond Cream (see Almond Log, page 297)
3 tablespoons granulated sugar
¹/₂ teaspoon ground cinnamon
¹/₂ stick (2 ounces) unsalted butter, chilled and cut into ¹/₄-inch pieces
4 ounces Pecorino Sardo or Pecorino Romano cheese

On a lightly floured work surface, roll the dough out to ¹/₈-inch thickness, flouring the surface of the dough as necessary. Using the fluted cutter and cutting as closely together as possible, cut out the circles. Gather the scraps, roll, and cut out the remaining dough. Using the smaller round cutter, being careful not to break through the dough, mark a centered circle, leaving a ³/₄-inch border. Place on two parchment-lined baking sheets, 1 inch apart, and chill until you have sliced all of your plums and the dough is firm.

Using a thin, very sharp knife, slice the plums in half, remove the pits and cut into paper-thin slices. You'll need approximately 25 slices per cookie.

Adjust the oven rack to the upper and lower positions and preheat the oven to 350 degrees.

Using an offset spatula or the back of a spoon, spread about 2 teaspoons of Almond Cream on each round, staying inside the smaller marked circle.

Starting at the edge of the Almond Cream, layer the plum slices working from the outside in. Form an outer ring with 5 to 6 slices of plums, allowing the tips of the fruit to overlap. Begin your next ring about ⅛ inch in from the first circle, working your way toward the center like a chrysanthemum. As you layer, the concentric rings will become smaller, tighter, and higher. Keep layering until you have a pile that is about 1 inch high.

In a small bowl, combine the sugar and cinnamon.

Dot each cookie with about 1 teaspoon of the butter and sprinkle with about ½ teaspoon of the cinnamon-sugar.

Bake for 20 to 25 minutes, until lightly browned, rotating the baking sheets halfway through to ensure even baking. Allow to cool. Shave a few thin pieces of the Pecorino cheese over the plums.

Yield: 14 large cookies

Pretty Pear Cookies

You may argue that it's not a cookie. You may want to call it a small tart. Call it what you like, but you can't argue about its looks—it's definitely very pretty.

Special Items: 4³⁄₄-INCH ROUND FLUTED CUTTER
4-INCH ROUND CUTTER

1 recipe (1½ pounds) Sweet Pastry Dough (page 219), chilled
1 recipe (1¼ cups) Almond Cream (see Almond Log, page 297), enough for 2 batches

FOR THE PEARS:
6 to 8 (3 pounds) unpeeled Bartlett pears, ripe but firm
3 tablespoons granulated sugar
1 teaspoon ground cinnamon
½ stick (2 ounces) unsalted butter, chilled and cut into ¼-inch cubes

Divide the dough in half and return one half to the refrigerator. On a lightly floured work surface, roll the dough out to ⅛-inch thickness, flouring the surface as necessary. Using the fluted cutter and cutting as closely together as possible, cut out the circles. Gather the scraps and set aside. Roll and cut out the remaining dough in the same manner. Gather the scraps together, chill, roll, and cut. Using the smaller round cutter, being careful not to break through the dough, mark a centered circle, leaving a ¾-inch border. Place on two parchment-lined baking sheets, 1 inch apart, and chill until firm.

To slice the pear, cut it vertically away from the core in 4 pieces, giving you 2 larger pieces and 2 smaller pieces. Using a thin, very sharp knife, cut the pear lengthwise into paper-thin slices. You should get about 50 slices per pear and will need approximately 25 slices per cookie.

Adjust the oven rack to the upper and lower positions and preheat the oven to 350 degrees.

Using an offset spatula or the back of a spoon, spread about 2 teaspoons of Almond Cream on each round, staying inside of the smaller marked circle.

"CALL THEM WHAT YOU LIKE—THEY'RE DEFINITELY VERY PRETTY."

Starting at the edge of the Almond Cream, layer the pear slices working from the outside in. Form the outer ring with 5 to 6 slices of pear, allowing the tips of the fruit to overlap. Begin your next ring about ⅛ inch in from the first circle, working your way toward the center like a chrysanthemum. As you layer, the concentric rings will become smaller, tighter, and higher. Keep layering until you have a pile that is about 1 inch high.

In a small bowl, combine the sugar and cinnamon.

Dot each cookie with about 1 teaspoon of the butter and sprinkle with about ½ teaspoon of the cinnamon-sugar.

Bake for 20 to 25 minutes, until lightly browned, rotating the baking sheets halfway through to ensure even baking.

Yield: 14 large cookies

Rugelach

My buddy Izzy knows everything about baking. He even knows that by folding this cream cheese dough in the same manner as puff pastry, you get the lightest, flakiest, best-tasting Rugelach dough ever. Once you've mastered the Raspberry Rugelach, try the chocolate or prune variations.

FOR THE CREAM CHEESE DOUGH:

2 sticks (8 ounces) unsalted butter, chilled and cut into 1-inch cubes
½ teaspoon kosher salt
1 cup (8 ounces) cream cheese
2 cups unbleached all-purpose flour or high-gluten flour

FOR THE RASPBERRY FILLING:

1 extra-large egg, lightly beaten
½ cup granulated sugar
Sourdough bread finely ground to equal 1 cup bread crumbs
¾ cup raspberry jam

FOR THE TOPPING:

3 tablespoons granulated sugar
½ teaspoon ground cinnamon

To prepare the dough: In the bowl of an electric mixer fitted with the paddle attachment, cream the butter, salt, and cream cheese on low, about 1 to 2 minutes, until combined. Turn the mixer off, add the flour, and mix on low, about 1 minute, until just incorporated.

Turn the dough out onto a lightly floured work surface and flatten slightly. Roll out to a 12 × 8-inch rectangle, ⅜ inch thick, flouring the surface of the dough as necessary. Brush off any excess flour and wrap in plastic to chill for at least 4 hours or overnight.

On a lightly floured surface, roll the dough into an 8 × 15-inch rectangle, flouring the surface of the dough as necessary and lifting the dough to square off the edges and corners to help maintain a rectangular shape. Lift and reposition the dough frequently while rolling to keep it from sticking to the work surface. Fold the dough into thirds by bringing the bottom third up to the middle and the top edge down to meet the bottom edge, as you would for a business letter. Turn the dough counterclockwise, so the open flap is on your right. Keeping your rolling pin and work surface well dusted with flour, press 4 to 5 horizontal ridges down the length of the rectangle, to help you roll straight. Press equally within the ridges as you roll the dough into an 8 × 15-inch rectangle. Repeat the letter fold in the same manner and turn the dough again, so the open flap is on your right. Roll and fold once more in the same manner, for a total of 3 turns. Wrap in plastic and chill for about 2 hours.

To make the Raspberry Rugelach: Cut the dough in half and return one half to the refrigerator. Cup your hands around the edges of the dough to round off the edges. On a lightly floured surface, roll the dough into a circle, ⅛ inch thick, flouring as necessary and rotating the dough to maintain the circular shape. Cut out a circle 12 inches in diameter. Brush a 1-inch border of beaten egg around the edge of the circle.

In a small bowl, combine the sugar and bread crumbs.

Place 6 tablespoons of the jam in the center of the circle and, using an offset spatula or the back of a spoon, spread the jam evenly up to the inner edge of the egg-washed border.

Sprinkle ½ cup of the bread-crumb mixture over the jam.

To make the topping: In a small bowl combine the sugar and cinnamon and set aside.

Cut the circle in half. Cut the circle in half again to make 4 quarters. Cut the quarters in half for 8 pieces and cut those 8 pieces in half to make a total of 16 small triangles.

Working with 1 piece at a time, slightly stretch out the pointed end of the triangle. Starting at the straight edge of the triangle, roll the dough toward the point until it's completely rolled up in a small crescent shape. Place on 2 parchment-lined baking sheets, about 1 inch apart. Continue with the remaining triangles. Chill for at least 3 hours or overnight, to allow the dough to relax.

Brush the rugelach with the remaining beaten egg and sprinkle with the cinnamon-sugar mixture. Repeat with the second half of dough.

Adjust the oven rack to the middle position and preheat the oven to 350 degrees. Bake for about 25 to 35 minutes, until nicely browned.

FOR THE CHOCOLATE FILLING:
½ cup walnuts
1 cup granulated sugar

Sourdough bread finely ground to equal 1 cup bread crumbs
½ teaspoon ground cinnamon
1 extra-large egg, lightly beaten
½ cup finely chopped bittersweet chocolate

FOR THE TOPPING:
3 tablespoons granulated sugar
½ teaspoon ground cinnamon

To make the Chocolate Rugelach: Adjust the oven rack to the middle position and preheat the oven to 325 degrees.

Spread the walnuts on a baking sheet and toast in the oven until lightly browned, about 10 to 12 minutes. Shake the pan halfway through to ensure that the nuts toast evenly. Cool, chop finely, and set aside.

In a small bowl combine the sugar, bread crumbs, and cinnamon.

Cut the dough in half and return one half to the refrigerator. On a lightly floured work surface, roll the dough into a 10 × 14-inch rectangle, flouring the surface as necessary. Place the shorter side parallel to the edge of the surface and brush a 1-inch border of the beaten egg along the bottom edge. Sprinkle half of the bread-crumb mixture, half of the walnuts, and half of the chocolate, evenly distributed, up to the egg-washed border. Using a rolling pin, gently roll over the surface to press the mixture into the dough.

Roll the dough into a log by folding the top edge over about ½ inch. Using both hands, roll the dough toward yourself, tucking it under with your thumbs to tighten as you work your way across the entire log. As you tuck, gently rock the dough back and forth to keep it taut and even. When you get to the end, roll the log back and forth to seal.

To make the topping: In a small bowl, combine the sugar and cinnamon. Brush the exposed surface of the log with the beaten egg and sprinkle with the topping. Slice the log into ten 1-inch pieces and place them, cut side down, on a parchment-lined baking sheet about 1 inch apart. Chill for at least 3 hours or overnight, to allow the dough to relax. Repeat with the remaining dough.

Preheat the oven to 350 degrees and bake in the same manner as the Raspberry Rugelach.

FOR THE PRUNE FILLING:
22 (about ¹⁄₂ pound) soft prunes
Sourdough bread finely ground to equal 1 cup bread crumbs
¹⁄₂ cup granulated sugar
1 extra-large egg, lightly beaten

FOR THE TOPPING:
3 tablespoons granulated sugar
¹⁄₂ teaspoon ground cinnamon

To make the Prune Rugelach: In a small bowl, cover the prunes with brandy and cover tightly with plastic wrap. Set aside in a warm place overnight to soften. Drain the prunes, setting aside the brandy for another use. Chop the prunes into quarters.

In a small bowl, combine the bread crumbs and sugar.

Cut the dough in half and return one half to the refrigerator. On a lightly floured work surface, roll the dough into a 10 × 14-inch rectangle, flouring the surface of the dough as necessary. Place the shorter side parallel to the edge of the surface and brush a 1-inch border with the beaten egg along the bottom edge. Sprinkle half of the bread-crumb mixture and half of the prunes over, evenly distributed up to the egg-washed border. Using a rolling pin, gently roll over the surface to press the mixture into the dough.

Roll the dough into a log by folding the top edge over about ¹⁄₂ inch. Using both hands, roll the dough toward yourself, tucking it under with your thumbs to tighten as you work your way across the entire log. As you tuck, gently rock the dough back and forth to keep it taut and even. When you get to the end, roll the log back and forth to seal.

To make the topping: In a small bowl, combine the sugar and cinnamon. Brush the exposed surface of the log with the beaten egg and sprinkle with the topping. Slice the log into 10 1-inch pieces and place them cut-side down, on a parchment-lined baking sheet, about 1 inch apart. Chill for at least 3 hours or overnight, to allow the dough to relax. Repeat with the remaining dough.

Adjust the oven rack to the middle position, preheat the oven to 350 degrees, and bake in the same manner as Raspberry Rugelach.

Yield: Raspberry: 38 pieces; Chocolate and Prune: 20 pieces

S Cookies

THIS SANDY-TEXTURED BUTTER COOKIE IS PIPED INTO CUTE, CURLY S SHAPES. For the minimalist cookie platter, arrange these with other butter cookies such as Almond Sunflowers (page 118), Shortbread (page 160), and Almond Slice-and-Bakes (page 115).

Special Item: PASTRY BAG FITTED WITH A #4 STAR TIP

> $^1\!/_2$ cup (2 ounces) whole unblanched almonds
> $^1\!/_2$ cup granulated sugar
> 2 sticks (8 ounces) unsalted butter, chilled and cut into 1-inch cubes
> 2 cups unbleached pastry flour or unbleached all-purpose flour
> 1 to 2 extra-large egg whites, to equal $^1\!/_4$ cup

Adjust the oven rack to the middle position and preheat the oven to 350 degrees.

In the bowl of a food processor fitted with the steel blade, combine the nuts with 2 tablespoons of the sugar and process until it's the consistency of a fine meal.

In the bowl of an electric mixer fitted with the paddle attachment, cream the butter on low, 2 to 3 minutes, until softened. Add the remaining sugar and nut mixture, turn the mixer up to medium, and mix for another 5 to 6 minutes until very light and fluffy, scraping down the sides of the bowl as needed.

Turn the mixer to low and add the flour and egg whites alternately in 3 batches. Mix until just combined.

Fill a pastry bag half full and pipe $1^1\!/_2$- to 2-inch-long tight S shapes onto a parchment-lined baking sheet, spaced 1 inch apart.

Bake for 25 minutes, until lightly browned and firm to the touch.

Yield: 30 cookies

Sbrisolona

Iᴛ'ꜱ ɴᴏ ꜱᴇᴄʀᴇᴛ ᴛʜᴀᴛ ᴛʜᴇ ʙᴇꜱᴛ ᴘᴀʀᴛ ᴏꜰ ᴄᴇʀᴛᴀɪɴ ꜱᴡᴇᴇᴛꜱ ɪꜱ ᴛʜᴀᴛ ᴄʀᴜᴍʙʟʏ streusel topping—plain, buttery, and crunchy. If you see me hanging around the baker's rack at La Brea Bakery, you can be sure it's those leftover crumbs of streusel clinging to the baking sheet that I'm after.

When my cousin Anette brought me her version of this Mantuan sweet, I saw stars. All the goodness of those choice crumbs was there, but in the form of a rustic, chunky cookie. I later discovered that the root of its name comes from *briciola*, which translated from Italian means "crumb." The method of crumbling a streusel mixture into a tart ring, dimpling it together, baking, cooling, and then breaking it into irregular chunks intrigued me. As much as I hate recipes that say "better the next day," this one really is.

Special Item: 12-ɪɴᴄʜ ꜰʟᴀɴ ʀɪɴɢ, ʟɪɢʜᴛʟʏ ᴄᴏᴀᴛᴇᴅ ᴡɪᴛʜ ᴍᴇʟᴛᴇᴅ ʙᴜᴛᴛᴇʀ

   1½ cups (8 ounces) whole unblanched almonds
   3 sticks (12 ounces) unsalted butter
   ¼ cup plus 2 tablespoons granulated sugar
   ¾ cup powdered sugar
   1¼ cups semolina flour
   1¾ cups unbleached all-purpose flour
   1 teaspoon kosher salt
   2 extra-large egg yolks
   3 tablespoons orange flower water

Adjust the oven rack to the middle position and preheat the oven to 325 degrees.

Spread the almonds on a baking sheet and toast in the oven until lightly browned, about 10 to 15 minutes. Shake the pan halfway through to ensure that the nuts toast evenly. Cool, then coarsely chop half of the almonds.

In a small saucepan, clarify the butter by heating it over medium-high heat until it boils with large, loud, rapidly bursting bubbles. Turn the heat down to medium and continue cooking about 5 to 7 more minutes, without letting it brown, until the butter becomes foamy and the bubbles are fewer and quieter. Remove from the heat and transfer to a bowl to cool. Skim the foam off the top and pour or spoon out 1 cup of the clarified butter, leaving the milk solids at the bottom of the bowl. Refrigerate any leftover butter for another use.

Turn the oven up to 350 degrees.

In the bowl of a food processor fitted with the steel blade, combine the whole almonds with half of the granulated sugar and process until it's the consistency of fine meal. Add the remaining sugars, flours, and salt, and pulse to incorporate. Add the egg yolks and flower water, and pulse just to combine.

Add the cup of clarified butter and pulse on and off a few times until the mixture is just moistened, but does not come together. Transfer the dough to a mixing bowl and toss in the remaining chopped almonds.

Place the flan ring on a parchment-lined baking sheet. Pick up a handful of dough, squeeze it together lightly in your fist, and crumble it, in large chunks, into the mold. Keeping your fingertips close together, dimple the dough to help press it together, making an uneven layer. Continue a handful at a time, crumbling and dimpling the remaining dough. The surface should be very bumpy and uneven. Once all of the dough is in the mold, dimple one final time to ensure that it holds together, but isn't tightly compressed.

Cover with foil and bake for 20 minutes. Remove the foil and return it to the oven for about 40 more minutes, until it is a medium straw color and firm to the touch.

Cool completely and break up into large, uneven chunks.

Yield: One 12-inch cookie, broken into several uneven pieces

Semolina-Fig Tiles

IF YOU APPRECIATE FIG NEWTONS, THIS IS THE COOKIE FOR YOU. RATHER than hiding inside the cookie, the sliced fig sits regally on top, framed by a delicate, scalloped edge. You'll recognize that familiar chewiness and crunch, but the subtle Mediterranean flavors of the fennel seeds and semolina will pleasantly surprise you. Although black mission figs would taste fine, the golden-flesh variety is more suited to the paler tones of this cookie.

Special Item: FLUTED PASTRY WHEEL, OPTIONAL

> *1 teaspoon fennel seeds*
> *1½ cups unbleached pastry flour or unbleached all-purpose flour*
> *½ cup semolina flour*
> *¼ cup granulated sugar*
> *¾ teaspoon baking powder*
> *2 sticks (8 ounces) unsalted butter, chilled and cut into 1-inch cubes*
> *1 extra-large egg yolk*
> *2 tablespoons white wine or champagne vinegar*
> *8 to 10 (4½ to 6½ ounces) large dried figs, Calimyrna or Smyrna, very moist, and refrigerated*
>   *until firm enough to slice*

In a small sauté pan, toast the fennel seeds over medium-low heat, stirring occasionally until they become aromatic and slightly browned, about 2 to 3 minutes. In a nut grinder or clean coffee grinder, grind the seeds to a fine powder.

In the bowl of a food processor fitted with the steel blade, or in the bowl of an electric mixer fitted with the paddle attachment, combine the flours, sugar, ground fennel, and baking powder, and pulse or mix on low to combine. Add the butter and pulse a few times or mix on low until the dough is the consistency of a coarse meal.

Add the egg yolk and vinegar, and mix on medium or pulse until the dough barely comes together.

Turn the dough out onto a lightly floured work surface. Dip the heel of your hand in flour and, working in small sections, smear the dough away from you, blending it together. When the dough has been all smeared out, use a dough scraper or spatula to scrape and gather the dough into a ball, divide it in half, and flatten into rectangles, 1 inch thick. Wrap each half in plastic and chill until firm, 2 to 4 hours or overnight.

Cut the figs vertically into ⅛-inch-thick slices.

Working with one piece of dough at a time, on a lightly floured surface, roll the dough into a large rectangle, ⅛ inch thick, flouring the surface as necessary. Transfer to a parchment-lined baking sheet and chill until firm, about 30 to 45 minutes. Repeat with the remaining dough.

Adjust the oven rack to the upper and lower positions and preheat the oven to 350 degrees.

Transfer the rectangle of dough to the work surface. Using the fluted wheel, trim the edges to make a large rectangle. Working with the shorter side parallel to the work surface, cut the rectangle vertically into 2-inch-wide strips. Cut the strips horizontally every 2½ inches to make the cookies. Transfer them to a parchment-lined baking sheet, spaced 1 inch apart. Place one slice of fig centered vertically on each cookie, firmly pressing down around the edges of the fig to keep it in place. If you're using the ends or smaller section of the fig, press two slices into the cookie, on a diagonal. Chill until firm, about 15–20 minutes. Repeat the process with the other rectangle of dough. Gather all the scraps of dough together, chill, roll, and cut in the same manner, working with a smaller rectangle.

Bake for about 20 minutes, until firm and lightly browned, rotating the baking sheets halfway through to ensure even baking.

Yield: About 3 dozen cookies

Shortbread

Don't turn the page just because you think you have enough shortbread recipes. I doubt yours is as rich, as buttery, and as perfectly salted as this one. Beware: If placed in a red plaid box, my Shortbread Bars, Wedges, and Buttons might be mistaken for Walker's—the best Scottish shortbread in the world.

Special Items: 2-inch round cutter, optional
#2 or #3 plain pastry tip, optional

2 sticks (8 ounces) unsalted butter, chilled and cut into 1-inch cubes
¼ teaspoon kosher salt
¼ cup powdered sugar
¼ cup granulated sugar
2 cups unbleached pastry flour or unbleached all-purpose flour

In the bowl of an electric mixer fitted with the paddle attachment, cream the butter and salt on low, 2 to 3 minutes, until softened. Add the sugars, turn the mixer up to medium, and mix for 3 to 4 minutes until light and fluffy, scraping down the sides of the bowl as needed.

Add the flour in 3 batches, turning the mixer off before each addition and mixing on low until just combined.

Turn the dough out onto a lightly floured work surface, gather into a ball, and flatten into a disc. Wrap in plastic and chill until firm, 2 hours or overnight.

For Shortbread Bars: On a lightly floured surface, roll the dough into a rectangle, ½ inch thick. Cut the dough into bars, about 1½ inches wide and 2¼ inches long, and place 1 inch apart on a parchment-lined baking sheet. Using a toothpick or bamboo skewer, poke the dough 6 times down the length of both sides of each bar. Chill until firm, about 30 minutes.

For Shortbread Wedges: On a lightly floured surface, roll the dough to ½-inch thickness. Cut the dough into a circle 8 inches in diameter and place on a parchment-lined baking sheet. Score the circle into 8 wedges, being careful not to break through the dough.

To form a pointed scalloped edge, gently make an impression on the edge of the circle with the tip of your finger. Using the thumb and index finger of the other hand, pinch the outer edge of dough together to make a small point on the edge. Move your index finger over to the other side of the first impression and repeat the process around the entire edge. Prick the perimeter of the circle with dots, $\frac{1}{4}$ inch from the edge. Continue to prick dots to form concentric rings, spaced $\frac{1}{2}$ inch apart. If you have leftover dough, shape into buttons or bars. Chill until firm, about 30 minutes.

For Shortbread Buttons: On a lightly floured surface, roll the dough to $\frac{1}{2}$-inch thickness. Using the 2-inch round cutter, cut out as many circles as possible, cutting as closely together as possible. Gather the scraps, reroll and cut out the remaining dough. Using the pastry tip, cut out 4 holes in the middle of each circle to resemble a button and place them 1 inch apart on 1–2 parchment-lined baking sheets. Chill until firm, about 30 minutes.

Adjust the oven rack to the middle position and preheat the oven to 350 degrees.

Bake for 15 minutes until the shortbread just starts to color. Rotate the baking sheets and turn the oven down to 300 degrees and bake for another 20 minutes.

Yield: 16 to 20 bars; or 8 wedge-shaped slices, with enough dough left over to make about 6 buttons; or 18 to 20 buttons

Swedish Ginger Wafers

As I was flipping through a food magazine, this recipe jumped off the page at me. I sensed this was the wafer version of Dutch almond windmill cookies, which I've been trying to duplicate for years. Thank you to Joyce Shinn, who sent this recipe to *Gourmet,* and thanks to her good friend Betty Boothe, who gave it to her many years ago.

I like to roll the dough out very thin and then cut out oversize rectangles. To roll this wet and sticky dough thin enough, Joyce suggests using a pastry cloth on the rolling surface and a rolling pin cover. At home, you might find it easier to form the dough into a bar, freeze it, and then slice it into thin wafers. The wafers won't be as large, but they will still be thin and crisp and dangerously addictive.

½ cup heavy cream, cold
1 stick (4 ounces) unsalted butter, softened
1½ teaspoons baking soda
1½ teaspoons ground cinnamon
1½ teaspoons ground ginger
1¼ teaspoons ground cloves
1 cup granulated sugar
1 teaspoon pure almond extract
½ cup light corn syrup
3 cups unbleached all-purpose flour

FOR DECORATING:
½ cup (1½ ounces) sliced unblanched almonds

In the bowl of an electric mixer fitted with the whisk attachment, beat the cream for a few minutes, until it holds stiff peaks. Transfer to another bowl and clean the mixing bowl.

In the bowl of an electric mixer fitted with the paddle attachment, cream the butter, baking soda, cinnamon, ginger, and cloves on low, 2 to 3 minutes, until incorporated. Add the sugar and turn the mixer up to medium, and mix for another 3 to 4 minutes until light and fluffy, scraping down the sides of the bowl as needed.

Turn the mixer off and add the almond extract, corn syrup, and whipped cream, mixing on low until just combined.

Add the flour in 3 batches, turning the mixer off before each addition and mixing on low until just combined.

Turn the dough out onto a floured work surface, gather into a ball and flatten into a 2-inch-thick rectangle. Wrap in plastic and chill until firm, at least 2 hours or overnight.

Divide the dough in half and return one half to the refrigerator. On a floured surface, roll the dough out to a large, very thin rectangle, about $\frac{1}{16}$ inch thick, flouring the rolling pin and surface of the dough as necessary. Cut into large wafers, $3\frac{1}{4}$ × $2\frac{1}{2}$ inches, and place them 1 inch apart on 2 parchment-lined baking sheets. Gather the scraps together, chill, reroll, and cut. Firmly press almond slices into the corners and centers of each cookie, being careful not to break the nuts. Chill until firm, about 30 minutes. Repeat the process with the other half of the dough.

Adjust the oven rack to the upper position and preheat the oven to 350 degrees.

Bake for about 6 to 8 minutes, until lightly browned and crisp, rotating the baking sheets halfway through to ensure even baking.

Alternately, for slice-and-bake cookies: Pat and shape each half of the dough into rectangular bars, 2 inches high. Drop each side of the rectangles against the work surface to help compress them, eliminating any air holes in the dough. Wrap the bars in plastic and place in the freezer until very firm, about 2 to 4 hours. Cut paper-thin slices and place them 1 inch apart on 2 parchment-lined baking sheets. Firmly press almond slices into the corners and centers of each cookie. Repeat with the remaining dough or wrap in plastic wrap and store in the freezer until ready to slice and bake.

Yield: 35 large wafers or 7 to 8 dozen smaller wafers

Walnut Toasts

I COULD'VE CALLED THEM WALNUT BISCOTTI BECAUSE REALLY, THAT'S WHAT they are—a twice-baked cookie. But with their unique nonbiscotti shape, I've given them a new nonbiscotti name. If you don't have a fresh, walnutty walnut oil, replace it with melted butter.

Special Item: 6-CUP-CAPACITY LOAF PAN, LIGHTLY COATED WITH MELTED BUTTER

2⅓ cups (8 ounces) walnut halves, plus 8 to 10 extra halves for placing down the center of the loaf
¾ stick (3 ounces) unsalted butter, melted
2 tablespoons walnut oil
1 cup granulated sugar
4¼ cups plus 2 tablespoons unbleached pastry flour or unbleached all-purpose flour
1½ teaspoons baking powder
1½ teaspoons baking soda
½ teaspoon kosher salt
½ teaspoon chopped rosemary
2 extra-large eggs
2 extra-large egg yolks
¼ cup plain yogurt

FOR THE TOPPING:
2 extra-large egg whites, lightly beaten
8 to 10 of the walnut halves from above

Adjust the oven rack to the middle position and preheat the oven to 325 degrees.
Spread the walnuts on a baking sheet and toast in the oven until browned, about 10 to 15 minutes. Shake the pan halfway through to ensure that the nuts toast evenly. Separate out 8 to 10 walnut halves and set aside for the topping.
Turn the oven up to 350 degrees.
In a medium bowl, combine the butter and walnut oil.
In the bowl of a food processor fitted with the steel blade, grind 1 cup of the wal-

nuts with half of the sugar until it's the consistency of a fine meal. Add the remaining sugar, flour, baking powder, baking soda, salt, and rosemary, and process to combine.

Transfer to a large mixing bowl and make a well in the center. Sprinkle the walnuts over the dry ingredients. Pour in the whole eggs, egg yolks, butter mixture, and yogurt and whisk together the liquids. Using one hand, slowly draw in the dry ingredients, mixing until combined.

Wash and dry your hands and dust them with flour. Turn the dough out onto a lightly floured work surface. Knead about 10 times until the dough is the texture of sticky modeling clay. Using your hands, flatten the dough into a rectangle about the same length as your loaf pan.

Transfer the dough to the prepared loaf pan and firmly pat it down with the flat side of your knuckles. Heavily coat the surface with the egg whites and firmly press the walnut halves into the dough, touching, to form a line down the center.

Bake until slightly firm, about 1 hour.

Invert the loaf and allow to cool completely, at least a couple of hours or overnight.

Adjust the oven rack to the middle position and preheat the oven to 200 degrees.

Using a serrated knife, slice the loaf into cookies, about ¼ inch thick. Arrange the cookies, closely spaced, on 1–2 parchment-lined baking sheets.

Bake until firm and dry, about 30 to 40 minutes.

Yield: 35 cookies

5. Scones

....

Believe it or not, when I was growing up there wasn't a Starbucks coffee bar on every corner. The morning repertoire at the local coffee shop was a greasy doughnut or a lousy danish. *Biscotti, espresso,* and *croissant* were words we mispronounced, and scones were exotic little biscuits served at teatime on the other side of the Atlantic. Times have certainly changed. We no longer mispronounce European pastries and are fluent with the names of our coffee drinks. Scones, albeit flavored with unusual combinations and eaten at all times of the day, have become a household word.

On this side of the Atlantic, we don't take the time for tea. Our ritual is a meal on the run. We want it fast and we want it full of flavor. My scones are richer, a little more buttery, and come in a variety of flavors: rosemary and cornmeal, mushrooms and onions, and dried fruits and nuts. Whether savory or sweet, fruity or nutty, they are a meal all in themselves.

There's nothing difficult about making scones. Just remember: For a tender, flaky scone, follow your grandmother's advice. Work quickly with gentle hands and once you've added your liquids, don't overmix. To incorporate the butter into the dry ingredients quickly and thoroughly, I use a food processor. To prevent overmixing, freeze the small cubes of butter for 10 to 15 minutes before adding to the dry ingredients. If you don't have a food processor, use a heavy-duty mixer or your hands. Whichever method you choose, work the butter into the dry ingredients until the mixture is a very fine meal. Once the butter is incorporated, I add the liquids and combine them by hand.

Normally, after cutting out the first round of scones, you would gather the scraps of dough and roll them out again. I found you get a much more delicate scone by skipping the rolling and simply reshaping the trimmings into one piece with your hands. Cut them out and repeat until you've used all of the dough.

Every day at the bakery, we make several kinds of scones. To distinguish the different flavors from one another, we make them in a variety of shapes and sizes. The Chocolate-Walnut Scones (page 171) are cut out and formed into clovers. Currant-Oat Paddles (page 173) are shaped into little ovals, while Dried Fruit and Nut Scones (page 175) are shaped into large wedges. Irish-Style Soda Bread (page 178) is more enchanting when made into a combination of triangles, rounds, and squares. At home, pick and choose whatever shapes you like.

Scones can be made ahead of time and stored in the freezer. Mix the dough, cut them out, and wrap well in plastic. When that last-minute party gets added to your hectic schedule, pull a few different types out of your freezer and within minutes, you'll have a tabletop full of fresh hot scones that beg for nothing more than a smile and a sigh of relief.

Buttermilk-Fruit Scones

Special Item: 2-INCH ROUND CUTTER

2¾ cups unbleached pastry flour or unbleached all-purpose flour
1 tablespoon baking powder
1 teaspoon baking soda
Pinch of salt
¼ cup plus 2 tablespoons granulated sugar, plus extra for sprinkling over the tops
1 tablespoon finely chopped lemon zest (about 1 lemon)
½ teaspoon freshly grated nutmeg, plus extra for garnishing
1½ sticks (6 ounces) unsalted butter, cut into 1-inch cubes and frozen
½ pound strawberries, sliced to equal 1½ cups, or 1½ cups (6 ounces) raspberries or blueberries
1 tablespoon pure vanilla extract
½ to ¾ cup buttermilk

Adjust the oven rack to the middle position and preheat the oven to 400 degrees.

In the bowl of a food processor fitted with the steel blade or in the bowl of an electric mixer fitted with the paddle attachment, combine the flour, baking powder, baking soda, salt, sugar, lemon zest, and nutmeg and pulse or mix on low until incorporated. Add the butter and pulse on and off a few times, or mix on low, until the mixture is pale yellow and the consistency of a fine meal.

Transfer the mixture to a large bowl and toss in the fruit. Make a large well in the center and pour in the vanilla extract and ½ cup of the buttermilk. Using one hand, draw in the dry ingredients, mixing until just combined. If the mixture feels dry, add a few more tablespoons of buttermilk.

Wash and dry your hands and dust them with flour. Turn the dough out onto a lightly floured work surface and gently knead a few times to gather it into a ball. Roll or pat the dough into a circle slightly thicker than ½ inch. Cut out the circles, cutting as closely together as possible and keeping the trimmings intact.

Gather the scraps, pat and press the pieces back together, and cut out the remaining dough. Place the circles 1 inch apart on a parchment-lined baking sheet. Sprinkle about ½ teaspoon of sugar and a few gratings of nutmeg over the top of each scone.

Bake for 25 minutes, until lightly browned.

Yield: 12 scones

Chocolate-Walnut Scones

Special Item: 1½-INCH ROUND CUTTER

1 cup (4 ounces) walnuts
¼ cup plus 2 tablespoons granulated sugar
2¾ cups unbleached pastry flour or unbleached all-purpose flour
1 tablespoon plus 1 teaspoon baking powder
Pinch of salt
1 stick plus 2 tablespoons (5 ounces) unsalted butter, cut into 1-inch cubes and frozen
1 cup (6 ounces) finely chopped bittersweet chocolate
1 cup heavy cream, plus extra for brushing the tops of the scones
¼ cup crème fraîche or sour cream
1 tablespoon pure vanilla extract

FOR THE TOPPING:
1 tablespoon granulated sugar
About ¼ cup walnuts

Adjust the oven rack to the middle position and preheat the oven to 325 degrees.

Spread the walnuts on a baking sheet and toast in the oven until lightly browned, about 4 to 6 minutes. Shake the pan halfway through to ensure that the nuts toast evenly.

Turn the oven up to 400 degrees.

In the bowl of a food processor fitted with the steel blade, combine the nuts with half of the sugar and process until the mixture is the consistency of a fine meal. Add the remaining sugar, flour, baking powder, and salt, and pulse to incorporate. Add the butter and pulse on and off until the mixture is the consistency of a fine meal.

Transfer the mixture to a large bowl and stir in the chocolate pieces. Make a large well in the center and pour in the cream, crème fraîche, and vanilla extract, and whisk together the liquids. Using one hand, draw in the dry ingredients, mixing until just combined.

Wash and dry your hands and dust them with flour. Turn the dough out onto a lightly floured work surface and gently knead a few times to gather it into a ball. Roll or pat the dough into a circle ¾ inch thick. Cut out the circles, cutting as closely together as possible and keeping the trimmings intact.

Gather the scraps, pat and press the pieces back together, and cut out the remaining dough. Place the circles in groups of three, gently pressing the edges together to form clovers, spaced 1 inch apart on a parchment-lined baking sheet.

Brush the tops with cream and sprinkle lightly with sugar. Using a Mouli grater, or the wide hole of a box grater, grate the nuts over the top of each scone.

Bake for 20 to 25 minutes, until slightly firm to the touch and lightly browned.

Yield: 12 scones

Currant-Oat Paddles

Sɪᴄᴋ ᴏꜰ ᴛʀɪᴀɴɢʟᴇꜱ ᴀɴᴅ ʀᴏᴜɴᴅꜱ, I ᴡᴀꜱ ᴅᴇꜱᴘᴇʀᴀᴛᴇ ꜰᴏʀ ᴀ ɴᴇᴡ ʟᴏᴏᴋ. Nᴀᴍᴇᴅ for their paddlelike shape, these scones are wholesome, oaty, and delectable.

1 cup (6 ounces) currants
½ cup whiskey
1 cup plus 2 tablespoons unbleached pastry flour or unbleached all-purpose flour
½ cup stone-ground whole-wheat flour
1 teaspoon baking powder
½ teaspoon plus ⅛ teaspoon baking soda
⅛ teaspoon kosher salt
3 tablespoons dark brown sugar, lightly packed
2 tablespoons granulated sugar
1¼ cups rolled oats
1 stick plus 2 tablespoons (5 ounces) unsalted butter, cut into ½-inch cubes and frozen
2½ tablespoons mild-flavored honey, such as clover
1 tablespoon pure vanilla extract
½ cup heavy cream, plus a little extra for brushing the tops of the scones

ꜰᴏʀ ᴛʜᴇ ᴛᴏᴘᴘɪɴɢ:
2 tablespoons granulated sugar
½ teaspoon ground cinnamon

Adjust the oven rack to the upper position and preheat the oven to 350 degrees.

In a small saucepan over low heat, simmer the currants with the whiskey until the liquid evaporates, about 2 to 3 minutes. Set aside to cool.

In the bowl of a food processor fitted with the steel blade or in the bowl of an electric mixer fitted with the paddle attachment, combine the flours, baking powder, baking soda, salt, sugars, and oats, and process or mix on low to incorporate. Add the butter and pulse on and off a few times, or mix on low, until the mixture is pale yellow and the consistency of a fine meal.

In a small bowl, whisk together the currants, honey, vanilla extract, and cream.

Transfer the flour mixture to a large bowl. Make a well in the center and pour the currant mixture into the well. Using one hand, draw in the dry ingredients, mixing until just combined.

Wash and dry your hands and dust them with flour. Turn the dough out onto a lightly floured work surface and gently knead a few times to gather it into a ball. Roll the dough into a 12-inch log. Flatten the log with the palm of your hand to form a long rectangle about 4 inches wide and 12 inches long. Cut into eight 1½-inch-wide pieces and place them 1 inch apart on a parchment-lined baking sheet.

Working with one at a time, flatten each piece with one hand while you cup the end with the other, rounding the corners to form an oval ½ inch thick and 3 to 4 inches long.

To prepare the topping: In a small bowl combine the sugar and cinnamon.

Brush the tops of the paddles with cream and sprinkle a fine, even layer of topping over each.

Bake for 35 to 45 minutes until firm and nicely browned.

Yield: 8 paddles

Dried Fruit and Nut Scones

WHATEVER YOU DO, DON'T INVITE ME HIKING (OR CAMPING), AND NEVER EVER offer me a granola bar. I hate them all. While I won't accompany you in the great outdoors, my granola-bar-like scones will keep you fed on the trail. They're my new favorite, packed full of flavor and crunch, and they give me more pleasure than any nature trail ever could.

Special Item: 10-INCH RING OR 10-INCH SPRINGFORM PAN, OPTIONAL

1 cup (5 ounces) whole unblanched almonds
³/₄ cup plus 2 tablespoons unbleached pastry flour or unbleached all-purpose flour
³/₄ cup stone-ground whole-wheat flour
1 teaspoon baking powder
³/₄ teaspoon baking soda
¹/₄ teaspoon kosher salt
¹/₄ cup plus 2 tablespoons granulated sugar
1¹/₄ cups rolled oats
1 stick plus 1 tablespoon (4¹/₂ ounces) unsalted butter, cut into ¹/₂-inch cubes and frozen
2 teaspoons finely chopped orange zest (about 1 orange)
¹/₂ cup (3 ounces) currants
1 cup (5 ounces) yellow raisins, coarsely chopped
1 cup (8 ounces) dried cherries, coarsely chopped
¹/₂ cup flax seeds
¹/₂ cup buttermilk

FOR DECORATING:
Powdered sugar

Adjust the oven rack to the middle position and preheat the oven to 325 degrees.
Spread the almonds on a baking sheet and toast in the oven until browned, about 10 to 15 minutes. Shake the pan halfway through to ensure that the nuts toast evenly. Cool, chop coarsely, and set aside.
Turn the oven up to 350 degrees.
In the bowl of a food processor fitted with the steel blade or in the bowl of an

electric mixer fitted with the paddle attachment, combine the flours, baking powder, baking soda, salt, sugar, and oats, and process or mix on low to incorporate. Add the butter and pulse on and off, or mix on low, until the mixture is pale yellow and the consistency of a fine meal.

Transfer the mixture to a large bowl and toss in the almonds, orange zest, currants, raisins, cherries, and flax seeds. Make a well in the center and pour in the buttermilk. Using one hand, draw in the dry ingredients, mixing until just combined.

Wash and dry your hands and dust them with flour. Turn the dough out onto a lightly floured work surface and gently knead a few times to gather it into a ball. Place the dough into the center of the ring. Using your palms, press the dough into a circle, until approximately 1 inch thick. (If you're not using a ring, form the dough by hand into a 10-inch circle.) Lift off the ring and cut the circle in half. Cut each section in half two more times, to form 8 triangles. Place them 1 inch apart on a parchment-lined baking sheet.

Bake for 35 to 45 minutes until firm and well browned.

When cooled, sift a fine layer of powdered sugar over the top.

Yield: 8 scones

Ginger Scones

CANDIED GINGER TURNS THIS TRADITIONAL CREAM SCONE INTO A SPICY AND addictive breakfast. After all these years, it's still our bestselling scone at the bakery.

Special Item: 3-INCH ROUND CUTTER

> 2¼ cups unbleached pastry flour or unbleached all-purpose flour
> ⅓ cup granulated sugar
> 1 tablespoon baking powder
> 1 teaspoon finely chopped lemon zest (about ½ lemon)
> 1½ sticks (6 ounces) unsalted butter, cut into 1-inch cubes and frozen
> 4½ ounces candied ginger, finely chopped into ¼-inch pieces to equal ⅔ cup
> ¾ cup heavy cream, plus extra for brushing the tops of the scones

Adjust the oven rack to the middle position and preheat the oven to 400 degrees.

In the bowl of a food processor fitted with the steel blade or in the bowl of an electric mixer fitted with the paddle attachment, combine the flour, sugar, and baking powder, and pulse or mix on low to incorporate. Add the lemon zest and butter, and pulse on and off, or mix on low, until the mixture is pale yellow and the consistency of a fine meal.

Transfer the mixture to a large bowl and stir in the ginger. Make a well in the center and pour in the cream. Using one hand, draw in the dry ingredients, mixing until just combined.

Wash and dry your hands and dust them with flour. Turn the dough out onto a lightly floured work surface and gently knead a few times to gather it into a ball. Roll or pat the dough into a circle about ¾ inch thick. Cut out the circles, cutting as closely together as possible and keeping the trimmings intact.

Gather the scraps, pat and press the pieces back together, and cut out the remaining dough. Place the scones 1 inch apart on a parchment-lined baking sheet.

Brush the tops with the remaining cream.

Bake for 12 to 16 minutes, until the surface cracks and they are slightly browned.

Yield: 8 scones

Irish-Style Soda Bread

MADE IN THE EXACT SAME MANNER AS A SCONE, THESE INDIVIDUAL LOAVES OF Irish-Style Soda Bread are hearty and comforting. Though this is an ancient tried-and-true recipe, I've added a little baking powder for lighter texture and chopped rye flakes for a little crunch. Work quickly, and as soon as the dough is shaped, it should be "slipped into the oven still quivering from the final pat," to quote John Thorne in *The Outlaw Cook*. Traditionally made on the farmhouse hearth, soda bread came to symbolize the warmth and hospitality of the Irish home. Continue the tradition and serve it warm, smeared with sweet butter, for all of your friends.

3³/₄ cups unbleached pastry flour or unbleached all-purpose flour

¹/₂ cup stone-ground whole-wheat flour

¹/₄ cup granulated sugar

¹/₂ cup wheat flakes or rye flakes, plus extra for sprinkling on top of the loaves

1¹/₂ teaspoons kosher salt

1 tablespoon baking powder

1 teaspoon baking soda

1 tablespoon finely chopped lemon zest (about 1¹/₂ lemons)

2 tablespoons caraway seeds

¹/₂ stick (2 ounces) unsalted butter, cut into ¹/₂-inch cubes and frozen

1³/₄ cups buttermilk

1 extra-large egg

Adjust the oven rack to the upper position and preheat the oven to 375 degrees. In the bowl of a food processor fitted with the steel blade or in the bowl of an electric mixer fitted with the paddle attachment, combine the flours, sugar, wheat or rye flakes, salt, baking powder, baking soda, lemon zest, and caraway seeds, and pulse or mix on low to incorporate. Add the butter and pulse on and off a few times, or mix on low, until the mixture is the consistency of a fine meal.

Transfer the mixture to a large bowl and make a well in the center. Pour in the buttermilk and egg, and whisk the liquids together. Using one hand, draw in the dry ingredients, mixing until just incorporated. The dough will be wet and sticky.

Wash and dry your hands and dust them with flour. Turn the dough out onto a lightly floured work surface and gather it into a ball. Pat the dough into a rectangle about 1 inch thick, flouring the surface of the dough as necessary. Using a cutter or shaping with your hands, form twelve 3-inch triangles, rectangles, circles, or a combination of all three, using about ½ cup of dough for each.

Gather the scraps, pat and press the pieces back together, and cut out the remaining dough. Place them 1 inch apart on a parchment-lined baking sheet.

Brush the tops with water and sprinkle ½ teaspoon of wheat flakes or rye flakes over each one.

Bake for about 35 to 40 minutes, until lightly colored and firm to the touch.

Yield: 10 to 12 mini breads

Michelle's Southern Sweet Biscuits

CALL IT WHAT YOU LIKE, A BISCUIT OR A SUGARED SCONE. THE SWEETNESS comes from the layer of sugar it's baked on. Its light, airy texture is a combination of White Lily flour (see "Sources," page 393), a touch of yeast, and extra-gentle hands. These are truly at their best when hot, so serve them straight out of the oven.

Special Item: 2-INCH ROUND CUTTER

1¾ teaspoons (0.4 ounce) packed fresh yeast or 2⅛ teaspoons active dry yeast
½ teaspoon granulated sugar
⅔ cup buttermilk
2 cups White Lily flour, unbleached pastry flour, or unbleached all-purpose flour
½ teaspoon kosher salt
2 teaspoons baking powder
½ teaspoon baking soda
2 sticks (8 ounces) unsalted butter, cut into 1-inch cubes and frozen
A few gratings of fresh nutmeg

FOR THE BOTTOM:
¾ stick (3 ounces) unsalted butter, melted, to prepare baking sheet and brush on the tops of the
    biscuits
¼ cup plus 2 tablespoons light brown sugar, lightly packed
½ teaspoon ground cinnamon

Place the yeast in a small mixing bowl, sprinkle in the sugar, pour in the buttermilk, and add 4 tablespoons of the flour. Allow to soften a few minutes, without stirring. Whisk together and cover the bowl tightly with plastic wrap. Set aside in a warm place until it rises slightly and tiny bubbles appear on the surface, about 30 minutes.

In the bowl of a food processor fitted with the steel blade or in the bowl of an electric mixer fitted with the paddle attachment, combine the remaining flour, salt, baking powder, and baking soda, and process or mix on low to incorporate. Add the butter and pulse on and off a few times, or mix on low, until the mixture is pale yellow and the consistency of a fine meal.

Transfer the mixture to a bowl, make a large well in the center, and pour in the yeast mixture. Using one hand, gently draw in the dry ingredients, mixing until just combined. The mixture will be very sticky.

Wash and dry your hands and dust them with flour. Turn the dough out onto a lightly floured work surface and gently knead to gather into a ball. Roll or pat the dough to ¾-inch thickness. Dip your cutter in flour and cut out the circles, cutting as closely together as possible and keeping the trimmings intact.

Gather the scraps, pat and press them back together, and cut out the remaining biscuits.

Dot each biscuit with melted butter and grate a few strokes of nutmeg over the tops. Set them aside on a lightly floured surface to rest for about 45 minutes.

Adjust the oven rack to the middle position and preheat the oven to 400 degrees.

Meanwhile, pour the remaining melted butter onto the baking sheets, and chill or freeze in a level position for about 10 to 15 minutes, until the butter hardens.

In a small bowl, combine the brown sugar and cinnamon. Evenly distribute the cinnamon mixture over the surface of the sheets. Place the biscuits ½ inch apart on the prepared baking sheets.

Bake for about 20 minutes, until lightly browned, rotating the baking sheets halfway through to ensure even baking.

Yield: 20 biscuits

Mushroom–Onion Scones

Not everyone likes sweets in the morning. At the bakery, we like to offer lots of savories to keep all those customers satisfied. Like the Parmesan Scones (page 184), these are a scrumptious meal on the run or the perfect substitute biscuit with lunch or dinner.

Special Item: 2-INCH ROUND CUTTER

FOR THE MUSHROOMS:
¼ cup extra-virgin olive oil
8 ounces Crimini or white button mushrooms, cut vertically into ¼-inch slices to equal 3 cups
Pinch of salt
A few grindings fresh black pepper
¼ cup dry sherry
2 tablespoons finely chopped fresh thyme

FOR THE ONIONS:
2 to 3 small (2-inch-diameter) yellow onions, peeled
¼ cup extra-virgin olive oil

FOR THE DOUGH:
2¼ cups unbleached pastry flour or unbleached all-purpose flour
½ cup stone-ground whole-wheat flour
½ teaspoon kosher salt, plus extra for sprinkling
1 tablespoon plus 1 teaspoon baking powder
4 tablespoons plus 1½ teaspoons (2½ ounces) unsalted butter, cut into 1-inch cubes and frozen
¼ cup extra-virgin olive oil
1 cup heavy cream, plus extra for brushing on top of the scones

FOR GARNISHING:
Ten 1-inch sprigs of fresh thyme

In a large sauté pan, over medium-high heat, heat the olive oil. Add the mushrooms, salt, and pepper, and sauté until browned, about 10 minutes. Remove from the heat, add the sherry, and return to the stove. Over high heat, reduce the liquid until evaporated, about 1 to 2 minutes. Transfer to a bowl and stir in the chopped thyme.

Adjust the oven rack to the middle position and preheat the oven to 375 degrees.

Slice the onions into ⅛-inch-thick rings, keeping the concentric rings intact, if possible. In the same large sauté pan, heat the olive oil over low heat, add the onions in 1 or 2 batches in a single layer and cook about 10 to 15 minutes, covered, until they're slightly softened but not colored. Using a spatula, carefully transfer the onions to a baking sheet or flat surface to cool, keeping the rings intact. Pour the remaining olive oil into a measuring cup and add more to equal ¼ cup. Set aside to use for the dough.

To prepare the dough: In the bowl of a food processor fitted with the steel blade or in the bowl of an electric mixer fitted with the paddle attachment, combine the flours, salt, and baking powder, and process or mix on low to incorporate. Add the butter and olive oil and pulse on and off a few times or mix on low until it's the consistency of a fine meal.

Transfer the mixture to a large bowl and toss in the mushrooms. Make a well in the center and pour in the cream. Using one hand, draw in the dry ingredients, mixing until just combined.

Wash and dry your hands and dust them with flour. Turn the dough out onto a lightly floured work surface and gently knead a few times to gather it into a ball. Roll or pat the dough into a circle slightly thicker than ½ inch. Cut out the circles, cutting as closely together as possible and keeping the trimmings intact.

Gather the scraps, pat and press the pieces back together, and cut out the remaining dough. Place the scones 1 inch apart on a parchment-lined baking sheet.

Brush the tops with the remaining cream. Place an onion ring on the top of each scone, and gently press down on the onion with your fingertips. If the rings are bigger than the scone, twist them into a figure eight. Sprinkle each scone with a pinch of salt and poke a sprig of thyme into the center.

Bake for 35 to 40 minutes, until firm to the touch and nicely browned.

Yield: 10 scones

Parmesan Scones

For a quick fix, you can't beat these biscuitlike savories. Eat them on the run or as an afternoon snack, or serve them with supper as you would any cheese biscuit.

Special Item: 1½-inch round cutter

2¾ cups unbleached pastry flour or unbleached all-purpose flour
1 tablespoon plus 1 teaspoon baking powder
2 teaspoons kosher salt
¾ cup (3 ounces) grated Parmesan Reggiano cheese
1 stick plus 1 tablespoon (4½ ounces) unsalted butter, cut into ½-inch cubes and frozen
½ cup (about 1 ounce) minced chives
1 cup crème fraîche or sour cream

FOR THE TOPPING:
2 tablespoons (1 ounce) unsalted butter, melted
2 tablespoons grated Parmesan Reggiano cheese
1 teaspoon fresh cracked black pepper

Adjust the oven rack to the upper position and preheat the oven to 400 degrees. In the bowl of a food processor fitted with the steel blade or in the bowl of an electric mixer fitted with the paddle attachment, combine the flour, baking powder, salt, and cheese and process or mix on low to incorporate. Add the butter and pulse on and off a few times, or mix on low, until it's the consistency of a fine meal.

Transfer the mixture to a large bowl, toss in the chives, and make a well in the center. Add the crème fraîche and, using one hand, draw in the dry ingredients, mixing until just combined. The mixture will be a bit dry and crumbly.

Wash and dry your hands and dust them with flour. Turn the dough out onto a lightly floured work surface and gently knead a few times to gather it into a ball. Roll or pat the dough into a circle slightly thicker than ½ inch. Cut out the circles, cutting as closely together as possible and keeping the trimmings intact.

Gather the scraps, pat and press the pieces back together and cut out the remaining dough. Place the circles in groups of three, with the edges touching to form a clover shape, and place 1 inch apart on a parchment-lined baking sheet.

Brush the tops with the melted butter. Sprinkle with a pinch of the Parmesan and a few grindings of fresh black pepper.

Bake for 25 minutes, until firm to the touch and lightly browned.

Yield: 16 scones

Rosemary Corncakes

Moist and crumbly at the same time, these unusually tasty scones are somewhere between a sweet and a savory. I want to give credit where credit is due, but unfortunately I can't remember who brought me this recipe. Thanks, whoever you are—we love it.

Special Item: 3-INCH ROUND CUTTER

3¾ cups unbleached pastry flour or unbleached all-purpose flour
1¾ cups stone-ground yellow cornmeal
1 tablespoon plus ½ teaspoon baking powder
2 teaspoons finely chopped fresh rosemary
¾ cup light brown sugar, lightly packed
3 sticks (12 ounces) unsalted butter, cut into ½-inch cubes and frozen
1 extra-large egg
1 extra-large egg yolk
2 tablespoons plus 2 teaspoons mild-flavored honey, such as clover
½ cup plus 2 teaspoons heavy cream, plus a little extra for brushing the tops of the scones

FOR GARNISHING:
24 small tufts of fresh rosemary

Adjust the oven rack to the middle position and preheat the oven to 350 degrees.

In the bowl of a food processor fitted with the steel blade or in the bowl of an electric mixer fitted with the paddle attachment, combine the flour, cornmeal, baking powder, rosemary, and brown sugar, and process or mix on low to incorporate. Add the butter and pulse on and off a few times, or mix on low, until the mixture is pale yellow and the consistency of a fine meal.

Transfer the mixture to a large bowl and make a well in the center. Pour in the eggs, honey, and cream, and whisk together the liquids. Using one hand, draw in the dry ingredients, mixing until just combined.

Wash and dry your hands and dust them with flour. Turn the dough out onto a lightly floured work surface and gently knead a few times to gather it into a ball. Roll or pat the dough into a circle about ¾ inch thick. Cut out the scones, cutting as closely together as possible and keeping the trimmings intact.

Gather the scraps, pat and press the pieces back together and cut out the remaining dough. Place them 1 inch apart on a parchment-lined baking sheet.

Brush the tops with the remaining cream and poke 2 small tufts of rosemary into the center of each.

Bake for 30 minutes, until slightly browned and firm to the touch.

Yield: 12 scones

6. Muffins

....

Muffins are the simpletons of the cake world. No fancy tricks, tools, or ingredients are required. Electric mixers and food processors do speed up your prep time, but are by no means a necessity. As long as you have a bowl, a baking tin, and an oven, you'll succeed.

Don't confuse these muffins with the mass-produced, generic-formula muffin. Thoughtfully tailored around specific flavors and ingredients, each one of these is unique and different from the next. In one recipe, browned butter intensifies the nuttiness of the pecans and balances the sweetness of the dates. In another, buttermilk does its job by enhancing the tanginess of the lemon and ginger. At the store, we have a huge audience to please. We always make sure there is a little something for everyone. Banana-Cocoa Muffins (page 192), not too rich and not too chocolatey, are heavenly to kids, but grown-ups enjoy the intensely chocolate Crotin de Chocolat (page 203). The healthy, wholesome customer will of course request the Bran Muffin (page 199), sweetened with pureed raisins and made with plenty of bran. And as for the traditionalist, there's always the Blueberry-Almond (page 195), a better version of the all-American blueberry muffin.

A muffin shouldn't just taste good; it has to look good too. There's nothing worse than dry, matte-looking muffins, appearing stale as soon as they come out of the oven. A simple streusel topping or glaze instantly transforms a plain muffin into an irresistible delight. Toppings also add texture, flavor, and sometimes a sneak preview of what's to come. The Italian Dried-Plum Muffin (page 205) is crowned with brandy-soaked prunes and speckled with cinnamon-sugar. Lemon-Ginger Muffins (page 207) look as moist as they taste with a soaking of lemon juice and a dainty drizzle of white glaze.

Another attraction of these miniature cakes is their intimate scale and individual size. I'm not a big fan of those oversize, King Kong muffins littering the countertops of coffee bars and convenience stores. I get full just looking at them. At the bakery, we prefer the standard 1/2-cup-capacity muffin tin, which produces a muffin that is just the right size.

All of the batters can be made up to a few days ahead. The quickest method to fill the tins is by using a pastry bag with a 3/4-inch-wide opening. If you don't have one, simply spoon the batter into the tins. After the muffins come out of the oven, allow them to cool before you remove them from the tins.

Generally considered a morning sweet, these charming little cakes rise to the occasion as a last-minute dessert.

Banana-Cocoa Muffins

IF IT'S KIDS YOU'RE TRYING TO PLEASE, THE DYNAMIC DUO OF BANANA AND chocolate never fails. These muffins don't rise as high as the others, but after one bite, you'll have no regrets.

Special Items: ½-CUP-CAPACITY MUFFIN TIN, LIGHTLY COATED WITH
MELTED BUTTER
PASTRY BAG FITTED WITH A WIDE TIP, OPTIONAL

FOR GARNISHING:
½ cup (4 ounces) pecans

FOR THE MUFFINS:
5 extra-large eggs
1¼ cups vegetable oil
4 to 6 very ripe bananas, to equal 2½ cups mashed banana puree
3¾ cups unbleached pastry flour or unbleached all-purpose flour
3⅓ cups granulated sugar
2 teaspoons baking soda
1 teaspoon baking powder
1 cup unsweetened imported cocoa powder

Adjust the oven rack to the middle position and preheat the oven to 325 degrees.

Spread the pecans on a baking sheet and toast in the oven until lightly browned, about 8 to 10 minutes. Shake the pan halfway through to ensure that the nuts toast evenly. Cool, coarsely chop, and set aside.

Turn the oven up to 350 degrees.

In a small bowl combine the eggs and oil and stir in the banana puree.

In a large bowl, sift to combine the flour, sugar, baking soda, baking powder, and cocoa powder. Make a large well in the center and pour in the banana mixture. Gradually draw in the dry ingredients, whisking until incorporated.

Fill the pastry bag half full and pipe or spoon the batter into the prepared muffin tins to two-thirds full. Sprinkle 2 teaspoons of the pecans over the top of each.

Bake for 15 minutes, until firm to the touch.

Yield: 12 muffins

Birdseed Muffins

WHY BIRDSEED MUFFINS? THE ANSWER IS OBVIOUS: THESE NUTTY, CRUNCHY muffins have all of those healthy, seedy tidbits that your parakeet loves to pick at.

Special Items: ½-CUP-CAPACITY MUFFIN TIN, LIGHTLY COATED WITH
MELTED BUTTER
PASTRY BAG FITTED WITH A WIDE TIP, OPTIONAL

¼ cup plus 2 tablespoons (6 ounces) shelled, unsalted sunflower seeds
½ cup rolled oats
2 tablespoons wheat germ
¼ cup millet
¼ cup sesame seeds
1 tablespoon flax seeds
1½ cups unbleached pastry flour or unbleached all-purpose flour
½ cup stone-ground whole-wheat flour
1¼ teaspoons baking powder
½ teaspoon baking soda
¼ teaspoon kosher salt
1 tablespoon poppy seeds
1 stick (4 ounces) unsalted butter, chilled and cut into 1-inch cubes
½ cup granulated sugar
2 extra-large eggs, beaten
¼ cup mild-flavored honey, such as clover
1¼ cups buttermilk

FOR THE TOPPING:
2 tablespoons sesame seeds
2 tablespoons flax seeds
2 tablespoons millet
2 tablespoons poppy seeds

Adjust the oven rack to the middle position and preheat the oven to 325 degrees.
To prepare the batter: Spread the sunflower seeds, oats, and wheat germ in rows

on a baking sheet. On another baking sheet, spread the millet, the sesame seeds, and the flax seeds in rows. Toast both sheets in the oven for 6 to 8 minutes, until lightly toasted. Allow to cool.

Turn the oven up to 350 degrees.

In the bowl of a food processor fitted with the steel blade, combine the sunflower seeds, wheat germ, flours, baking powder, baking soda, and salt. Process until the sunflower seeds have the same consistency as the flour. Add the toasted oats, millet, sesame seeds, flax seeds, and poppy seeds and pulse on and off a few times, just to combine.

In the bowl of an electric mixer fitted with the paddle attachment, cream the butter on low, 2 to 3 minutes, until softened. Add the sugar and mix on medium, about 2 to 3 minutes, until light and fluffy, scraping down the sides of the bowl as needed. Add the eggs, 1 tablespoon at a time, mixing well between each addition.

Turn the mixer to medium-low, and add the honey. Slowly pour in the buttermilk, mixing until incorporated. Add the flour mixture in 3 batches, turning the mixer off before each addition and mixing on low until combined.

To prepare the topping: In a small bowl, toss together the seeds. Sprinkle $\frac{1}{2}$ teaspoon of the topping into the bottom of each prepared muffin cup. Fill the pastry bag half full and pipe or spoon the batter into the muffin tin, filling the cups completely to the rim. Sprinkle 1 teaspoon of the topping over the surface of each muffin.

Bake for about 25 minutes, until firm and golden brown.

Yield: 18 muffins

Blueberry–Almond Muffins

No muffin chapter would be complete without the ubiquitous blueberry muffin recipe. The ground almonds and crunchy almond topping just might sway you away from your old family favorite. Don't stop at blueberries; all other berries are delicious, and so are nectarines, peaches, and pears.

Special Items: ½-CUP-CAPACITY MUFFIN TIN, LIGHTLY COATED WITH
              MELTED BUTTER
              PASTRY BAG FITTED WITH A WIDE TIP, LARGE ENOUGH TO
              ACCOMMODATE THE FRUIT, OPTIONAL

½ cup (3 ounces) whole unblanched almonds
¾ cup granulated sugar
1 stick plus 2 tablespoons (5 ounces) unsalted butter, chilled and cut into 1-inch cubes
1 tablespoon finely chopped orange zest (about half of an orange)
1 tablespoon plus 1 teaspoon baking powder
¾ teaspoon baking soda
½ teaspoon kosher salt
3 extra-large eggs, lightly beaten
1½ cups buttermilk
3 cups unbleached pastry flour or unbleached all-purpose flour
2 cups blueberries or 1 to 1½ cups chopped strawberries, nectarines, peaches,
    or pears (½-inch chunks)

FOR THE TOPPING:
1 tablespoon egg white (½ extra-large egg white)
1 tablespoon granulated sugar
Pinch of ground cinnamon
A few gratings of fresh nutmeg
½ cup plus 2 tablespoons (about 2 ounces) sliced unblanched almonds

Adjust the oven rack to the middle position and preheat the oven to 325 degrees. To prepare the batter: Spread the whole almonds on a baking sheet and toast in the oven until lightly browned, about 15 to 20 minutes. Shake the pan halfway through to ensure that the nuts toast evenly.

Turn the oven up to 350 degrees.

In the bowl of a food processor fitted with the steel blade, combine the almonds with half of the granulated sugar and process until it's the consistency of a fine meal.

In the bowl of an electric mixer fitted with the paddle attachment, cream the butter, orange zest, baking powder, baking soda, and salt on low, 2 to 3 minutes, until softened. Add the remaining sugar and ground nut mixture, and mix on medium about 3 to 4 minutes, until light and fluffy, scraping down the sides of the bowl as needed. Add the eggs, 1 tablespoon at a time, mixing well between each addition. Slowly, pour in the buttermilk and mix on medium, just to combine.

Add the flour in 3 batches, turning the mixer off before each addition and mixing on low until just combined.

Remove the bowl from the mixer and fold in the fruit.

To prepare the topping: In a small bowl, whisk the egg white until frothy. Add the sugar, cinnamon, nutmeg, and almonds.

Fill the pastry bag half full and pipe or spoon the batter into the prepared muffin tin, filling the cups to the rim. Spoon about a tablespoon of topping over each muffin, concentrating the almonds in the center of each muffin.

Bake for about 20 to 25 minutes, until the topping is nicely browned and the muffin is firm to the touch. If the batter has cracked through the topping, gently press it down with your fingertips to deflate.

Yield: 12 muffins

Bobka Muffins

THESE HAVE ALL THE SWEET, YEASTY FLAVOR AND IRRESISTIBLY TENDER TEX-
ture of a Russian Coffee Cake (page 284), but they're baked into individual muffins.
Yet another good reason to save those chocolate cake or cookie crumbs to use in the
filling.

Special Item: ½-CUP-CAPACITY MUFFIN TIN, LIGHTLY COATED WITH
                            MELTED BUTTER

*1 recipe Russian Coffee Cake, following the directions for free-form coffee cakes up to the point of
    forming the 24-inch log and sealing it (see page 284)*

FOR THE TOPPING:
1¼ cups unbleached pastry flour or unbleached all-purpose flour
¼ cup granulated sugar
½ teaspoon kosher salt
¾ teaspoon baking powder
5 tablespoons (2½ ounces) unsalted butter, cut into ½-inch pieces and frozen
1 extra-large egg

Slice the log into fourteen 1½-inch pieces. Working with one slice at a time, tuck
the tail end of dough in between the coil, gently pinching it to ensure that it sticks.
Place the slice, tail side down, in the prepared muffin tin.

Set aside in a warm place for about 2 hours, until doubled in size and soft and
spongy to the touch.

Meanwhile, to prepare the topping: In the bowl of a food processor fitted with
the steel blade, or in the bowl of an electric mixer fitted with the paddle attachment,
combine the flour, sugar, salt, and baking powder. Add the butter and pulse on and
off or mix on low until it's the consistency of a coarse meal.

In a small bowl, whisk the egg. Measure out 2 tablespoons for brushing on the
muffins, and set aside.

Transfer the butter mixture to a large bowl. Pour in the egg and gradually draw in
the dry ingredients, mixing to incorporate. It should be crumbly and uneven. Chill
until ready to use.

Adjust the oven rack to the middle position and preheat the oven to 350 degrees.

Brush the surface of the muffins with the reserved egg and sprinkle 2 tablespoons topping over each one.

Bake for 30 minutes, until firm to the touch.

Yield: 14 muffins

Bran Muffins

EVERY BAKER HAS HER VERSION OF A BRAN MUFFIN, AND I HAVE MINE. MOST recipes call for sweetened bran cereals and lots of sugar, defeating the purpose of this healthier style of muffin. I make mine the way they should be, with lots of toasted unprocessed bran and pureed raisins. When toasted, bran adds a distinctive, nutty flavor. The cooked and pureed raisins saturate the muffins, giving them their unusually dark color and moist, fruity quality.

I think you'll like this recycled classic of mine, and if you don't believe me, ask the dessert and muffin maven herself, Maida Heatter. She says they're the best she's ever had.

Special Items: ½-CUP-CAPACITY MUFFIN TIN, LIGHTLY COATED WITH
                MELTED BUTTER
                PASTRY BAG FITTED WITH A WIDE TIP, OPTIONAL

2 cups unprocessed bran
1½ cups raisins
1½ cups water
½ cup buttermilk
1 teaspoon orange zest, finely chopped (about one-third of an orange)
½ cup light brown sugar, lightly packed
½ cup vegetable oil
1 extra-large egg
1 extra-large egg white
½ cup unbleached all-purpose flour
¼ cup stone-ground whole-wheat flour
1 teaspoon baking powder
1 teaspoon baking soda
½ teaspoon kosher salt

Adjust the oven rack to the middle position and preheat the oven to 350 degrees.

Spread the bran on a baking sheet and toast for 6 to 8 minutes, until toasted, stirring halfway through to ensure that it doesn't burn.

In a small saucepan, stir together 1 cup of the raisins and 1 cup of the water and simmer on low heat until the water is absorbed, about 15 minutes. Place in a blender or in the bowl of a food processor fitted with the steel blade, and process until pureed.

Pour the bran into a large bowl, add the buttermilk and remaining ½ cup of water, and stir to combine. Stir in the raisin puree, orange zest, and brown sugar.

Add the oil, whole egg, and egg white, mixing well to incorporate.

Sift the flours, baking powder, baking soda, and salt into the raisin mixture. Add the remaining whole raisins and stir to combine.

Fill the pastry bag half full and pipe or spoon the batter into the prepared muffin tins, filling the cups to just over the rim and mounding the batter slightly.

Bake for about 25 minutes, until the muffins are well browned and firm to the touch.

Yield: 10 muffins

Browned Butter—Pecan Muffins

In case you haven't noticed, I have a thing for browned butter. I've never seen a muffin recipe that called for it, so I figured it was about time. When you brown the butter with a vanilla bean, the butter takes on a unique, nutty richness and is a truly perfect accompaniment to the dates and pecans.

Special Items: ½-CUP-CAPACITY MUFFIN TIN, LIGHTLY COATED WITH
MELTED BUTTER
PASTRY BAG FITTED WITH A WIDE TIP, OPTIONAL

1 cup plus 2 tablespoons (5 ounces) pecans
2 sticks (8 ounces) unsalted butter
1 vanilla bean
10 large soft Medjool dates
¼ cup plus 2 tablespoons granulated sugar
2½ cups unbleached all-purpose flour
1 tablespoon baking powder
½ teaspoon kosher salt
1½ teaspoons ground cinnamon
¾ cup light brown sugar, lightly packed
1 cup buttermilk
2 extra-large eggs

FOR THE STREUSEL TOPPING:
2 tablespoons of the toasted pecans
3 tablespoons unbleached all-purpose flour
2 tablespoons light brown sugar, lightly packed
1 tablespoon of the browned butter

Adjust the oven rack to the middle position and preheat the oven to 325 degrees. Spread the pecans on a baking sheet and toast in the oven until lightly browned, about 8 to 10 minutes. Shake the pan halfway through to ensure that the nuts toast evenly. Allow to cool, measure out 1 cup for the batter, and set aside the remaining 2 tablespoons for the topping.

Turn the oven up to 350 degrees.

To prepare the batter: In a medium saucepan, over medium-high heat, begin to melt the butter. Using a small paring knife, split the vanilla bean lengthwise. With the back of the knife, scrape out the pulp and the seeds and add the scrapings and the pod to the butter. Swirl the pan to ensure the butter cooks evenly and doesn't burn. It will bubble somewhat vigorously as it browns. Continue cooking 3 to 5 more minutes until the bubbles subside and the liquid is dark brown with a nutty, toasty aroma. Remove the vanilla bean. Measure out ¾ cup plus 1 tablespoon of the butter and dark flecks and allow to cool completely. Set the remaining browned butter aside for the topping and to brush the tops of the muffins.

Cut the dates in half, remove the pits, and slice into thin slivers. Set aside.

In the bowl of a food processor fitted with the steel blade, combine 1 cup of nuts with half of the granulated sugar and process until it's the consistency of a fine meal. Add the remaining sugar, the flour, baking powder, salt, cinnamon, and brown sugar and pulse to combine.

Transfer to a large bowl and make a well in the center. Pour in the buttermilk, eggs, and ¾ cup plus 1 tablespoon of the browned butter, and whisk together. Gradually draw in the dry ingredients, whisking until incorporated. Stir in the dates and set aside.

To prepare the topping: Chop the remaining 2 tablespoons of pecans. In a small bowl, combine the flour and brown sugar. Add 1 tablespoon of the reserved browned butter and stir in the pecans.

Fill the pastry bag half full and pipe or spoon the batter into the prepared muffin tin, filling the cups to the rim. Brush the tops with the remaining browned butter and sprinkle about 1 teaspoon of topping over each.

Bake for 35 minutes, until topping is browned and crisp.

Yield: 12 muffins

Crotin de Chocolat

I DON'T RECOMMEND THESE WITH YOUR FIRST CUP OF COFFEE IN THE MORNING, but I do recommend them as an afternoon pick-me-up. Dense without being heavy, and rich without being sweet, this could be the ultimate cupcake for grown-ups. For the true chocoholic, add an extra 2 ounces of chopped chocolate.

Special Items: ½-CUP-CAPACITY MUFFIN TIN, LIGHTLY COATED WITH
MELTED BUTTER
PASTRY BAG FITTED WITH A WIDE TIP, OPTIONAL

2 teaspoons (0.6 ounce) packed fresh yeast or 2¼ teaspoons
    active dry yeast
1 cup plus ½ teaspoon granulated sugar
½ cup plus 2 tablespoons lukewarm water
1½ cups unbleached pastry flour or unbleached all-purpose flour
½ cup 2 tablespoons unsweetened imported cocoa powder,
    plus extra for dusting the tops
2 sticks (8 ounces) unsalted butter, melted and cooled
4 extra-large eggs, lightly beaten
1 cup coarsely chopped bittersweet chocolate (6 ounces), or
    more according to taste

Place the yeast in a small bowl. Sprinkle in ½ teaspoon of the sugar and pour the water over to soften a few minutes. Stir in ¾ cup of the flour and cover the bowl tightly with plastic wrap. Set aside in a warm place until it becomes bubbly, about 30 minutes.

Adjust the oven rack to the middle position and preheat the oven to 350 degrees. In a large bowl, sift to combine the cocoa powder and the remaining sugar and flour.

Make a large well in the center and pour in the butter, eggs, and yeast mixture. Whisk together the liquids and gradually draw in the dry ingredients, whisking until incorporated. Stir in the chocolate.

CROTIN DE CHOCOLAT:
"THE ULTIMATE CUPCAKE FOR GROWN-UPS."

Fill the pastry bag half full and pipe or spoon the batter into the muffin tin, filling the cups to the rim.

Bake for 15 to 18 minutes, until almost firm to the touch.

While slightly warm, sift a fine layer of cocoa powder over the surface.

Yield: 12 muffins

Italian Dried-Plum Muffins

ONE OF MY FAVORITE COMBINATIONS IS PRUNES AND BRANDY. UNFORTUNATELY, most people turn their noses up when they hear the word *prune*. As far as I'm concerned, a prune is a prune is a prune. But, when we call them by a fancier name—say, "Italian dried plums"—not as many noses turn upward.

At least 1 day ahead, soak the prunes by covering them in brandy. Stored in an airtight container, they will keep indefinitely at room temperature. The strength of the brandy mellows after time and cuts through the richness of the prunes.

Special Items: ½-CUP-CAPACITY MUFFIN TIN, LIGHTLY COATED WITH
                     MELTED BUTTER
                   PASTRY BAG FITTED WITH A WIDE TIP, WIDE ENOUGH TO
                     ACCOMMODATE THE FRUIT, OPTIONAL

½ cup brandy
29 soft, plump pitted prunes
2½ cups unbleached pastry flour or unbleached
    all-purpose flour
¾ cup granulated sugar
2 teaspoons baking powder
1 teaspoon baking soda
2 tablespoons finely ground coffee
2 sticks (8 ounces) unsalted butter, cut into 1-inch
    cubes and frozen
1½ cups plain yogurt
2 extra-large eggs
1 tablespoon pure vanilla extract

FOR THE TOPPING:
3 teaspoons granulated sugar
¼ teaspoon ground cinnamon

In a small saucepan over medium heat, warm the brandy for a few minutes. Place the prunes in a bowl and pour the brandy over them. Add a touch more brandy if necessary to cover the prunes. Cover the bowl tightly with plastic wrap and soak the prunes overnight or longer.

Adjust the oven rack to the middle position and preheat the oven to 350 degrees.

To prepare the batter: Over a small bowl, strain the prunes through a fine-mesh sieve, setting aside the remaining brandy for another use. Slice the prunes into quarters, and set aside 36 slices to top the muffins.

In the bowl of a food processor fitted with the steel blade, or in the bowl of an electric mixer fitted with the paddle attachment, combine the flour, sugar, baking powder, baking soda, and ground coffee, and process or mix on low to incorporate. Add the butter and pulse on and off, or mix on low, until it's the consistency of a fine meal.

Transfer the mixture to a large bowl and make a well in the center. Pour in the yogurt, eggs, and vanilla extract, and whisk the liquids together. Gradually draw in the dry ingredients and mix to combine. Stir in the sliced prunes.

To prepare the topping: In a small bowl combine the sugar and cinnamon.

Fill the pastry half full and pipe or spoon the batter into the muffin tins, filling the cups to the rim. Place 3 pieces of sliced prune on top of each muffin and sprinkle with a pinch of cinnamon-sugar topping.

Bake for about 25 minutes, until lightly browned and slightly firm to the touch.

Yield: 12 muffins

Lemon-Ginger Muffins

By soaking the muffins in lemon juice and sugar after they're baked, you get a super-moist, super-lemony, and super-yummy muffin.

Special Items: ½-CUP-CAPACITY MUFFIN TIN, LIGHTLY COATED WITH MELTED BUTTER
PASTRY BAG FITTED WITH WIDE TIP, OPTIONAL

1 stick (4 ounces) unsalted butter, chilled and cut into 1-inch cubes
1 tablespoon plus 1 teaspoon finely chopped lemon zest (about 1 lemon)
1 teaspoon baking soda
2 tablespoons grated fresh ginger, approximately one 2-inch piece
1 cup granulated sugar
2 extra-large eggs
1 cup buttermilk
2 cups unbleached pastry flour or unbleached all-purpose flour

FOR SOAKING THE MUFFINS:
¼ cup lemon juice (1 to 2 lemons)
2 tablespoons granulated sugar

FOR THE GLAZE:
½ cup powdered sugar, sifted
2½ teaspoons water

Adjust the oven rack to the middle position and preheat the oven to 350 degrees.

To prepare the batter: In the bowl of an electric mixer fitted with the paddle attachment, cream the butter, lemon zest, baking soda, and ginger on low, 2 to 3 minutes, until combined. Add the sugar and turn the mixer up to medium, mixing another 2 to 3 minutes, until light and fluffy, scraping down the sides of the bowl as needed.

In a small bowl, whisk together the eggs and buttermilk.

Add the flour and the egg mixture to the butter mixture alternately in 3 batches, turning the mixer off before each addition and mixing on low to combine.

Fill a pastry bag half full and pipe or spoon the batter into the muffin tin, filling the cups two-thirds full.

Bake until firm to the touch, about 30 minutes. Allow to cool.

To prepare the soaking liquid: In a bowl, combine the lemon juice and sugar. Dip the top portion of the muffin three-quarters of the way into the liquid.

To prepare the glaze: In a small bowl, combine the powdered sugar and water.

Place the muffins on a work surface. Dip the fingers of one hand into the bowl of glaze. Holding your hand just above the muffin, quickly move it back and forth to drizzle the glaze over the surface, allowing it to run down the sides. Continue with the remaining muffins.

Yield: 15 muffins

Ricotta Muffins

WHEN YOU'RE IN THE MOOD FOR A MUFFIN THAT'S NOT TOO SWEET, THESE will do the trick. Hearty and satisfying, they have a hint of fennel and you'll be surprised by the rich and creamy ricotta center.

Special Items: ½-CUP-CAPACITY MUFFIN TIN, LIGHTLY COATED WITH
MELTED BUTTER
PASTRY BAG FITTED WITH A WIDE TIP, OPTIONAL

FOR GARNISHING:
½ cup (2 ounces) walnuts or pecans

FOR THE BATTER:
2 teaspoons fennel seeds
3 cups unbleached pastry flour or unbleached all-purpose flour
¾ cup granulated sugar
1 tablespoon plus 1 teaspoon baking powder
¾ teaspoon baking soda
1½ cups plain yogurt
¾ cup vegetable oil

FOR THE FILLING:
½ cup (4 ounces) ricotta cheese
6 tablespoons crème fraîche or sour cream
Kosher salt to taste

Adjust the oven rack to the middle position and preheat the oven to 325 degrees.

Spread the nuts on a baking sheet and toast in the oven until lightly browned, about 8 to 10 minutes. Shake the pan halfway through to ensure that the nuts toast evenly. Cool, chop finely, and set aside.

Turn the oven up to 350 degrees.

To prepare the batter: In a small sauté pan, over medium-low heat, toast the fennel seeds, stirring occasionally until they become aromatic and turn slightly brown, about 2 to 3 minutes. Allow to cool and finely chop, crush, or grind them in a spice grinder or clean coffee grinder.

In a large bowl, sift to combine the flour, sugar, baking powder, and baking soda. Sprinkle in the fennel seeds. Make a large well in the center and pour in the yogurt and oil. Whisk together the liquids and gradually draw in the dry ingredients, mixing until incorporated.

To prepare the filling: Place the ricotta in a mixing bowl and break it up a little with a rubber spatula to loosen. Stir in the crème fraîche and salt.

Fill the pastry bag half full and pipe or spoon the batter into the muffin tin, filling the cups one-third full. Place about 1 tablespoon of the filling into the center of each muffin. Pipe or spoon the remaining batter into the cups, filling them to just below the rim. Sprinkle about 1 teaspoon of the nuts over the top of each.

Bake for 25 to 30 minutes, until lightly browned and firm to the touch.

Yield: 12 muffins

Yam Muffins

Tʜᴇsᴇ sᴘɪᴄʏ, ᴍᴏɪsᴛ ᴍᴜꜰꜰɪɴs ᴀʀᴇ ʙʀɪɢʜᴛ ᴏʀᴀɴɢᴇ ʟɪᴋᴇ ᴀ ᴘᴜᴍᴘᴋɪɴ, ᴡɪᴛʜ all of the sweet goodness of baked yams. I couldn't decide which variation I liked better, the currants cooked in brandy, or the dried cranberries. I've included both, so you can decide for yourself.

Special Items: ¹/₂-ᴄᴜᴘ-ᴄᴀᴘᴀᴄɪᴛʏ ᴍᴜꜰꜰɪɴ ᴛɪɴ, ʟɪɢʜᴛʟʏ ᴄᴏᴀᴛᴇᴅ ᴡɪᴛʜ
ᴍᴇʟᴛᴇᴅ ʙᴜᴛᴛᴇʀ
ᴘᴀsᴛʀʏ ʙᴀɢ ꜰɪᴛᴛᴇᴅ ᴡɪᴛʜ ᴀ ᴡɪᴅᴇ ᴛɪᴘ, ᴏᴘᴛɪᴏɴᴀʟ

2 to 3 (¹/₂ pound) Jewel or Garnet yams
³/₄ cup plus 2 tablespoons currants or dried cranberries
¹/₄ cup brandy (if using currants)
2 cups plus 2 tablespoons unbleached pastry flour or unbleached all-purpose flour
¹/₂ cup granulated sugar
¹/₂ cup light brown sugar, lightly packed
¹/₄ teaspoon baking powder
¹/₄ teaspoon baking soda
Scant ¹/₂ teaspoon kosher salt
¹/₂ teaspoon ground cinnamon
¹/₄ teaspoon freshly grated nutmeg
¹/₄ teaspoon ground cloves
Scant ¹/₂ teaspoon ground ginger
¹/₂ cup vegetable oil
2 extra-large eggs, lightly beaten

ꜰᴏʀ ᴛʜᴇ ᴛᴏᴘᴘɪɴɢ:
¹/₂ cup plus 2 tablespoons (3 ounces) hulled pumpkin seeds
¹/₂ extra-large egg white, about 1 tablespoon
1 tablespoon granulated sugar
Pinch of ground cloves
A few gratings of fresh nutmeg

Adjust the oven rack to the middle position and preheat the oven to 400 degrees.

To prepare the batter: Place the yams directly on the oven rack and bake them until they are very soft and starting to burst, about 45 minutes to an hour. Allow to cool, remove the skins, and set aside.

Turn the oven down to 325 degrees.

In the bowl of a food processor fitted with the steel blade, puree the yams. Measure out 1½ cups of the puree and store the leftovers for another use.

Spread the pumpkin seeds on a baking sheet and toast in the oven until lightly toasted, puffed up, but still green, about 8 to 10 minutes. Shake the pan halfway through to ensure that the seeds toast evenly. Cool and chop very coarsely.

Turn the oven up to 350 degrees.

If you're using currants, place them in a small saucepan with the brandy and simmer over low heat until the liquid evaporates, about 3 to 5 minutes. Set aside to cool. If you're using cranberries, chop them coarsely and set aside.

In a large mixing bowl, sift to combine the flour, sugars, baking powder, baking soda, salt, cinnamon, nutmeg, cloves, and ginger. Make a large well in the center and pour in the oil, eggs, and 1½ cups yam puree. Whisk together the liquid ingredients and slowly draw in the dry ingredients, mixing until combined. Stir in the currants or cranberries.

Fill the pastry bag half full and pipe or spoon the batter into the muffin tin, filling the cups to the rim.

To prepare the topping: In a small bowl, whisk the egg white until frothy. Add the sugar, cloves, nutmeg, and pumpkin seeds.

Spoon about 1 tablespoon of the topping over each muffin, spreading to evenly cover the surface.

Bake for 25 minutes, until the muffins are firm to the touch and the tops are nicely browned and crunchy.

Yield: 10 muffins

7. Tarts

I fell in love with tarts when I was fifteen years old, on my first trip to France. Proudly displayed in the window of every Parisian bakery, those round, low showpiece pies were unlike anything I'd ever seen before. Compared to the swollen, two-crusted fruit or mile-high cream pies typical in America, these tarts seemed quintessentially French—slim and sleek and civilized, with just enough attitude. It seemed a crime to eat them—covered as they were with perfectly symmetrical rows of shiny glazed fruit, custard-filled with random scorched edges, or bejeweled with a necklace of sliced almonds and powdered sugar. Once I got over thinking of tarts as works of art and realized how good they tasted, I was a convert for life.

As I baked my way through the classical school of tart making, duplicating those French standards like Tarte aux Pommes, Tarte aux Noix, and Tarte aux Cerises, I figured out the secret to a great-tasting tart: The ingredients must be fresh and the flavors simple and well-balanced, but equally important is the correct ratio of crust to filling, and the resulting contrast of textures. With those principles in mind, I was free to experiment with a variety of shapes and nontraditional crusts. A yeasty croissant dough paired with a soft, eggy custard or pears baked on top of a flaky, buttery disc of puff pastry makes perfect sense to me. Though the tarts at La Brea Bakery aren't conventional, they're still rooted in that French tradition.

When you want to achieve that classic, low form, you have to use a French tart mold. There are two types. Most people find the fluted tart pan with a removable bottom easier to line and easy to transfer. But I prefer the finished look of a tart baked in a smooth-sided, bottomless flan ring. If you use this type of mold, keep in mind you'll need to slide a flat piece of cardboard underneath the tart to move it from baking sheet to platter. Or try baking the tart on the reverse side of a baking sheet, making it easy to slide off. Both types of molds are available in a multitude of sizes (see "Sources," page 393). If you change the size of the mold I call for, don't forget to adjust the amount of filling and the baking time as well.

For a thin and even good-looking crust, the dough must be

handled as little as possible and rolled out properly. Rolling out the dough for a tart is not a difficult procedure, but a few extra tips never hurt. Most important is the temperature of the room and the temperature of the dough. The oven should be turned off, and when possible, a cool room is best. A large, smooth counter-top, marble slab, or Formica board are all good surfaces for rolling. If the weather is extremely warm and your rolling surface isn't mobile or is too large to chill in the refrigerator, cool the surface down by placing a baking sheet covered in ice, frozen food packages, or portable frozen ice packs over the surface for 10 minutes before rolling your dough. The dough should be cold but pliable when rolling it out. Take the pastry directly from the refrigerator, cut it into a few pieces and pound it with a rolling pin to soften. Use your fingertips (not your palms) to work it quickly into a smooth, pliable ball. Before you roll, brush your ring or mold with melted butter. Have a small bowl of flour nearby. Place the dough in the center of your floured work surface. Pound the ball of dough with a rolling pin to flatten it into a disc about 1 inch thick. Begin rolling it from the center of the disc, turning it slightly clockwise after each stroke to make an even circle, keeping the dough and the work surface lightly floured as necessary. If the dough cracks, it's too cold; warm it briefly with the palm of your hand. If it is too soft, it will stick to the surface. If that's the case, you may need to return it to the refrigerator. Roll the dough at least 2 inches larger in diameter than the ring or pan to be lined, to a thickness of $\frac{1}{8}$ to $\frac{1}{4}$ inch depending on the dough and recipe. Roll in short strokes, stopping short of the edges of the dough so they don't get too thin. Lift and turn the circle frequently to keep it from sticking to the work surface.

To line the mold, place it on a parchment-lined baking sheet. Gently fold the circle of dough into quarters, placing the counterpoint in the center of the mold, and carefully unfold. Alternately, you may roll the dough completely around the rolling pin to pick it up, and set it over the mold to unroll. If the dough is too soft to move, then chill it on a baking sheet until firm enough to handle. If it gets too firm and is rigid, let it soften a few minutes. To fit the dough into the pan, work your way around the edges, gently lifting up the dough and easing it down so that it fits into the corners and sides of the mold. It's important that you don't stretch the dough to fit, or it will shrink later during baking. Dip the knuckle of your index finger in flour and run it around the inside of the pan, gently pressing the dough into the corners with the flat part of your knuckle. Using the three middle fingers of one hand, press the dough into the sides of the pan, pinching slightly if necessary to make sure that the dough comes up slightly above the top of the rim and is an even thickness all around. The side of the pastry must be at a sharp right angle to the bottom at this point or you'll lose the height of the shell, and corners will be too thick, when it shrinks during baking. Trim the pastry even with the edge of the mold and chill or freeze until firm, 30 minutes to an hour. Allowing the dough to rest will prevent shrinking while it bakes.

Because the filling of some tarts bakes more quickly than the crust, you may need to "blind-bake" the shell without the filling to give the crust a head start. To blind-bake, you must weigh down the dough so it doesn't rise as it cooks. Line your mold and chill the tart shell as above. Brush the entire surface of the shell lightly with melted butter. Line the bottom and sides with coffee filters or parchment paper. (I like the large, flat-bottomed coffee filters from automatic drip coffeemakers; they're pliable, reusable, and soft. If the filters aren't large enough to line the entire shell, arrange three or four of them in an overlapping pattern to completely cover the bottom and drape over the sides.) Fill the lining, up to the top of the rim of your mold, with dried beans or metal pie weights (see "Sources," page 393), both of which can be saved and reused. Make sure the beans or weights are pressed tightly into the corners of the dough. Bake in a preheated 350-degree oven for 25 minutes, until the top of the crust is golden brown. Cool completely and remove beans or weights with a large spoon and carefully peel off paper lining. If the bottom of the pastry is not uniformly browned, return it unlined to the oven for a few minutes until fully cooked. Before you fill the shell, check for cracks in the dough. If there are some, smear a small amount of raw dough over the cracks to repair them.

If you too have become a tart convert, do as we do at the bakery. Keep your doughs in the freezer and your fillings in the refrigerator and you'll be ready to bake a Cherry Bundle (page 231) or a Florentine Wedge (page 238) whenever the mood strikes.

Sweet Pastry Dough

THIS IS THE FIRST SWEET CRUSTY PASTRY I LEARNED TO MAKE, AND TO THIS day, I still think it's the best. Leftover dough can be rolled, cut out, and baked into sugar cookies.

> 2³/₄ cups unbleached pastry flour or unbleached all-purpose flour
> ¹/₂ cup granulated sugar
> 2 sticks (8 ounces) unsalted butter, cut into ¹/₂-inch cubes and frozen
> 2 extra-large egg yolks
> ¹/₄ cup heavy cream

In the bowl of a food processor fitted with the steel blade or in the bowl of an electric mixer fitted with the paddle attachment, combine the flour and sugar and pulse or mix on low to incorporate. Add the butter, and pulse on and off or mix on low until it's the consistency of a fine meal.

In a small bowl, whisk together the egg yolks and cream. Add to the butter mixture and pulse a few times or mix on low until the dough barely comes together.

Turn the dough out onto a lightly floured work surface. Dip the heel of your hand in flour and, working with small sections, smear the dough away from you to blend it together. When the dough has been all smeared out, using a metal scraper or spatula, scrape and gather it together. Divide the dough in half and gently knead each half to gather into a ball. Flatten into discs and wrap in plastic to chill at least 2 hours, until firm. Freeze for longer storage.

Yield: 1¹/₂ pounds dough: enough for two 10- to 12-inch tarts or
ten 4³/₄-inch individual tarts

Banana Cream Tart

Everyone loves this Banana Cream Tart. An offshoot of that classic American pie, ours is made in a low tart shell with pastry cream and crème fraîche. To customize your Banana Cream Tart, sprinkle it with shaved chocolate, coconut, or toasted nuts.

Special Item: 10-INCH FLAN RING, LIGHTLY COATED WITH MELTED BUTTER

> ½ recipe (¾ pound) Sweet Pastry Dough (see page 219), chilled
> 1 recipe Pastry Cream (see Kinder Pies, page 245)
> 3 ripe, firm bananas (about 1½ pounds), sliced into ¼-inch round slices
> 2 cups heavy cream
> ¾ cup crème fraîche

Adjust the oven rack to the middle position and preheat the oven to 350 degrees.

On a lightly floured work surface, roll the dough out to a 12-inch circle, ⅛ inch thick, flouring the surface of the dough as necessary. Line the tart ring, chill, and blind-bake according to the directions on page 217.

Spread about 2 tablespoons of Pastry Cream on the bottom of the tart shell. Layer with 1¼ cups of the sliced bananas to cover the entire bottom.

In the bowl of an electric mixer fitted with the whisk attachment, whip the cream and crème fraîche on low until the cream thickens enough not to spatter. Increase the speed to medium-high and continue to whip until the cream holds soft peaks.

In a medium bowl, combine the remaining Pastry Cream with 1 cup of the whipped cream and return the remaining 3 cups of whipped cream to the refrigerator, covered, until ready to serve. Fold the rest of the bananas into the Pastry Cream mixture and fill the tart shell, spreading evenly. Cover and chill until ready to serve.

Before serving, check the consistency of the whipped cream. If necessary, whisk a few times to stiffen slightly. Spoon the whipped cream onto the top of the pie in a dome, spreading it with the back of a large spoon to form uneven peaks.

Yield: One 10-inch tart

Belgian Sugar Pie

SIMPLICITY IS THE SECRET IN THIS DELICIOUS TART. EGGS, CREAM, AND SUGAR are whisked together and poured into a croissant dough shell and baked to perfection. Creamy and buttery with a crispy crust, it tastes like the sweetest, richest French toast you've ever had.

Special Item: ONE 10-INCH FLAN RING, OR SPRINGFORM PAN

About ⅓ recipe (1 pound) Croissant dough (page 294), chilled for at least 3 hours

FOR THE FILLING:
1 extra-large egg
¾ cup heavy cream
1 tablespoon pure vanilla extract
1 extra-large egg white, lightly beaten
½ cup plus 2 tablespoons granulated sugar
2 tablespoons unsalted butter, softened

On a lightly floured work surface, roll the dough out to a 12-inch circle about ¼ inch thick, flouring the surface as necessary. Center the flan ring on the circle of dough and gently press down to score a circle into the dough. Place the flan ring on a parchment-lined baking sheet.

To form a scalloped edge, pick up a small ½-inch section of the dough and fold the dough over to meet the marked line and firmly press the dough to seal. Place your thumb on the folded edge pointing inward toward the center. Using your other hand, pick up a small section of dough, fold it over and press down to seal. Move your thumb to the other side of the newly formed pleat. Keeping your thumb in place, pick up another piece of dough and fold it over, pressing down to seal. Repeat around the entire edge, rotating the circle of dough as you work your way around to form diagonal pleats.

Lift the dough into the ring and gently press it outward to reach the edge of the mold. Using your fingertips, dimple the dough about 10 times. Set aside in a warm place to rise, until slightly puffy and spongy to the touch, about 1 to 1½ hours.

Adjust the oven rack to the middle position and preheat the oven to 350 degrees.

To make the filling: In a large bowl, whisk together the whole egg, cream, and vanilla extract.

Brush the edge of dough with egg white. Sprinkle over $\frac{1}{2}$ cup of the sugar over the entire tart shell. Dimple the bottom a few more times and pour in the filling. Dot the top with butter and sprinkle the remaining sugar around the edge.

Bake for about 45 minutes, until the custard is set and the crust is lightly browned.

Yield: One 10-inch tart

Black Currant Silk Tart

Perforated wedges of pastry arranged on top add a fresh and modern touch to this classic tart. Vivid colorful fruit peeking through the holes gives a sneak preview of what's to come. I prefer cassis (black currants) but if you can't find it, try raspberries, huckleberries, blackberries, or passion fruit. Fresh fruit is always better, but if it's out of season, frozen fruit purees are available at Latin markets, upscale markets, and restaurant supply stores (see "Sources," page 393) all year round.

Special Items: 10-INCH FLAN RING, LIGHTLY COATED WITH MELTED BUTTER
THREE GRADUATED ROUND CUTTERS, 1/2 INCH TO 1 INCH

1 recipe (1½ pounds) Sweet Pastry Dough (see page 219), chilled

FOR THE FILLING:
1½ quarts fresh fruit or ½ pound frozen fruit puree
2 extra-large eggs
1 cup plus 2 tablespoons heavy cream
½ cup granulated sugar

Adjust the oven rack to the middle position and preheat the oven to 350 degrees. Divide the dough in half and return the other half to the refrigerator.

On a lightly floured work surface, roll the dough out to a 12-inch circle, ⅛ inch thick, flouring the surface of the dough as necessary. Line the tart ring, chill, and blind-bake according to the directions on pages 217.

On a lightly floured surface, roll the remaining dough out to a circle, ⅛ inch thick. Cut out a 9-inch circle and transfer to a parchment-lined baking sheet. Chill until firm, about 15 to 20 minutes. Cut the circle into quarters and cut the quarters in half to make 8 wedges. Separate the slices and using the small cutters, cut out 3 graduated circles in each wedge. Bake for 20 minutes until golden brown. Set aside to use as the top crust.

To prepare the filling using fresh fruit: In the bowl of a food processor fitted with the steel blade, pulse until the fruit is pureed. Place the fruit in a fine-mesh sieve and press the fruit through, straining out the seeds and skin. Measure the puree. You should have 1½ cups.

To prepare the filling using frozen fruit puree: Thaw the fruit puree and strain through a fine-mesh sieve.

In a large bowl, whisk together the eggs, cream, sugar, and fruit puree to combine. Pour into the tart shell and bake for 20 to 25 minutes until set. When done, the filling should no longer quiver when you gently shake the baking sheet, and the surface should be a deep purple.

Allow to cool and arrange the perforated wedges on top of the custard, leaving room to slice in between each.

Yield: One 10-inch tart

Breakfast Bars

THIS MAY BE THE SINGLE MOST ADDICTIVE PASTRY WE MAKE. FRUITY JAM sandwiched between a tender crust and streusel topping—crunchy, buttery, and salty. The edges that burn and caramelize are what I nibble at early in the morning as I pass by the baker's rack.

FOR THE STREUSEL TOPPING:
2½ cups unbleached pastry flour or unbleached all-purpose flour
½ cup plus 2 tablespoons granulated sugar
1 teaspoon kosher salt
1¼ teaspoons baking powder
1 stick plus 2 tablespoons (5 ounces) unsalted butter, cut into 1-inch cubes and frozen
1 extra-large egg, beaten

FOR THE DOUGH:
4 cups unbleached pastry flour or unbleached all-purpose flour
½ cup granulated sugar
½ cup light brown sugar, lightly packed
½ cup cornstarch
1 teaspoon kosher salt
4 sticks (1 pound) unsalted butter, chilled and cut into 1-inch cubes

FOR THE FILLING:
2 cups raspberry jam

To prepare the topping: In the bowl of a food processor fitted with the steel blade or in the bowl of an electric mixer fitted with the paddle attachment, combine the flour, sugar, salt, and baking powder, and pulse, or mix on low, to incorporate. Add the butter and pulse on and off or mix on low until it's the consistency of a coarse meal.

Transfer the mixture to a bowl and add the egg, tossing with your hands to incorporate. It should be crumbly and uneven. Chill until ready to use.

To prepare the dough: In the bowl of a food processor fitted with the steel blade or in the bowl of an electric mixer fitted with the paddle attachment, combine the flour, sugars, cornstarch, and salt. Add the butter and pulse on and off, or mix on low, until the dough barely comes together.

Turn the dough out onto a lightly floured work surface and gently knead to gather into a ball. Flatten into a disc and wrap in plastic to chill until firm, at least 2 hours or overnight.

Adjust the oven rack to the middle position and preheat the oven to 350 degrees.

On a lightly floured surface, roll the dough into a 10 × 16-inch rectangle, $\frac{1}{4}$ inch thick, flouring the surface as needed. Place on a parchment-lined baking sheet and bake until lightly browned, about 20 to 25 minutes. Allow to cool.

Spread the jam over the surface of the crust and crumble a heavy layer of topping over the jam.

Bake for about 40 minutes, until the topping is nicely browned.

When cool, cut into squares.

Yield: 16 pieces

Caramelized Banana Puffs

T HOUGH YOU WON'T FIND THIS RECIPE IN YOUR CLASSIC FRENCH COOKBOOKS, I think you'll agree that bananas and puff pastry is a match made in heaven. If you have your puff pastry ready, they're unbelievably quick to make. Cut out a few circles of pastry, slice the bananas, and sprinkle on some sugar—that's all there is to it. If you don't have the 4-inch cake pans, substitute any individual-size pan, making sure you cut the puff pastry 1 inch larger.

Special Items: 5-INCH ROUND CUTTER
EIGHT 4-INCH-DIAMETER, ³/₄-INCH-HIGH MINI TEFLON
    CAKE PANS (SEE "SOURCES," PAGE 393) OR DISPOSABLE
    ALUMINUM PIE PANS (I-CUP CAPACITY), LIGHTLY
    COATED WITH MELTED BUTTER

½ recipe (2 pounds) Puff Pastry (see page 330), chilled
¼ cup water
1 cup sugar plus extra for sprinkling
8 (3½ pounds) ripe, firm bananas, sliced into ¼-inch round slices

Cut the Puff Pastry in half and return one half to the refrigerator. On a lightly floured work surface, roll out the Puff Pastry ⅛ inch thick, flouring the surface of the pastry as necessary. Cut out four 5-inch circles. Place them on a baking sheet and freeze for 30 minutes until firm. Repeat with the remaining dough.

In a heavy-duty small, deep saucepan, stir together the water and sugar. Over medium-high heat, bring the mixture to a boil without stirring. Using a pastry brush dipped in water, brush down the sides of the pan to remove any undissolved sugar granules. Continue cooking without stirring. When the sugar begins to color, after 5 to 7 minutes, begin to tilt and swirl the pan to cook evenly. When it reaches an amber color, remove from the heat and immediately pour a tablespoon or so of the hot caramel mixture into each of the cake pans, swirling the pan with tongs or a heat pad to evenly coat the bottom. Allow to cool.

Adjust the oven rack to the upper position and preheat the oven to 375 degrees.

Place 3 banana slices, slightly overlapping, in the center of each pan and, working your way outward, arrange the banana slices in concentric circles (this is the layer you will see when serving, so be sure it's neatly arranged). Continue layering the slices, using one whole banana for each pan. The bananas should reach about $\frac{1}{4}$ inch above the rim of the pan.

Place a circle of Puff Pastry over the top of each pan. Transfer to the baking sheets and invert the tarts by placing your hand on the pastry and quickly flipping it over, gently removing your hand after they've been inverted, leaving the pan on top.

Sprinkle the edges of each pastry with about $\frac{1}{2}$ teaspoon granulated sugar.

Bake for about 35 minutes, until the pastry starts to color and rise and the sugar begins to melt. Remove the baking sheet from the oven. Using tongs or 2 forks, remove the pans, leaving the tarts on the baking sheet. Return them to the oven to bake for another 15 minutes, until the pastry is nicely browned.

Yield: 8 tarts

Cheese Bars

I_F THERE'S ONE RULE IN COOKING, IT IS NEVER INTERFERE TOO MUCH WITH the classics. Made with a crispy graham cracker crust and a smooth cream cheese filling, my Cheese Bars are still based on that classic cheesecake recipe, but changed just enough to call them my own.

Rectangular and square molds are available at some kitchen stores. If you have no luck finding them, bake the bars in the traditional round springform pan and call them cheese slices.

Special Item: RECTANGULAR FLAN RING (SEE "SOURCES," PAGE 393), 12 × 4 INCHES, WITH 2-INCH SIDES, LIGHTLY COATED WITH MELTED BUTTER

About ⅓ recipe Graham Cracker dough (see page 124), chilled

FOR THE FILLING:
2¼ cups (13½ ounces) cream cheese
½ cup granulated sugar
½ teaspoon kosher salt
½ cup crème fraîche
2 extra-large eggs
1 tablespoon lemon juice
1 tablespoon pure vanilla extract
2 teaspoons poppy seeds

Adjust the oven rack to the middle position and preheat the oven to 350 degrees.

To prepare the crust: On a lightly floured work surface, roll the dough out to a rectangle slightly larger than 12 × 4 inches, ⅛ inch thick, flouring the surface of the dough as necessary. Transfer to a parchment-lined baking sheet and trim the edges of the dough by placing the rectangular mold over it, pressing down to cut through. If the dough shrinks away from the mold, use your fingers to press it out, eliminating any gaps. Remove the trimmings on the outside of the mold and set aside to use for patching the crust. Bake for about 20 to 25 minutes, until browned and slightly firm to the touch. Allow to cool. If there are any gaps where the dough shrank while baking, use some of the leftover dough to patch it, so that the filling doesn't leak through.

Meanwhile, to prepare the filling: In the bowl of an electric mixer fitted with the paddle attachment, combine the cream cheese, sugar, and salt, and mix on medium for about 2 to 3 minutes, until smooth and creamy. Add the crème fraîche and mix another minute to combine.

In a medium bowl whisk together the eggs, lemon juice, and vanilla extract. Slowly add the liquid to the cheese mixture, mixing on medium, until completely incorporated.

Strain the mixture through a fine-mesh sieve and stir in the poppy seeds. Pour into the mold and spread evenly. The filling should fill the mold three-quarters full.

Bake for 30 minutes, until the sides are set and the center of the cheesecake moves ever so slightly.

Cool for 10 minutes and place in the refrigerator for at least 1½ to 2 hours until set and cold. Slice into 1-inch bars.

Yield: 12 to 14 slices

Cherry Bundles

DEFINITELY NOT YOUR TRADITIONAL TART, THESE LITTLE PURSES OF FRUIT still have all the necessary elements to be a tart: a crust and a filling. The crust is made of a rich cream cheese dough, perfectly complementing the tangy cherry compote inside. If cherries are out of season, substitute the cranberry compote from Cranberry Crumble Tart (see page 236).

Special Items: 5-INCH ROUND CUTTER
TWELVE 10-INCH PIECES OF KITCHEN STRING OR TWINE

1 recipe cream cheese dough with the turns and folds (see Rugelach, page 151) or
  1½ pounds Puff Pastry Dough (page 330), chilled

FOR THE CHERRY COMPOTE:
1½ cups granulated sugar
½ cup water
1 vanilla bean
1 cinnamon stick
2¼ pounds fresh red sweet cherries, stemmed and pitted to equal 6 cups
1½ cups (12 ounces) dried sour cherries
¼ cup brandy
1 tablespoon plus 1 teaspoon cornstarch, dissolved in 2 tablespoons water
1 tablespoon balsamic vinegar

FOR THE TOPPING:
1 to 2 extra-large egg whites, lightly beaten
¼ cup granulated sugar

Divide the dough in half and return one half to the refrigerator. On a lightly floured work surface, roll the dough out to ⅛-inch thickness, flouring the surface of the dough as necessary. Cut out six 5-inch circles. Place them on a parchment-lined baking sheet and chill until firm, about 30 minutes to an hour. Repeat with the remaining dough.

To prepare the cherry compote: In a large, heavy-duty, deep saucepan, stir together the sugar and water. Using a small paring knife, split the vanilla bean lengthwise. With the back of the knife, scrape out the pulp and the seeds and add the scrapings and the pod to the sugar mixture. Add the cinnamon stick. Over medium-high heat, bring the mixture to a boil without stirring. Using a pastry brush dipped in water, brush down the sides of the pan to remove any undissolved sugar granules. When the sugar begins to color, after 3 to 4 minutes, tilt and swirl the pan to cook evenly. When the mixture reaches an even medium caramel color, remove from the heat.

Add the fresh cherries. The mixture will spatter and the sugar may seize and harden. Add the dried sour cherries and brandy, and return to the heat to cook about 5 more minutes, until the cherries are tender and the hardened sugar has dissolved.

Place a fine-mesh sieve over a large bowl, and pour in the fruit, straining the liquid into the bowl. Pour the liquid back into the saucepan and transfer the fruit to the bowl. Over high heat, bring the liquid to a boil, remove from the heat, and whisk in the cornstarch mixture. Cook for another 1 to 2 minutes, over medium-high heat, until the juice is shiny, bubbly, and slightly thickened. Add the balsamic vinegar and combine with the fruit. Allow the filling to cool and remove the vanilla bean and the cinnamon stick.

On a lightly floured surface, roll to enlarge each circle to a 7- to 7½-inch diameter, keeping it as round as possible, flouring the surface of the dough as necessary.

Working with one circle at a time, place about ⅓ cup of the compote in the center. Bring the two opposite sides of the circle to meet in the middle. Holding the two halves together with the thumb and index finger of one hand, pleat the remaining edges of dough, gathering the edges above the fruit to form the top of the bundle. Holding it together with one hand, wrap a piece of the twine around the center and tie it tightly. It will look like a small drawstring purse. Place the bundles on 1 or 2 parchment-lined baking sheets, 2 inches apart. Freeze until frozen, at least 1 hour.

Adjust the oven racks to the upper and lower positions and preheat the oven to 400 degrees.

Brush the bundles with the egg white and sprinkle with sugar.

Bake for about 35 to 40 minutes, until nicely browned and the filling begins to bubble out, rotating the baking sheets halfway through to ensure even baking. Allow to cool and cut off the string.

Yield: 12 bundles

Cinnamon-Custard Tart

NO TART CHAPTER WOULD BE COMPLETE WITHOUT A CUSTARD TART. OURS IS more like a flan, not too rich and sprinkled with cinnamon.

Special Item: 10-INCH FLAN RING

> ½ *recipe (¾ pound) Sweet Pastry Dough (see page 219), chilled*
> 1½ *cups heavy cream*
> 1 *cinnamon stick*
> 1 *vanilla bean*
> ½ *tablespoon finely chopped orange zest (about 1 orange)*
> 2 *extra-large eggs*
> ½ *cup granulated sugar*
> 1 *tablespoon unsalted butter*
> ¼ *teaspoon ground cinnamon*

On a lightly floured work surface, roll the dough out to a 12-inch circle, ⅛ inch thick, flouring the surface of the dough as necessary. Line the tart ring, chill, and blind-bake according to the directions on page 217.

Adjust the oven rack to the middle position and preheat the oven to 350 degrees.

Meanwhile, in a medium saucepan over medium-high heat, combine the cream and cinnamon stick. Using a small paring knife, split the vanilla bean lengthwise. With the back of the knife, scrape out the pulp and the seeds and add the scrapings and the pod to the cream. Add the orange zest and bring to a boil. Remove the pan from the heat and allow the cream to steep and the flavors to infuse for 30 minutes to an hour.

Strain the cream mixture through a fine-mesh sieve to remove the zest, and return the cream to the pot.

In a small mixing bowl, whisk together the eggs and sugar.

Bring the cream back to a boil, then slowly pour it over the egg mixture, whisking continuously as you pour.

Pour the custard into the tart shell, dot with butter, and sprinkle with cinnamon.

Bake for about 30 minutes until just set.

Yield: One 10-inch tart

Cinnamon-Milk Tart

DON'T LET THE NAME OR INGREDIENTS DECEIVE YOU; THIS TART TASTES MUCH better than it sounds. I first heard about milk tart through Beatrice, a pastry chef I worked with many years ago at Spago. She reminisced about this South African dessert, the way we do when we're homesick and hungry for that all-American apple pie. Made in every household, it's a dessert that South Africans take pride in.

During a recent visit to South Africa, I tasted many milk tarts. After several mediocre versions of this regional specialty, I finally hit the jackpot on a game reserve in Shawamari. Pure white and covered in a blanket of cinnamon, this Milk Tart was plain and creamy, delicious and comforting like a good rice pudding.

Special Items: 10-INCH FLAN RING, LIGHTLY COATED WITH MELTED BUTTER
3-INCH-DIAMETER CARDBOARD GUIDE OR PAPER PLATE

FOR THE DOUGH:
2½ cups unbleached pastry flour or unbleached all-purpose flour
1¼ cups powdered sugar
2 sticks (8 ounces) unsalted butter, chilled and cut into 1-inch cubes
1 extra-large egg
1 extra-large egg yolk

FOR THE FILLING:
4 cups whole milk
½ cup plus 1 tablespoon granulated sugar
1 vanilla bean
¼ cup plus 2 tablespoons cornstarch

FOR DECORATING:
¼ cup ground cinnamon

To prepare the dough: In the bowl of a food processor fitted with the steel blade or in the bowl of an electric mixer fitted with the paddle attachment, combine the flour and sugar and pulse, or mix on low, to incorporate. Add the butter and pulse on and off or mix on low, until it's the consistency of a coarse meal.

In a small bowl, whisk together the whole egg and egg yolk, and pour into the flour mixture. Pulse or mix on low until the dough barely comes together.

Turn the dough out onto a lightly floured work surface. Dip the heel of your hand in flour and working with small sections, smear the dough away from you to blend it together. When the dough has been all smeared out, use a metal scraper or spatula to scrape and gather it together. Divide the dough in half and gently knead each half and gather into a ball. Flatten into 2 discs and wrap in plastic. Chill one piece until firm, at least 2 hours, and freeze the other for later use.

On a lightly floured work surface, roll the dough out to a 10-inch circle, $\frac{1}{8}$ inch thick, flouring the surface of the dough as necessary. Line the tart ring, chill, and blind-bake according to the directions on page 217.

To prepare the filling: In a deep stainless-steel saucepan over low heat, warm $3\frac{1}{2}$ cups of the milk with the granulated sugar. Using a small paring knife, split the vanilla bean lengthwise. With the back of the knife, scrape out the pulp and the seeds and add the scrapings and the pod to the milk. Turn the heat to medium and bring to a boil.

Meanwhile, in a large bowl, whisk together the remaining milk and the cornstarch.

When the milk comes to a boil, pour it into the cornstarch mixture and whisk together. Return it to the saucepan and bring it back to a boil over medium heat, stirring occasionally, so it doesn't color. Continue cooking, allowing it to bubble and thicken, about 2 minutes. Remove the vanilla bean and pour the filling into the baked tart shell. Chill until set and cold, about 45 minutes.

Place the 3-inch guide in the center of the tart and sift an even layer of cinnamon over the top of the tart, to make an outer circle of cinnamon.

Yield: One 10-inch tart

Cranberry Crumble Tart

THIS FALL DESSERT HAS ALL THE HOMINESS OF A COBBLER COMBINED WITH the refined sophistication of a tart.

Special Item: 10-INCH FLAN RING, LIGHTLY COATED WITH MELTED BUTTER

½ recipe (¾ pound) Sweet Pastry Dough (see page 219), chilled

FOR THE COMPOTE:
½ cup water
¾ cup granulated sugar
1 vanilla bean
1 cinnamon stick
1 cup fresh cranberries (or frozen, if fresh aren't available)
¾ cup plus 2 tablespoons (4 ounces) dried cranberries
¾ cup orange juice
1 tablespoon cornstarch, dissolved in 1 tablespoon water

FOR THE STREUSEL TOPPING:
¾ cup unbleached pastry flour or unbleached all-purpose flour
¾ cup granulated sugar
¾ teaspoon ground cinnamon
1½ sticks unsalted butter, cut into 1-inch cubes and frozen
½ extra-large egg, lightly beaten, 2 tablespoons

On a lightly floured work surface, roll the dough out to a 12-inch circle, ⅛ inch thick, flouring the surface of the dough as necessary. Line the tart ring and chill according to the directions on page 215.

To prepare the compote: In a large, heavy-duty, deep saucepan, stir together the water and sugar. Using a small paring knife, split the vanilla bean lengthwise. With the back of the knife, scrape out the pulp and the seeds and add the scrapings and the pod to the sugar mixture. Add the cinnamon stick. Over medium-high heat, bring the mixture to a boil without stirring. Using a pastry brush dipped in water, brush down the sides of the pan to remove any undissolved sugar granules. When the sugar begins to color, after 3 to 4 minutes, begin to tilt and swirl the pan to cook evenly. When the mixture reaches an even medium caramel color, remove from the heat.

Add the fresh cranberries, dried cranberries, and orange juice. The mixture will spatter and the sugar may seize and harden. Return to the heat and cook 5 to 8 more minutes, until the cranberries swell and begin to pop and the hardened sugar has dissolved.

Place a fine-mesh strainer over a large bowl and pour in the fruit, straining the liquid into the bowl. You should have about 1¾ cups liquid. Pour the liquid back into the saucepan and transfer the fruit to the mixing bowl. Over high heat, bring the liquid to a boil, remove from the heat, and whisk in the cornstarch mixture. Cook for another 1 to 2 minutes, until the juice is shiny, bubbly, and slightly thickened. Combine with the fruit. Allow the filling to cool and remove the vanilla bean and the cinnamon stick. You'll have about 3 cups of filling.

Adjust the oven rack to the middle position and preheat the oven to 350 degrees.

To prepare the topping: In a food processor fitted with the steel blade or the bowl of an electric mixer fitted with the paddle attachment, combine the flour, sugar, and cinnamon and process or mix on low to incorporate. Add the butter and pulse on and off, or mix on low, until it's the consistency of a coarse meal. Add the measured beaten egg and pulse or mix on low, just to combine. Refrigerate until ready to use.

Remove the tart shell from the refrigerator and pour in the compote. Crumble the topping evenly over the top.

Bake for 45 minutes, until the compote is bubbling and the topping is nicely browned.

Yield: 8 to 10 servings

Florentine Wedges

INSPIRED BY THOSE CRUNCHY CANDYLIKE FLORENTINE COOKIES, I ADDED A crust and made a tart. Tasty and eye-catching, the honey-caramel layer is studded with green pistachios, red cranberries, and candied lemon zest. Use your favorite tiny cookie cutters to create a decorative border on the tart. For the traditionalist, cut the dough into small circles and you'll have your Florentine cookie.

Special Items: 2³/₄-INCH ROUND CUTTER (FOR COOKIES)
1-INCH ROUND OR SHAPED CUTTER (FOR DECORATIVE BORDER ON TARTS)
CANDY THERMOMETER (CHECK YOUR THERMOMETER'S ACCURACY IN BOILING WATER; IT SHOULD READ 212 DEGREES)

1 recipe (1¹/₂ pounds) Sweet Pastry Dough (see page 219), chilled

FOR THE FILLING (ENOUGH FOR 2 TARTS OR 24 COOKIES):
¹/₂ cup plus 2 tablespoons (2 ounces) unblanched sliced almonds
¹/₃ cup heavy cream
3 tablespoons mild-flavored honey, such as clover
3 tablespoons granulated sugar
1 vanilla bean
2 tablespoons (1 ounce) unsalted butter
3 tablespoons unbleached pastry flour or unbleached all-purpose flour
2 tablespoons Candied Lemon Zest (see page 374), syrup drained off
¹/₄ cup (1 ounce) raw shelled unsalted pistachios, coarsely chopped
¹/₄ cup (1 ounce) dried cranberries, coarsely chopped

Adjust the oven racks to the upper and lower positions and preheat the oven to 325 degrees.

For the tarts: Divide the dough in half and return one half to the refrigerator. On a lightly floured work surface, roll the dough out to a 12-inch circle, ¹/₄ inch thick, flouring the surface of the dough as necessary. Cut out a 10-inch circle, leaving the scraps intact. Transfer the circle to a parchment-lined baking sheet and prick the surface of the circle about 10 times with the tines of a fork. Using the 1-inch cut-

ter, cut out small circles or shapes from the scraps of dough. Brush the edge of the large circle of dough with water and place the cut-out shapes, touching, around the entire edge to form a decorative border. Chill until firm, about 30 minutes to an hour. Repeat the process with the remaining dough.

For the cookies: Divide the dough in half and return one half to the refrigerator for another use. On a lightly floured surface, roll the dough out ¼ inch thick, flouring the surface of the dough as necessary. Using the 2¾-inch cutter, cutting as closely together as possible, cut out about 24 cookies. Place them on 1–2 parchment-lined baking sheets, spaced ½ inch apart, and chill until firm.

Spread the almonds on a baking sheet and toast in the oven on the lower rack until lightly toasted, about 5 to 7 minutes. Shake the pan halfway through to ensure that the nuts toast evenly.

Turn the oven up to 350 degrees.

To prepare the filling: In a medium-size heavy-duty saucepan, stir together the cream, honey, and sugar. Using a small paring knife, split the vanilla bean lengthwise and with the back of the knife, scrape out the pulp and the seeds and add the scrapings and the pod to the mixture. Add the butter and, over medium heat, bring the mixture to a boil without stirring, tilting and swirling the pan to ensure it cooks evenly without coloring. Cook the mixture 5 to 6 minutes, until it reaches 230 degrees on a candy thermometer (thread stage). Remove from the heat and sift in the flour, whisking to combine. Remove the vanilla bean. Stir in the candied zest, almonds, pistachios, and cranberries.

For the tarts: Using the back of a spoon or an offset spatula, spread half of the filling onto each tart shell, up to the decorative border.

For the cookies: Allow the mixture to sit until it's cool enough to handle. With your hands, pick up a heaping teaspoon of the filling and roll it between your palms to form a ¾-inch ball. Flatten to a 2¼-inch disc and place on top of the cookie. It should be about ½ inch from the edge of the cookie. To make sure you have the right amount of filling, bake a test cookie. The filling should bubble and spread into a thin candied surface, running over the sides in a few places.

Bake the tarts for 20 to 25 minutes, and the cookies for about 15 minutes, rotating the baking sheets halfway through to ensure even baking. The crust should be nicely browned and the filling an even, deep caramel color. Allow to cool completely. Slice the tarts into wedges, slicing between the decorative shapes.

Yield: Two 10-inch tarts or about 2 dozen cookies

Gâteau Basque

Iғ you're at the kitchen counter, trimming sliver after sliver of this irresistible almond tart (and you've lost count of the slivers), not to worry. According to Calvin Trillin, noted food writer and humorist, as long as you're standing up, not using a fork, or eating off of someone else's plate, the calories never count.

Special Item: 10-INCH TART RING, LIGHTLY COATED WITH MELTED BUTTER

1 recipe cream cheese dough with the turns and folds (see Rugelach, page 151), chilled

FOR THE FILLING:
1 cup plus 2 tablespoons (6 ounces) unblanched almonds
1 cup powdered sugar
1 stick plus 1 tablespoon (4½ ounces) unsalted butter, chilled and cut
  into 1-inch cubes
1 extra-large egg
1 extra-large egg yolk
2 tablespoons dark rum
1 tablespoon pure almond extract
1 recipe Pastry Cream (see Kinder Pies, page 245)

FOR THE TOPPING:
1 extra-large egg white, lightly beaten
2 tablespoons granulated sugar

To prepare the filling: In the bowl of a food processor fitted with the steel blade, grind the almonds with half of the powdered sugar until it's the consistency of a fine meal.

In the bowl of an electric mixer, cream the butter on low, 2 to 3 minutes, until softened. Add the remaining powdered sugar and mix on medium 3 to 4 minutes until light and fluffy, scraping down the sides of the bowl as needed. Add the almond mixture and mix another minute, until combined.

In a medium bowl, whisk together the whole eggs, egg yolk, rum, and almond extract. Turn the mixer to low and slowly pour in the egg mixture a few teaspoons at a time and mix until incorporated. Add the Pastry Cream and mix on low until just combined. Refrigerate until set, about an hour.

Cut the dough into 2 unequal parts, one slightly larger than the other, and return the smaller part to the refrigerator. On a lightly floured work surface, roll the larger half of the dough out to a 12-inch circle, ⅛ inch thick, flouring the surface of the dough as necessary. Line the tart ring according to the directions on page 215, but don't trim the excess dough. Chill until firm, about 30 minutes to an hour.

Roll the other half of the dough out to a circle, ¼ inch thick, flouring the surface of the dough as necessary. Cut out a circle slightly larger than 11 inches. Place it on a baking sheet, and, using a straight-edge razor or very sharp knife, score the dough with diagonal lines, spaced ¼ inch apart, to cover the entire surface, being careful not to cut all the way through. Score diagonal lines going in the other direction to make a diagonal grid. Chill until firm, 30 minutes to an hour.

Adjust the oven rack to the middle position and preheat the oven to 350 degrees.

Remove the tart shell and top crust from the refrigerator. Spoon the filling into the tart shell and spread evenly. Brush the edge of the tart shell with the egg white and center the top over the tart, pressing down gently. Using a rolling pin, roll over the edge gently to seal the top crust to the bottom crust and remove the excess dough. Brush the top with egg white and sprinkle the surface with sugar.

Bake for 1 hour and 20 minutes, until nicely browned.

Yield: One 10-inch tart

Hazelnut–Banana Tart

EVERY BAKERY NEEDS A FEW YEAR-ROUND FRUIT TARTS, AND THIS IS ONE OF our favorites. The individual flavors of the bananas and hazelnuts, sweet, rich and nutty, complement without overshadowing one another. When plums go out of season and you're waiting for tangerines to hit the markets, this banana standby won't disappoint.

Special Item: 12-INCH TART RING, LIGHTLY COATED WITH MELTED BUTTER

½ recipe (¾ pound) Sweet Pastry Dough (see page 219), chilled

FOR THE FILLING:
½ cup (2½ ounces) hazelnuts
1¼ cups plus 1 tablespoon powdered sugar
½ cup unbleached pastry flour or unbleached all-purpose flour
5 extra-large egg whites
2 sticks (8 ounces) unsalted butter
1 vanilla bean

FOR THE TOPPING:
4 to 5 bananas, ripe yet firm and sliced at an angle, ¼ inch thick and about
    1½ inches in diameter
2 teaspoons granulated sugar

On a lightly floured work surface, roll the dough out to a 13-inch circle, ⅛ inch thick, flouring the surface of the dough as necessary. Line the tart ring and chill according to the directions on page 215.

Adjust the oven rack to the middle position and preheat the oven to 325 degrees.

To prepare the filling: Spread the hazelnuts on a baking sheet and toast in the oven until lightly browned, about 10 to 15 minutes. Shake the pan halfway through to ensure that the nuts toast evenly. Allow to cool. Gather the nuts into a kitchen towel and rub together to remove the skins.

Turn the oven up to 350 degrees.

In the bowl of a food processor fitted with the steel blade, combine the hazelnuts with half of the powdered sugar, and process until it's the consistency of a fine meal. Add the remaining sugar and flour, and pulse to combine. Pour in about two-thirds of the egg whites and process until a smooth paste. Add the remaining egg whites and pulse on and off until combined. Transfer to a large bowl.

In a medium saucepan over high heat, begin to melt the butter. Using a small paring knife, split the vanilla bean lengthwise. With the back of the knife, scrape out the pulp and the seeds and add the scrapings and the pod to the butter. Swirl the pan to ensure the butter cooks evenly and doesn't burn. It will bubble somewhat vigorously as it browns. Continue to cook 3 to 5 more minutes until the bubbles subside and the butter is dark brown and has a nutty aroma. Remove the vanilla bean.

Slowly pour the browned butter and dark flecks into the nut mixture, whisking to incorporate.

Pour the mixture into the tart shell. Starting from the outer edge, arrange the bananas, slightly overlapping, in concentric circles to cover the entire surface of the tart. Sprinkle with the sugar and bake for about an hour, until the filling is firm and the crust is nicely browned.

Yield: One 12-inch tart

Kinder Pies

I**F THERE HASN'T BEEN A NURSERY RHYME NAMED AFTER THESE CHARMING LIT-**tle pies, then there should be. Decorated with whimsical cutout shapes of dough and filled with chocolate and vanilla cream and sweet rice, Kinder Pies are irresistible to both kids and adults. Kids can't resist their playful appeal and adults can't resist their buttery crust and creamy rich center. If you don't have enough rings, you can always make a smaller batch.

Special Items: TWELVE 3½-INCH FLAN RINGS, WITH ½-INCH SIDES, LIGHTLY
           COATED WITH MELTED BUTTER
      5-INCH ROUND CUTTER
      2-INCH ROUND OR DECORATIVE COOKIE CUTTERS (STARS,
           HEARTS, ANIMALS)

FOR THE DOUGH:
4 cups unbleached pastry flour or unbleached all-purpose flour
2 teaspoons kosher salt
4 sticks (1 pound) unsalted butter, chilled and cut into 1-inch cubes
2 extra-large eggs
4 extra-large egg yolks

FOR THE RICE:
½ cup Arborio rice
2 cups whole milk
¼ cup granulated sugar
¼ teaspoon kosher salt

FOR THE PASTRY CREAM:
7 extra-large egg yolks
½ cup granulated sugar
2 tablespoons cornstarch
2 tablespoons unbleached pastry flour or unbleached
    all-purpose flour
2 cups whole milk
1 vanilla bean

2 tablespoons (1 ounce) unsalted butter

2 ounces bittersweet chocolate, melted and set aside

2 extra-large egg yolks, lightly beaten with a few drops of water
½ cup granulated sugar

Adjust the oven rack to the middle position and preheat the oven to 350 degrees.

To prepare the dough: In the bowl of a food processor fitted with the steel blade or in the bowl of an electric mixer fitted with the paddle attachment, combine the flour and salt and process or mix on low to incorporate. Add the butter and pulse a few times, or mix on low, until it's the consistency of a fine meal.

In a small bowl, whisk together the whole eggs and egg yolks. Add to the flour mixture and pulse a few times, or mix on low, until the dough barely comes together.

Turn the dough out onto a lightly floured work surface. Dip the heel of your hand in flour and working with small sections at a time, smear the dough away from you to blend it together. When the dough has been all smeared out, using a metal scraper or spatula, scrape and gather it together and knead a few times to gather into a ball. Flatten into a disc, wrap in plastic, and chill until firm, at least 2 hours or overnight.

To make the rice: In a small ovenproof saucepan combine the rice, milk, sugar, and salt. Over high heat, bring to a boil. Remove from the heat, cover, and cook in the oven until the rice is tender and the liquid is absorbed, about 30 to 35 minutes.

To make the Pastry Cream: In the bowl of an electric mixer fitted with the whisk attachment, beat the egg yolks and sugar on high until the mixture is very thick, pale yellow, and forms a ribbon when the beater is lifted from the bowl. Remove the bowl from the mixer and sift in the cornstarch and flour, whisking to combine.

In a medium stainless-steel saucepan over high heat, begin to warm the milk. Using a small paring knife, split the vanilla bean lengthwise. With the back of the knife, scrape out the pulp and the seeds and add the scrapings and the pod to the milk. Bring the milk to a boil. Slowly pour about one quarter of the hot milk into the egg mixture, whisking constantly. Return the egg-milk mixture to the saucepan to combine with the remaining milk. Cook over medium heat, whisking the mixture until it's thickened and bubbles in the center. Over a medium bowl, strain the cream through a fine-mesh sieve. Stir in the rice. Divide half the mixture into another bowl. Whisk the butter into one and the melted chocolate into the other. Cover each with plastic wrap, pressing it against the surface of the cream to prevent a skin from forming. Chill in the refrigerator until cold.

Divide the dough in half and return one half to the refrigerator. On a lightly floured surface, roll the dough out to ⅛ inch thick, flouring the surface of the dough as necessary. Cutting as closely together as possible, cut out 12 circles and place them on a parchment-lined baking sheet to chill until firm, about 30 minutes to an hour. Set the scraps aside.

Roll and cut out the remaining dough in the same manner.

Gather all of the scraps together and chill. Roll the dough out ¼ inch thick and, using your shaped cutters, cut out 12 shapes and chill.

Place the flan rings on two parchment-lined baking sheets. Line the rings according to the directions on page 215, but don't trim off the excess dough. Fill the shells halfway with the vanilla cream. Top with the chocolate cream filling to just below the rim.

Adjust the oven rack to the upper and lower position and preheat the oven to 350 degrees.

Remove the other 12 circles of dough from the refrigerator. Brush the edge of the filled tart shells with the egg yolk and center a circle over each tart. With your fingers or using a rolling pin, press or roll around the rim to seal the top crust to the bottom crust and to trim the excess dough. Continue this process with the remaining tarts.

Brush the tops of the tarts with the egg yolk and place the cutout shapes in the center of each, gently pressing down to ensure that they stay in place. Brush again with the egg yolk and sprinkle the entire top of each tart with about 2 teaspoons of sugar.

Bake for 40 to 45 minutes, until the crust is nicely browned, rotating the baking sheets halfway through to ensure even baking.

Yield: 12 small tarts

Lemon Cups

THESE DELICIOUS, PRETTY LITTLE TARTS USE THE ENTIRE LEMON—EVERYTHING but the seeds. Their deep, buttery crust is coated with raspberry jam and filled with zingy lemon batter. This untraditional "lemon tart" is very elegant and easily made year round.

Special Item: EIGHT 2-INCH-TALL, 3-INCH-DIAMETER CAKE RINGS (SEE "SOURCES," PAGE 393), COATED WITH MELTED BUTTER

1 recipe (1½ pounds) Sweet Pastry Dough (see page 219), chilled
2 tablespoons raspberry jam
1 whole lemon, washed and cut into quarters, seeds removed
3 cups powdered sugar
2 tablespoons light corn syrup
1¼ cups (7 ounces) whole blanched almonds
¾ cup cornstarch
4 extra-large eggs, lightly beaten
1½ sticks (6 ounces) unsalted butter

FOR THE GLAZE:
¼ cup plus 2 tablespoons powdered sugar
2 tablespoons buttermilk
1 tablespoon corn syrup

To line the molds: Separate out one third of the dough and return the rest to the refrigerator. On a lightly floured work surface, roll the dough into a rectangle, ⅛ inch thick, flouring the surface of the dough as necessary. Using an offset spatula or the back of a spoon, spread a thin, even layer of raspberry jam over the dough. Using your cake ring as a cutter, cut out 8 circles, cutting as closely together as possible. Transfer the rings and dough onto a parchment-lined baking sheet, spaced 2 inches apart.

On a lightly floured surface, roll the remaining dough into a rectangle about 18 × 9½ inches, trimming the edges straight. Working with the longer side parallel to the edge of the counter, cut vertically every 2 inches to make eight 2 × 9-inch strips.

Line the insides of the cake rings, pressing gently with your fingers to help the dough stick to the sides of the molds. (It may be necessary to brush on more melted butter if the dough has trouble sticking.) If they don't fit perfectly, patch with dough scraps and smooth to even. Trim off the excess dough from the tops and chill until firm, about 30 minutes to an hour.

Adjust the oven rack to the middle position and preheat the oven to 350 degrees.

To prepare the batter: In the bowl of a food processor fitted with the steel blade, combine the lemon, 1 cup of the powdered sugar, and the corn syrup, and process for 2 to 3 minutes until coarsely ground. Transfer to a large mixing bowl.

In the bowl of a food processor fitted with the steel blade, combine the remaining powdered sugar with the almonds and process until it's the consistency of a fine meal. Add the cornstarch and pulse to combine.

Add about ¼ cup of the beaten eggs to the nut mixture and pulse on and off a few times to combine. Add the remaining eggs in two more batches, pulsing on and off until smooth. Add to the lemon mixture, and whisk to combine.

In a small saucepan over medium heat, melt the butter. Bring it to a boil and remove from the heat. Skim off and discard the milk solids accumulated on the top and measure the butter. You should have ½ cup. Pour the hot butter over the lemon-nut mixture, whisking to combine.

Fill the molds with the lemon filling to three-quarters full.

Bake for 40 to 50 minutes until firm and nicely browned. After the first 20 to 25 minutes of baking, when the crust begins to color and the cake is slightly firm, remove from the oven. Using a small paring knife, make an X in the center of each cake, cutting all the way through the top surface. Return to the oven to finish baking. The batter will rise up through the X for an uneven, risen surface.

To prepare the glaze: In a small bowl whisk together the powdered sugar, buttermilk, and corn syrup. Set aside.

Allow the tarts to cool slightly, about 15 minutes, and brush them with the glaze or cool completely and sift a fine layer of powdered sugar over the top.

Yield: 8 individual tarts

Normandy Apple Tart

LARGE, SUCCULENT CHUNKS OF APPLES BATHED IN BROWNED BUTTER COVER the surface of this rustic free-form tart. The walnut filling is a pleasing surprise, nestled inside the crispy browned puff pastry crust. It's rich and delicious and very attractive. Make 1 large tart or 12 smaller tarts.

Special Item: 6-INCH CUTTER

FOR THE NUT FILLING:
2 cups (8 ounces) walnuts
¾ cup powdered sugar
2 tablespoons light corn syrup
1 extra-large egg white

About ⅔ recipe (3 pounds) Puff Pastry (see page 330), chilled
3 large (about 1 pound) Granny Smith apples, peeled
¼ cup granulated sugar
½ stick plus 2 tablespoons (3 ounces) unsalted butter
1 vanilla bean

To prepare the nut filling: Adjust the oven rack to the middle position and preheat the oven to 325 degrees.

Spread the walnuts on a baking sheet and toast in the oven until lightly browned, about 8 to 10 minutes. Shake the pan halfway through to ensure that the nuts toast evenly.

In the bowl of a food processor fitted with the steel blade, combine the nuts with half the powdered sugar and process until it's the consistency of a fine meal. Add the remaining sugar, corn syrup, and egg white, and pulse on and off a few times until it's a smooth paste. Chill until firm, about 1 hour.

For the large tart: On a lightly floured work surface, roll the Puff Pastry to a 12 × 14-inch rectangle, ¼ inch thick, flouring the surface of the dough as necessary. Trim the edges straight and place on a parchment-lined baking sheet and chill until firm, 30 minutes to an hour.

Divide the filling into 5 pieces. Roll two of the pieces into 10-inch-long ropes, 1 inch thick, and two of the pieces into 12-inch-long ropes, 1 inch thick, setting the remaining piece aside. Place the ropes on the Puff Pastry to form a square, about an inch from the edge, pinching the ropes together at the ends to form corners. Don't worry if your ropes of filling break; simply pinch them back together. Fold the edges of the Puff Pastry over the ropes of filling, firmly pressing down with your fingertips to seal. Smear the remaining walnut filling over the bottom of the Puff Pastry and place in the freezer for at least an hour until frozen.

To make small tarts: Divide the dough in half and return one half to the refrigerator. On a lightly floured work surface, roll the Puff Pastry out ¼ inch thick, flouring the surface as necessary. Cut out 5 to 6 circles and place them on a parchment-lined baking sheet. It may be necessary to gather the scraps and stack them to reroll. Smear about 1–2 tablespoons of the filling into the center of each circle, leaving a ½-inch border. Make a scalloped edge by pushing the thumb of one hand against the thumb and index finger of the other hand. Continue around the entire edge of each circle and then freeze at least 1 hour until frozen. Repeat the process with the remaining dough.

Cut the apples away from their cores, in four pieces. For the large tart, cut the apples flat side down, into ¾-inch slices. For the small tarts, slice the apples flat side down, a little less than ½ inch thick. Place the apples in a medium bowl and sprinkle with 2 tablespoons of the sugar and chill until cold, about 15 minutes.

Adjust the oven rack to the upper position for the large tart and the upper and lower positions for the small tarts and preheat the oven to 375 degrees.

In a medium saucepan over medium-high heat, begin to melt the butter. Using a small paring knife, split the vanilla bean lengthwise. With the back of the knife, scrape out the pulp and the seeds and add the scrapings and the pod to the butter. Swirl the pan to ensure the butter cooks evenly and doesn't burn. It will bubble somewhat vigorously as it browns. Continue to cook 3 to 5 more minutes, until the bubbles subside and the butter is dark brown and has a nutty aroma. Remove the vanilla bean. Pour the butter over the apples and toss to coat. Allow to cool. Store the extra butter that settles in the bottom of the bowl in the refrigerator for another use.

For the large tart: Place the apple wedges on the bottom of the tart, curved side up, packed closely together in three rows with 5 or 6 wedges in each row. Pile the leftover wedges on top of the rows and sprinkle the entire tart with the remaining 2 tablespoons of sugar.

For the small tarts: Place 6 to 8 apple slices, curved side up, onto the bottom of each tart. Sprinkle about a teaspoon of sugar over each.

Bake the tarts for 45 minutes, until the crust is well browned and the apples are cooked.

Yield: One 12 × 14-inch tart or 12 individual tarts

Nut Slices

Everyone who bites into this tart instantly starts talking about their grandmother. It's nutty and sweet, could that be why? Use the leftover dough to make nut cookies.

Special Item: RECTANGULAR FLAN RING (SEE "SOURCES," PAGE 393), 12 × 4 INCHES, LIGHTLY COATED WITH MELTED BUTTER, OPTIONAL

FOR THE DOUGH:
1/3 cup (1 3/4 ounces) whole unblanched almonds
3/4 cup powdered sugar
2 cups plus 2 tablespoons unbleached pastry flour or unbleached all-purpose flour
1 1/2 teaspoons baking powder
1/2 teaspoon kosher salt
1 1/2 sticks (6 ounces) unsalted butter, chilled and cut into 1-inch cubes
1 extra-large egg yolk
2 tablespoons heavy cream, half and half, or whole milk
1 tablespoon orange flower water

FOR THE FILLING:
1/4 cup plus 2 tablespoons (2 1/2 ounces) whole unblanched almonds
1/2 cup powdered sugar
1/2 teaspoon ground cardamom
1/2 teaspoon ground cinnamon
1/8 teaspoon freshly grated nutmeg
2 to 3 extra-large egg whites
1 to 2 tablespoons orange marmalade

Adjust the oven rack to the middle position and preheat the oven to 325 degrees.
Spread the almonds for both the dough and the filling on a baking sheet and toast in the oven until lightly browned, about 15 to 20 minutes. Shake the pan halfway through to ensure that the nuts toast evenly. Allow the nuts to cool. Separate out 1/4 cup plus 2 tablespoons of the nuts for the filling and set aside.
To prepare the dough: In the bowl of a food processor fitted with the steel blade,

combine ⅓ cup of the almonds and half of the powdered sugar and process until it's the consistency of a fine meal. Add the remaining sugar, the flour, baking powder, and salt, and pulse a few times to combine. Add the butter and pulse on and off for about half a minute, until it's the consistency of a fine meal.

In a small bowl, whisk together the egg yolk, cream, and orange flower water. Add to the flour mixture and pulse until the dough barely comes together.

Turn the dough out onto a lightly floured work surface. Dip the heel of your hand in flour and, working with small sections, smear the dough away from you to blend it together. When the dough has been all smeared out, using a metal scraper or spatula scrape and gather it together. Divide the dough in half and gently knead each half together. Flatten into two rectangles, wrap in plastic, and chill until firm, at least 2 hours or overnight.

To prepare the filling: In the bowl of a food processor fitted with the steel blade, combine the almonds with ½ cup of the powdered sugar and process until it's the consistency of a fine meal. Add the remaining sugar, cardamom, cinnamon, and nutmeg, and pulse to combine. Transfer to a bowl. Make a well in the center and pour in two of the egg whites, whisking to combine. Gradually draw in the dry ingredients, and whisk until thoroughly incorporated. The mixture should be shiny, smooth, and spreadable. If it seems too stiff, add a few drops of the extra egg white. Set aside.

Preheat the oven to 350 degrees.

Remove half of the dough from the refrigerator and turn onto a lightly floured surface. Roll the dough into a rectangle, 13 × 5 inches, about ¼ inch thick and transfer to a parchment-lined baking sheet. Set the mold on top of the dough and press down, cutting all the way through the dough. Remove the mold and set it aside. If you're not using a mold, shape the rectangle free-form and trim the edges to 12 × 4 inches.

Using an offset spatula or the back of a spoon, spread the orange marmalade evenly over the dough. Spread the nut filling over the marmalade. Chill the bottom while you roll out the remaining dough.

On a lightly floured surface, roll the dough into a 15 × 6-inch rectangle, ⅛ inch thick. Cut the dough into 12 strips, ¾ inch wide. Remove the bottom from the refrigerator. Layer 6 strips diagonally across the filling, at 1-inch intervals, using the shorter pieces toward the short ends of the rectangle. To form the second layer of lattice, place the remaining strips over the first layer, crisscrossing diagonally.

Place the mold over the dough and press down to trim the strips, and bake with the mold in place. If you aren't using a mold, trim the strips with a knife. (Wrap these and freeze for another use.)

Allow to cool and slice.

Gather the scraps, chill, and roll out to make cookies.

Bake 40 minutes, until nicely browned.

Yield: 8 to 10 slices

Pear Puffs

Our pear tart is probably very different from yours. For ours, we cut the pear in half, leaving its core, seeds, and stem intact. We cut off a section of the rounded bottom of the fruit, so it sits upright on the puff pastry, providing a lovely cross-section view of the pear's interior. Look for small pears, about 2¼ inches long. If you can't find them, large pears will work; just make them small by slicing off a larger section of the rounded bottom of the pear. Like a minimalist sculpture, the beauty of this tart is its pure formal simplicity. Oh yeah, it tastes good too.

Special Item: 5-inch round cutter

> ½ recipe (about 2 pounds) Puff Pastry, chilled (page 330)
> 5 small Bartlett pears (about 1¼ pounds), small and ripe, yet firm
> 1 extra-large egg white, lightly beaten
> 3 tablespoons plus 1 teaspoon granulated sugar

Divide the Puff Pastry in half and return one half to the refrigerator. On a lightly floured work surface, roll the pastry out to about ⅛ inch thick, lightly flouring the surface as necessary. Cutting as closely together as possible, cut out 5 circles and place them on a parchment-lined baking sheet to chill in the freezer until firm, about 30 minutes to an hour. Gather the scraps of dough, stack them on each other, and wrap in plastic wrap and freeze for another use. Repeat with the remaining Puff Pastry.

Adjust the oven rack to the upper and lower positions and preheat the oven to 375 degrees.

On a cutting board, lay each pear on its side. Starting at the base of the stem, using a small, sharp knife, carefully slice the stem in half vertically. Slice the pear in half, keeping each half of the stem intact and leaving the core and seeds in place. Continue with the remaining pears.

Shave off a 1-inch circular piece of the pear's bottom third, to create a flat area so that the pear can sit upright on the tart. If your pear is large, shave off more of the pear to scale it down a little. Place the pear halves upright, in the center of each circle.

Brush the pastry with the egg white and sprinkle the entire surface of each tart with about 1 teaspoon of the sugar.

Bake for 30 to 40 minutes, until the pear is thoroughly cooked and shiny and the puff pastry is a deep golden brown. Rotate the baking sheets halfway through to ensure even baking.

Yield: 10 tarts

PICNIC TARTS: "THEY'RE SO SMALL YOU CAN SAMPLE ALL FIVE FLAVORS."

Picnic Tarts

Picnic Tarts is the name these cute little tartlets go by at La Brea Bakery. Made daily in a variety of flavors, Pistachio-Currant, Brown Butter and Fruit, Lemon, Nut, and Mini Pear Rustics, these 2-bite-maximum tarts take the place of a cookie. They're so small you can sample all five flavors.

All of the fillings, except that for the Nut Tarts, can be made in advance. With a little planning, you can easily make the entire assortment.

Hopefully you'll have at least 12 molds; if not, line as many as you have, bake them, and reuse the molds for the next batch after you remove the tarts.

Special Items: AT LEAST SIX OR UP TO TWENTY-FOUR 2¾-INCH TARTLET MOLDS (SEE "SOURCES," PAGE 393), ¼-CUP CAPACITY, LIGHTLY COATED WITH MELTED BUTTER

3-INCH ROUND CUTTER

1 recipe (1½ pounds) Sweet Pastry Dough, chilled (see page 219)

To prepare the tart shells for the Pistachio-Currant, Brown Butter and Fruit, Lemon, and Nut Tarts: On a lightly floured work surface, roll one half of the dough out to ⅛ inch thick, flouring the surface of the dough as necessary. Cutting as closely together as possible, cut out the circles. Place them on a parchment-lined baking sheet, not overlapping, and chill until firm, 30 minutes to an hour. Set the scraps aside.

Roll and cut out the remaining dough in the same manner. Gather all the scraps together, chill, roll, and cut.

Working with one at a time, soften the edge of the circle by gently pinching and stretching it with your fingers to make it pliable. Line the tart molds, pressing the dough into the corners with your fingers. If the dough shrinks below the rim of the mold, press the dough slightly to force it up to the rim. If there's excess dough, trim it even with the rim. Chill until firm, about 30 minutes.

Pistachio-Currant Picnic Tarts

Special Item: SEVERAL DOUGH-LINED TARTLET MOLDS, UP TO 24 (SEE PICNIC
TARTS, PAGE 257)

1½ cups (6½ ounces) raw, shelled, unsalted pistachios
3 cups powdered sugar
1 cup plus 2 teaspoons unbleached pastry flour or unbleached all-purpose flour
6 extra-large egg whites, minus 2 tablespoons
2 sticks plus 2 tablespoons (9 ounces) unsalted butter
1 vanilla bean
¼ cup plus 2 tablespoons (3 ounces) currants

Adjust the oven rack to the upper and lower positions and preheat the oven to
350 degrees.

In the bowl of a food processor fitted with the steel blade, grind the nuts with half
of the sugar and process until it's the consistency of a fine meal. Add the flour and
remaining sugar, and pulse to combine. Pour in about two-thirds of the egg whites
and process until a smooth paste. Add the remaining egg whites, and pulse on and off
until combined. Transfer the nut mixture to a large bowl.

In a small saucepan, over medium-high heat, begin to melt the butter. Using a
small paring knife, split the vanilla bean lengthwise and, with the back of the knife,
scrape out the pulp and the seeds and add the scrapings and the pod to the butter.
After a few minutes, the butter will become foamy and begin to darken. Swirl the pan
to promote even browning, taking care that it doesn't burn. Continue cooking about
5–7 more minutes until the bubbles subside and the liquid is dark brown with a
nutty, toasty aroma. Remove the vanilla bean.

Slowly pour the browned butter and dark flecks into the nut mixture, whisking
continuously. Stir in the currants.

Spoon about 2 tablespoons of filling into each tart shell, place the molds on 1–2
baking sheets, ½ inch apart, and bake for 25 minutes, until the crust is nicely
browned and the filling is firm to the touch. Halfway through, rotate the baking
sheets to ensure even baking.

Yield: 24 tartlets

Brown Butter and Fruit Picnic Tarts

Special Item: SEVERAL DOUGH-LINED TARTLET MOLDS, UP TO 24 (SEE PICNIC
                  TARTS, PAGE 257)

3 extra-large eggs
1¼ cups granulated sugar, plus extra for sprinkling
Scant ½ cup unbleached pastry flour or unbleached all-purpose flour, sifted
1½ sticks (6 ounces) unsalted butter
1 vanilla bean
1½ cups (¾ pound) strawberries, sliced in half vertically, or raspberries, blueberries, or ¼-inch
    chunks of pears

Adjust the oven rack to the upper and lower positions and preheat the oven to
350 degrees.

In a large bowl, whisk together the eggs and sugar. Stir in the flour and whisk
until combined.

In a small saucepan, over medium-high heat, begin to melt the butter. Using a
small paring knife, split the vanilla bean lengthwise. With the back of the knife,
scrape out the pulp and the seeds and add the scrapings and the pod to the butter.
Swirl the pan to ensure the butter cooks evenly and doesn't burn. It will bubble
somewhat vigorously as it browns. Continue cooking 3 to 5 more minutes, until the
bubbles subside and the liquid is dark brown with a nutty, toasty aroma. Remove the
vanilla bean.

Slowly, pour the browned butter and dark flecks in a steady stream into the egg
mixture, whisking continuously.

Place half a strawberry, or 3 to 5 raspberries, or 5 blueberries, or 3 chunks of
pear into each tart shell and pour 2 tablespoons of the filling into each shell. Sprinkle a pinch of sugar over each, place the molds on 1–2 baking sheets, spaced ½ inch
apart, and bake for 25 minutes until the crust is nicely browned. Halfway through,
rotate the baking sheets to ensure even baking.

Yield: 24 tartlets

Nut Picnic Tarts

I'M TORN BETWEEN THE LOOK OF AN OPEN-FACED TART WITH ALL OF THE NUTS exposed and the appealing texture of a pie with a top crust. You be the judge. If you make the two-crusted-pie version, you'll need to have more dough on hand or make fewer tarts.

Special Items: CANDY THERMOMETER (CHECK YOUR THERMOMETER'S ACCURACY
IN BOILING WATER; IT SHOULD READ 212 DEGREES)
SEVERAL DOUGH-LINED TARTLET MOLDS, UP TO 24 (SEE PICNIC
TARTS, PAGE 257)

3/4 cup (3 ounces) hulled pumpkin seeds
3/4 cup (3 ounces) whole unblanched almonds
Scant 3/4 cup (3 ounces) whole unsalted macadamia nuts
Scant 3/4 cup (3 ounces) hazelnuts
1 1/2 sticks (6 ounces) unsalted butter
1 vanilla bean
1 cup plus 2 tablespoons heavy cream
1/4 teaspoon kosher salt
1 cup plus 2 tablespoons water
1 1/2 cups granulated sugar
3 tablespoons light corn syrup

Adjust the oven rack to the middle position and preheat the oven to 325 degrees.

Spread the pumpkin seeds on a baking sheet and toast until lightly browned, about 8 to 10 minutes. On another baking sheet spread the nuts in separate rows and toast in the oven until lightly browned, about 15 to 20 minutes. Shake the pans halfway through to ensure that the nuts and seeds toast evenly. Allow the nuts to cool. Gather the hazelnuts into a kitchen towel and rub them together to remove the skins. Cut the macadamia nuts into rough halves.

Turn the oven up to 350 degrees.

Pour the cream and the salt into a medium bowl and set aside.

In a small saucepan over medium-high heat, begin to melt the butter. Using a small paring knife, split the vanilla bean lengthwise. With the back of the knife, scrape out the pulp and the seeds and add the scrapings and the pod to the butter. Swirl the pan to ensure the butter cooks evenly and doesn't burn. It will bubble somewhat vigorously as it browns. Continue cooking about 3 to 5 more minutes until the bubbles subside and the liquid is dark brown with a nutty, toasty aroma. Remove the vanilla bean, pour over the cream and whisk to combine.

In a medium saucepan, over medium-high heat, heat the water, sugar, and corn syrup. When the mixture comes to a boil, using a pastry brush dipped in water, wash down the sides of the pan to dissolve any sugar granules. Allow the caramel to cook, without stirring, for about 10 to 15 minutes. The mixture will begin to turn a light amber color, and will be covered with slowly bursting bubbles. Continue to cook, swirling the pan to ensure even coloring, to 268 degrees on a candy thermometer (hard ball stage). If you don't have a candy thermometer, dip your fingers into ice water, pick up a very small piece of the sugar syrup, and immediately plunge your fingers and the syrup into ice water. Remove the sugar and pinch it together with your fingers. It should form a hard ball. Remove from the heat and immediately stir in the cream mixture and nuts. Be careful; the mixture may spatter. Return to the heat and simmer on medium-low for another 3 to 5 minutes, stirring occasionally until the temperature reaches 210 degrees on a candy thermometer. The mixture should be slightly thickened and reduced and a pale caramel color. Remove from the heat, pour into a bowl, and allow to cool slightly for about 15 to 20 minutes, until barely warm. (As the nut mixture cools, it frequently crystallizes and turns grainy. Although the caramel needs to cool down a bit so it doesn't melt the crust, it's important that the molds are filled while the mixture is still smooth.)

Fill each tart shell with 2 tablespoons of the caramel mixture and, if using a top crust, center it over the filling, cupping with your hands and pressing down to seal the top and bottom crusts together, and trim the excess dough. With a sharp knife, score the top with 4 lines, like a sunburst, not meeting in the middle, and score 4 small lines in between the large ones.

Place the molds on 1–2 baking sheets, spaced ½ inch apart, and bake for about 25 minutes, until the crust is nicely browned, rotating the baking sheets halfway through to ensure even baking.

Yield: 24 tartlets

Lemon Picnic Tarts

Special Item: SEVERAL LINED TARTLET MOLDS, UP TO 24 (SEE PICNIC TARTS, PAGE 257)

4 to 5 extra-large eggs, beaten to measure 1 cup plus 2 tablespoons
¾ cup lemon juice (about 4 to 5 lemons)
1 tablespoon lemon zest, finely chopped (about 1 lemon)
2¼ cups granulated sugar
¼ cup plus 2 tablespoons unbleached pastry flour or unbleached all-purpose flour

Adjust the oven rack to the middle position and preheat the oven to 350 degrees.

In a large bowl, whisk together the eggs, lemon juice, lemon zest, and sugar. Sift in the flour and mix until combined.

Fill each tart shell with 3½ tablespoons of the filling, and place the molds on 1–2 baking sheets, ½ inch apart.

Bake for 25 minutes, until the crust is nicely browned and the filling is set, rotating the baking sheets halfway through to ensure even baking.

Yield: 24 tartlets

Mini Pear Rustics

The filling is partially enclosed by folding up the edge of the dough into a six-sided stop sign. These interesting shapes add decor to your platter of assorted mini picnic tarts.

Special Item: 4-INCH ROUND CUTTER

FOR THE DOUGH:
3 cups unbleached pastry flour or unbleached all-purpose flour
¼ cup plus 2 tablespoons granulated sugar
3 sticks (12 ounces) unsalted butter, chilled and cut into 1-inch cubes
2 tablespoons pure vanilla extract

FOR THE STREUSEL TOPPING:
1 cup plus 2 tablespoons unbleached pastry flour or unbleached all-purpose flour
1 cup plus 2 tablespoons granulated sugar
2 sticks plus 2 tablespoons (9 ounces) unsalted butter, cut into 1-inch cubes and frozen

FOR THE FILLING:
4 to 5 Bartlett pears, unpeeled, or 4 to 5 apples (about 2¼ pounds), peeled and cut into
    tiny ¼-inch cubes
2 tablespoons granulated sugar

To prepare the dough: In the bowl of a food processor fitted with the steel blade or in the bowl of an electric mixer fitted with the paddle attachment, combine the flour and sugar, and pulse or mix on low to incorporate. Add the butter and vanilla extract, and pulse on and off a few times or mix on low until the mixture barely comes together.

Turn the dough out onto a lightly floured surface. Dip the heel of your hand in flour, and working with small sections, smear the dough away from you to blend it together. When the dough has been all smeared out, using a metal scraper or spatula, scrape and gather it together. Knead the dough a few times and flatten into a disc. Wrap in plastic wrap and chill until firm, at least 2 hours or overnight.

To prepare the topping: In the bowl of a food processor fitted with the steel blade, or in the bowl of an electric mixer fitted with the paddle attachment, combine the flour and sugar and pulse or mix on low to incorporate. Add the butter and pulse on and off or mix on low until it's the consistency of a coarse meal. Chill until ready to use.

For the filling: In a medium mixing bowl, toss the cubed pears or apples with the sugar and allow to sit for about an hour, until the fruit begins to release some of its juices.

Divide the dough in half and return one half to the refrigerator. On a lightly floured surface, roll the dough out 1/4 inch thick, flouring the surface of the dough as necessary. Cutting as closely together as possible, cut out the circles. Place the circles on two parchment-lined baking sheets, not overlapping, and chill until firm, at least 30 minutes to an hour. Set the scraps aside.

Roll and cut out the remaining dough in the same manner. Gather all the scraps together, chill, roll, and cut.

Remove the circles from the refrigerator. Working with one at a time (it may be necessary to chill some of the circles so the dough doesn't become too soft), mound 2 tablespoons of the fruit into the center. Fold a very small section of the edge of the dough (about the size of your fingertip) up toward the filling and press down to seal. Fold another small section of the dough up toward the filling, allowing the dough to pleat as you fold. Press down where the two edges overlap to ensure that the dough holds the folded shape. Continue to work your way around the tart, to make about 6 folds. Gently cup your hand over the entire tart and press down the pleats to ensure that they seal well and will not unfold while baking. Repeat with the remaining circles and place them on two parchment-lined baking sheets, 2 inches apart. Chill until firm, about 30 minutes to an hour.

Adjust the oven racks to the upper and lower positions and preheat the oven to 375 degrees.

Spoon a heaping tablespoon of the streusel topping over the exposed fruit and press down gently so that it adheres.

Bake for 20 to 25 minutes, until the crust is golden brown, rotating the baking sheets halfway through to ensure even baking.

Yield: Twenty-four 4-inch tarts

Plum Puffs

COOKED FRUIT ENCASED IN PUFF PASTRY MAY SOUND SIMPLE TO YOU, BUT ONCE you've tasted these Plum Puffs you'll see how incredibly sophisticated and luxurious it can be. Try other compotes too, like the strawberry-rhubarb compote (see Strawberry-Rhubarb Cobbler with Brown Butter Biscuit, page 107).

Folding the dough is necessary to keep the compote in the tart during the early stages of baking. Don't worry if the folds aren't perfect. As the Plum Puffs bake, the folds will open and the tarts will take on a shape all their own.

Special Item: 5-INCH ROUND CUTTER

FOR THE COMPOTE:
2 tablespoons water
¼ cup plus 2 tablespoons granulated sugar
1 vanilla bean
4 (¾ pound) plums, peaches, or nectarines, pitted and cut into eighths,
    to equal about 3 to 4 cups
1 tablespoon brandy
2 teaspoons cornstarch, dissolved in 1 tablespoon of water

½ recipe (about 2 pounds) Puff Pastry (see page 330), chilled

FOR THE TOPPING:
1 extra-large egg white, lightly beaten
1 tablespoon plus 1 teaspoon granulated sugar

To prepare the compote: In a large, heavy-duty, deep saucepan, stir together the water and sugar. Using a small paring knife, split the vanilla bean lengthwise. With the back of the knife, scrape out the pulp and the seeds and add the scrapings and the pod to the sugar mixture. Over medium-high heat, bring the mixture to a boil without stirring. Using a pastry brush dipped in water, brush down the sides of the pan to remove any undissolved sugar granules. When the sugar begins to color, after 3 to 4 minutes, begin to tilt and swirl the pan to cook evenly. When the mixture reaches an even medium caramel color, remove from the heat.

Add the fruit. The mixture may spatter and the sugar may seize and harden. Remove from the heat, add the brandy, and return to medium-high heat for 4 to 6 more minutes, until the fruit is tender and the hardened sugar has dissolved.

Place a large strainer over a bowl and pour in the fruit, straining the liquid into the bowl. Remove the vanilla bean. Pour the liquid back into the saucepan and transfer the fruit to the bowl. Over high heat, bring the liquid to a boil, remove from the heat and whisk in the cornstarch mixture. Cook, whisking constantly, for another 1 to 2 minutes, until the juice is shiny, bubbly, and slightly thickened. Combine with the fruit and allow to cool.

Divide the Puff Pastry in half and return one half to the refrigerator. On a lightly floured work surface, roll the pastry out about 1/8 inch thick, lightly flouring the surface as necessary. Cutting as closely together as possible, cut out the circles and place them on a parchment-lined baking sheet to chill until firm, about 30 minutes to an hour. Gather the scraps of pastry, stack them on each other, and wrap in plastic wrap to freeze for another use. Repeat with the other half of Puff Pastry.

Working with one circle at a time (it may be necessary to chill some of the circles so the dough doesn't become too soft), mound about 1/4 cup of compote into the center of the circle. Fold a 3/4-inch section of the edge of the circle up toward the filling and press down to seal. Fold another small section up toward the filling, allowing the pastry to pleat as you fold. Press down where the 2 edges overlap to ensure that the pastry holds the folded shape. Continue to work your way around the tart, making 6 folds. Gently cup your hand over the entire tart and press down the pleats to ensure that they seal. Repeat with the remaining circles and place them on a parchment-lined baking sheet, 2 inches apart. Chill for at least 30 minutes, until firm.

Adjust the oven rack to the upper position and preheat the oven to 375 degrees.

Brush the pastry with the egg white and sprinkle with the sugar. Bake for about 30 minutes, until the crust is nicely browned.

Yield: 9 puffs

Pumpkin Pie

I HATE PUMPKIN PIES. THEY ARE ALWAYS OVERSEASONED WITH PUMPKIN-friendly spices and the texture is inevitably watery and mealy. Unfortunately, they are in high demand over the holidays, and at the bakery, we are forced to make hundreds of them. This got me thinking: What can I do to make a great pumpkin pie that even I would enjoy eating? Yams came to mind first. Though sturdier in texture, they would still be creamy and sweet. Yams led to melted butter, melted butter led to vanilla, and vanilla led to maple. I don't think there's a better pumpkin pie out there. If you like more spice in yours, go ahead and spice it up.

Special Item: 10-INCH PIE PAN

FOR THE DOUGH:
1 stick (4 ounces) unsalted butter, chilled and cut into 1-inch cubes
³⁄₄ cup vegetable shortening, chilled
1¹⁄₂ teaspoons kosher salt
2³⁄₄ cups unbleached pastry flour or unbleached all-purpose flour
¹⁄₄ cup ice water

FOR THE FILLING:
2 medium Jewel or Garnet yams
¹⁄₂ cup canned pumpkin
¹⁄₂ stick (2 ounces) unsalted butter
1 vanilla bean
2 extra-large eggs
1 extra-large egg yolk
³⁄₄ cup heavy cream
2 tablespoons whole milk
¹⁄₃ cup pure maple syrup
3 tablespoons light brown sugar, lightly packed
1 tablespoon brandy
¹⁄₂ teaspoon ground ginger
¹⁄₄ teaspoon kosher salt
1 very small pinch ground cloves
1 small pinch white pepper

FOR GARNISHING:

2 tablespoons milk or water

1 tablespoon granulated sugar

⅛ teaspoon ground cinnamon

4 to 5 gratings of fresh whole nutmeg

Adjust the oven rack to the middle position and preheat the oven to 400 degrees.

To prepare the dough: In the bowl of an electric mixer fitted with the paddle attachment, combine the butter, shortening, and salt and mix on low 2 to 3 minutes until softened. Turn the mixer up to medium and mix another 1 to 2 minutes, scraping down the sides of the bowl as needed. Add the flour in 3 batches, mixing on low until it's the consistency of a coarse meal. Add the ice water, mixing just until the dough comes together.

Turn the dough out onto a lightly floured work surface and knead a few times to gather it into a ball. Divide the dough in half, flatten each into a disc, and wrap in plastic. Chill one of the discs until firm, at least 2 hours or overnight. Freeze the remaining dough for another use.

To prepare the filling: Place the yams directly on the oven rack and bake them until they are very soft and starting to burst, about 45 minutes to an hour. Allow to cool, remove the skins, and set aside.

On a lightly floured surface, roll the dough out to an 11-inch circle, about ¼ inch thick, flouring the surface of the dough as necessary. Fold the dough into quarters and place the counterpoint in the middle of the pie pan. Unfold the dough and arrange it evenly in the pan, allowing the excess dough to hang over the edges. Trim the dough, leaving ½ inch of dough hanging over the edge. Fold the ½-inch section of dough underneath so it's even with the rim of the pan to create a thicker edge. Make a scalloped edge by pushing the thumb of one hand against the thumb and index finger of the other hand. Continue around the entire edge of the dough. Chill until firm, 30 minutes to an hour.

Turn the oven down to 350 degrees.

Blind-bake the crust according to the directions on page 217.

In the bowl of a food processor fitted with the steel blade, puree the yams with the pumpkin. Transfer the mixture to a small saucepan. Over medium heat, stirring constantly, allow the moisture to evaporate as the mixture bubbles and cooks, about 5 to 7 minutes. Remove from the heat.

In a small saucepan over medium-high heat, begin to melt the butter. Using a small paring knife, split the vanilla bean lengthwise. With the back of the knife, scrape out the pulp and the seeds and add the scrapings and the pod to the butter. Swirl the pan to ensure the butter cooks evenly and doesn't burn. Continue cooking about 3 to 5 more minutes, until the bubbles subside and the butter is dark brown and has a nutty aroma. Remove the vanilla bean.

Add the browned butter and dark flecks to the pumpkin-yam mixture and combine. Strain the mixture into a large bowl.

In a medium bowl, whisk the whole eggs, egg yolk, cream, milk, maple syrup, brown sugar, brandy, ginger, salt, cloves, and pepper. Add to the pumpkin mixture, whisking to combine.

Brush the scalloped rim with the milk or water and pour in the filling to just below the rim.

In a small bowl combine the granulated sugar, cinnamon, and nutmeg. Sprinkle the topping over the filling.

Bake for about 1 to 1½ hours, until the filling is set and the crust is nicely browned. When done, the filling should no longer quiver when you gently shake the baking sheet.

Yield: One 10-inch pie

Red Plum Tart

RED-FLESHED PLUMS, SUCH AS SANTA ROSA, ELEPHANT HEARTS, OR PLUOTS, are one of my favorite summer fruits, never overly sweet and always full of flavor. When baked, their true character is revealed. That concentrated plum flavor magically emerges and the wrinkled skin and vibrant purple tones seem almost unreal. As you pull this tart out of the oven, please don't even think of ruining it with that awful gooey traditional fruit tart glaze.

Special Item: ONE 12-INCH TART RING, LIGHTLY COATED WITH MELTED BUTTER

FOR THE DOUGH:
1 tablespoon anise seeds
1¼ cups unbleached pastry flour or unbleached all-purpose flour
¼ cup granulated sugar
½ teaspoon baking powder
1 stick (4 ounces) unsalted butter, chilled and cut into 1-inch cubes
2 extra-large egg yolks
¼ cup heavy cream
1 tablespoon pure vanilla extract

1 recipe hazelnut filling (see Hazelnut-Banana Tarts, page 243)

FOR THE TOPPING:
10 to 12 (about 2 pounds) Santa Rosa, Elephant Heart, or Pluot plums,
   ripe yet firm, cut into eighths
1 tablespoon granulated sugar, for sprinkling

To prepare the dough: In a small sauté pan over medium-low heat, toast the anise seeds, stirring occasionally until they become aromatic and are lightly browned, about 2 to 3 minutes. Allow to cool and coarsely chop, crush, or grind in a spice mill.

In the bowl of a food processor fitted with the steel blade or in the bowl of an electric mixer fitted with the paddle attachment, combine the flour, sugar, baking powder, and anise seeds and pulse or mix on low to incorporate. Add the butter and pulse on and off, or mix on low, until it is the consistency of a coarse meal.

In a small bowl, whisk together the egg yolks, cream, and vanilla extract. Add to the butter mixture and pulse or mix on low until the dough barely comes together.

Turn the dough out onto a lightly floured surface. Dip the heel of your hand in flour and, working with small sections, smear the dough away from you to blend it together. When all the dough has been smeared out, scrape and gather it together using a metal scraper or spatula. Knead it a few times to gather it into a ball and flatten it into a disc. Wrap in plastic and chill until firm, about 2 hours or overnight.

On a lightly floured surface roll the dough out to a 13-inch circle, ⅛ inch thick, flouring the surface of the dough as necessary. Line the tart ring and chill according to the directions on page 215.

Adjust the oven rack to the middle position and preheat the oven to 350 degrees.

Pour the hazelnut filling into the tart shell. Then, starting from the outer edge, arrange the plums skin side down in concentric circles, covering the entire surface of the tart. Sprinkle the plums with the sugar.

Bake for about 40 minutes until the filling is bubbly. Turn the oven down to 325 degrees and continue to bake for another 20 minutes, until the filling is firm and the crust is nicely browned.

Yield: One 12-inch tart

Triple Almond Tart

ALMONDS ARE DEFINITELY ONE OF THE SEVEN WONDERS OF THE WORLD. THEY make their presence known in every aspect of this tart. Extract of almond adds a hint of flavor to the crust, while the ground almonds give the filling a crunchy texture with a robust, nutty flavor. A small ring of chocolate subtly marks the center, and sliced almonds festively decorate the top. As the name implies, this is three times as good as any almond tart you've had. If you're not a huge chocolate lover, use half the amount of glaze for a thinner coating of chocolate.

Special Items: 10-INCH FLAN RING, LIGHTLY COATED WITH MELTED BUTTER
5- TO 6-INCH RING FOR DECORATING, OPTIONAL

FOR THE DOUGH:
1 cup unbleached pastry flour or unbleached all-purpose flour
2 tablespoons granulated sugar
2 tablespoons light brown sugar, lightly packed
2 tablespoons cornstarch
1 stick (4 ounces) unsalted butter, chilled and cut into ½-inch cubes
2 tablespoons pure almond extract

FOR THE FILLING:
¾ cup (3½ ounces) whole unblanched almonds
½ cup granulated sugar
¾ cup powdered sugar
½ cup unbleached pastry flour or unbleached all-purpose flour
½ cup egg whites, 3 to 4 extra-large eggs
1 tablespoon plus 1 teaspoon pure almond extract
1½ sticks (6 ounces) unsalted butter
1 vanilla bean

FOR THE GLAZE:
2 tablespoons water
2 tablespoons brewed coffee or ½ teaspoon instant espresso powder
3 tablespoons unsweetened cocoa powder

1 tablespoon granulated sugar
1 tablespoon light corn syrup
2 ounces bittersweet chocolate, melted
1 tablespoon brandy

FOR DECORATING:
26 sliced unblanched almonds

To prepare the dough: In the bowl of a food processor fitted with the steel blade, or in the bowl of an electric mixer fitted with the paddle attachment, combine the flour, sugars, and cornstarch and pulse on and off or mix on low to incorporate. Add the butter and almond extract, and pulse on and off or mix on low until the dough barely comes together.

Turn the mixture out onto a lightly floured work surface. Dip the heel of your hand in flour and, working with small sections, smear the dough away from you to blend it together. When the dough has been all smeared out, scrape and gather the dough together using a metal scraper or spatula.

Knead a few times to gather into a ball and flatten into a disc. Wrap in plastic and chill until firm, about 2 hours or overnight.

On a lightly floured surface, roll the dough into a 12-inch circle, ⅛ inch thick, flouring the surface of the dough as necessary. Line the flan ring and chill according to the directions on page 215.

Adjust the oven rack to the middle position and preheat the oven to 325 degrees.

To prepare the filling: Spread the whole almonds on a baking sheet and toast in the oven until lightly browned, about 15 to 20 minutes. Shake the pan halfway through to ensure that the nuts toast evenly.

For the garnish: On a separate baking sheet, spread the sliced almonds and toast for about 5 to 7 minutes, until lightly browned.

Turn the oven up to 350 degrees.

In the bowl of a food processor fitted with a steel blade, combine the whole almonds with half of the granulated sugar and process until it's the consistency of a fine meal. Add the remaining sugar, powdered sugar, and flour, and pulse to combine.

In a small bowl, whisk the egg whites and the almond extract together. Add about two-thirds of the egg whites and process until a smooth paste. Add the remaining egg whites and pulse on and off until combined. Transfer to a large bowl.

In a medium saucepan over high heat, begin to melt the butter. Using a small paring knife, split the vanilla bean lengthwise. With the back of the knife, scrape out the pulp and the seeds and add the scrapings and the pod to the butter. Swirl the pan to ensure the butter cooks evenly and doesn't burn. Continue cooking 3 to 5 more minutes, until the bubbles subside and the butter is dark brown and has a toasty, nutty aroma. Remove the vanilla bean and allow to cool.

Slowly pour the browned butter and dark flecks into the nut mixture, whisking to incorporate.

Pour the mixture into the tart and smooth to even. Bake for about 25 to 30 minutes. If the surface of the tart bubbles up, prick it in a few places to deflate, and continue baking until firm to the touch and lightly browned.

Allow to cool completely before glazing.

To make the glaze: In a small saucepan over medium high heat, combine the water, coffee, cocoa powder, sugar, and corn syrup. Bring to a boil, stirring constantly to prevent the sauce from burning on the bottom. Remove from the heat, whisk in the melted chocolate and stir in the brandy. Allow to cool to lukewarm.

To glaze the tart, center the 6-inch ring over the tart. Pour the chocolate glaze into the center of the ring, smoothing to even with an offset spatula or the back of a spoon. Allow to set for about 10 minutes. (If you are not using a 6-inch ring as a guide, spread the glaze in a free-form circle.) Lift off the ring and place the sliced almonds at a slight diagonal, touching, around the entire outer edge of chocolate.

Yield: One 10-inch tart

8. Morning Pastries

....

If you've ever walked the streets of Paris in the early morning hours, then you've probably smelled that irresistible aroma wafting up through sidewalk grills from underground. What you might not realize is that you're standing above the workshop of a French bakery, where the day's hot pastries are being pulled out of the ovens. Down below, small armies of bakers work in subterranean kitchens, preparing for the masses who arrive every morning to retrieve their breakfast of a croissant, a brioche, or maybe a raisin roll; eating baked breakfast treats is a national pastime for the French. Meanwhile, kilos of dough are proofing as busy hands pat and roll, fold and turn, and shape, coil, and curl what will be tomorrow's morning treats. They're impossible to resist, so just follow your nose. Whether you come out with a traditional croissant, an apple turnover, or any one of the multitudes of these morning pastries, you can be sure that they all share that memorable smell of sweet, buttery yeasted pastry.

Three main categories of doughs make up this chapter's morning pastries. Croissants (page 294) and Danish Dough (page 318) are made with yeast and layered with butter. Brioche (page 287) and Bobka (page 281) also have yeast, but in their case the butter is mixed directly into the dough. That leaves Puff Pastry (page 330), the crispiest, flakiest dough of all. Yeast-free, it gets its rise from repeated folding and layering of the buttery dough.

No matter which dough or method, these classic pastries are all about butter. Not margarine—*butter!* My preference is imported Normandy butter. It's high in butterfat with a low water content, a deep yellow color, and unmistakably superior flavor. Look for it in specialty markets or ask your local cheese seller to track some down for you. Some of the best domestic butters are made by small dairies across the country: Strauss Family Creamery on the West Coast and Egg Farm Dairy on the East Coast are two good choices. Supermarket varieties such as Plugra and Land O Lakes are also good quality and widely available.

Butter, when folded into dough, acts as the separating agent, miraculously turning a solid slab into hundreds of flaky layers. For butter to work its magic, a few simple rules must be applied. Do your preparation in a cool room, preferably on a chilled work surface that's large enough to accommodate the dough as you roll it out. Most important, the dough and butter must be the same consistency; neither one should be colder or harder than the other. To be sure, beat the butter and knead it by hand or soften it in a mixer with the paddle attachment. The butter should remain cool but malleable. If it's too soft and greasy, it will ooze out of the dough; if it's too firm, it might break through the dough. As you roll it out, work quickly and handle the dough as little as possible, so the heat of your hands doesn't melt the butter. Allow the dough its resting time for easy, stress-free rolling and to help maintain the layers.

The buttery doughs that get an extra boost from yeast need time to rise, or, as we say in the baking world, *proof.* Proofing time will vary, depending on the weather, the temperature of your kitchen, and the size of the dough. Keep an eye on your dough— when it's slightly puffy and spongy to the touch, it's ready to be baked.

All of these doughs have a fairly long shelf life when properly stored. Yeasted doughs should never be kept longer than one to two days in the refrigerator; they become overly sour and the yeast loses its strength. They can, however, be divided in half and frozen for up to two months. The method I prefer is to make the dough, assemble the pastries, and freeze them. When you're ready to bake they must be brought up to room temperature (or defrosted in the refrigerator overnight) and then allowed to proof. Puff Pastry, with all that butter, will also keep only a couple of days in the refrigerator before spotting and turning gray. For longer storage of Puff Pastry, it also must be frozen. However, these pastries made from Puff Pastry (and those made with cream cheese dough) can be assembled, frozen, and baked directly out of the freezer.

Take a deep breath and set aside your old fears and preconceived notions. Don't be afraid to get the pages of this chapter good and messy, and remember to organize your time and resist the temptation to take shortcuts. This is not as difficult as you think. The satisfaction of baking these elegant pastries definitely outweighs the time and effort required. They are the classics of European pastry-making, as well as the heart and soul of our pastries at La Brea Bakery.

Bobka Pastries

....

Morning pastries made from this sweet yeasted dough can be as satisfying as those made from Croissant or Danish dough, but without the extra time and effort of rolling and folding in the butter. Like a pie dough, Bobka Dough comes together in minutes. Chill overnight (or freeze for longer storage) and use this rich and buttery dough to make a homey Russian Coffee Cake (page 284), Chocolate Armadillos (page 282), Bobka Muffins (page 197), or a not quite as flaky Cinnamon Bun (see page 303).

Bobka Dough

1 ounce (1 tablespoon plus 1 teaspoon, packed) fresh yeast or 3¼ teaspoons
    active dry yeast
½ cup whole milk, cold
3 cups plus 3 tablespoons unbleached all-purpose flour
¼ cup granulated sugar
1 teaspoon kosher salt
12 gratings fresh whole nutmeg
¼ teaspoon baking powder
2 sticks (8 ounces) unsalted butter, chilled and cut into ½-inch cubes
2 extra-large eggs, lightly beaten

Place the yeast in a medium bowl and pour the milk over to soften for a few minutes.

In the bowl of a food processor fitted with the steel blade, or in an electric mixer fitted with the paddle attachment, combine the flour, sugar, salt, nutmeg, and baking powder, and pulse or mix on low to incorporate. Add the butter and pulse on and off or mix on low until it's the consistency of a coarse meal, with pieces about the size of garbanzo beans.

Whisk the eggs into the yeast mixture and add to the flour mixture. Pulse a few times or mix on low until the dough barely comes together.

Turn the dough out onto a lightly floured work surface and knead a few times to form a ball. Pat the dough into an oval about ½ inch thick, and fold all 4 sides into the center to form a rough rectangle. Dust the surface of the dough with flour, turn the dough over and roll it out to an 8 × 9-inch rectangle, ¾ inch thick. Wrap in plastic and chill at least 6 to 8 hours, or overnight.

Yield: 2 pounds

Chocolate Armadillos

YOU MAY HAVE SEEN THESE AT YOUR LOCAL JEWISH DELI UNDER THE GUISE OF Chocolate Cigars, but I can promise you, those aren't as good as these (and neither is the name). With some help from my old friend Izzy Cohen, these are as tasty as an armadillo could be.

Save your old chocolate cake crumbs or stale Brownies (see page 17) in the freezer or make a batch of Chocolate Madeleines (see page 41) in a cake pan to grind up and use in the filling. Once you've spread the filling, roll them up at an angle, in the shape of an extended paper Chinese yo-yo. For a super rich and gooey center, add more chocolate to the filling.

1 recipe (2 pounds) Bobka Dough (see page 281), chilled
1 cup crème fraîche or sour cream
1 cup chocolate cake crumbs
½ cup bittersweet chocolate, finely chopped
½ recipe Streusel Topping (see Breakfast Bars, page 225)
2 tablespoons unsalted butter, melted

Divide the dough in half, and return one half to the refrigerator. On a lightly floured work surface, roll the dough into an 11 × 15-inch rectangle, just under ¼ inch thick, flouring the surface of the dough as necessary. Trim the edges straight, saving the trimmings. Cut the trimmings into several 2- to 3-inch pieces to use as reinforcement strips when rolling the dough into armadillos.

Working with the longer side parallel to the edge of the surface, spread ½ cup of the crème fraîche over the dough. Sprinkle half of the cake crumbs and half of the chocolate over the surface and gently roll over with a rolling pin. Make nine vertical cuts 1½ inches wide and gently stretch each piece to elongate slightly. Working with one piece of dough at a time, place the end of a reinforcement strip along the bottom edge of the dough, parallel to the work surface. Using the reinforcement strip as a guide to roll the dough around, roll the dough in an upward direction, veering off to the left at a 45-degree angle. As you roll up the dough, anchor it with your thumbs, tucking it under with your index fingers to help maintain that 45-degree angle. The strip will eventually be completely encased in the roll. As you roll, gently rock back and forth, stretching the dough slightly to make a taut roll, about 4 to 5 inches long. Place on a parchment-lined baking sheet and continue with the remaining pieces of dough.

Place the topping in a flat, wide container. Brush the armadillos with the melted butter and roll them in the topping to heavily coat. Place them on a parchment-lined baking sheet, topping side up, $1\frac{1}{2}$ inches apart. Set aside in a warm place to proof until slightly puffy and spongy to the touch, about 1 hour and 15 minutes.

Repeat the process with the remaining dough.

Adjust the oven rack to the upper and lower positions and preheat the oven to 350 degrees.

Bake for about 40 minutes, until nicely browned.

Yield: 18 armadillos

Russian Coffee Cake

LAYERS OF YEASTY DOUGH SURROUND A SOUR CREAM AND CHOCOLATE CRUMB filling in this Old World classic. Whether baked free-form or in a loaf pan, it's rich, satisfying, and dangerously addictive. If you come from the same part of the world as I do, this coffee cake will bring back happy memories of your grandmother's kitchen.

As in the Chocolate Armadillos (see page 282), save your stale Brownies (page 17), Chocolate Madeleines (page 41), or your favorite chocolate cake scraps and grind them into crumbs in a food processor for the filling.

Special Item: TWO 6-CUP-CAPACITY LOAF PANS, OPTIONAL

>   *1 recipe (2 pounds) Bobka Dough (see page 281), chilled*
>   *1 cup crème fraîche or sour cream*
>   *1 cup chocolate cake crumbs*
>   *½ cup (2½ ounces) bittersweet chocolate, coarsely chopped*
>   *1 extra-large egg, lightly beaten*
>   *1 to 2 tablespoons unsalted butter, melted*
>   *½ recipe (2 cups) Streusel Topping (see Breakfast Bars, page 225), chilled*

For free-form coffee cakes: On a lightly floured work surface roll the dough into an 18 × 14-inch rectangle, about ¼ inch thick, flouring the surface of the dough as necessary and lifting the dough to square off the edges and corners to help maintain a rectangular shape and an even thickness. Trim the edges straight and brush off any excess flour.

Working with the longer side parallel to the edge of the surface, spread the crème fraîche, cake crumbs, and chocolate over the dough, leaving a 1-inch border along the bottom. Gently roll over the filling a few times with a rolling pin. Brush the bottom edge with the beaten egg.

Fold the top edge of dough over about 1 inch. Using both hands, roll the dough toward yourself, tucking it under with your thumbs to tighten and working your way across the entire log. As you tuck, gently rock the log back and forth to keep it taut and even. Rock the log back and forth to seal. Position it seam side down and trim the ends straight to about 24 inches long.

Cut the log in half. Working with one half at a time, place the longer side parallel to the edge of the surface and cut it down the center horizontally. Place one piece, filling side up, on a parchment-lined baking sheet. Place the other piece on top of that, filling side up, crossing the 2 ends on a diagonal. Twist the 2 halves around each other twice, pinching the ends together to seal. Place on a parchment-lined baking sheet and repeat with the other half of the log. Set them aside in a warm place to proof until slightly puffy and spongy to the touch, about 2½ hours. Brush the surface with melted butter and sprinkle a heavy layer of the streusel over the top before baking.

For loaves: Divide the dough in half and return one half to the refrigerator. On a lightly floured work surface, roll the dough into an 18 × 8-inch rectangle, about ¼ inch thick, flouring the surface of the dough as necessary and lifting the dough to square off the edges and corners to help maintain a rectangular shape and an even thickness. Trim the edges straight and brush off any excess flour.

Working with the longer side parallel to the edge of the surface, spread half of the crème fraîche, cake crumbs, and chocolate over the surface, leaving a 1-inch border along the bottom edge. Gently roll over the filling a few times with a rolling pin. Brush the bottom edge with the beaten egg.

Roll the dough into a log in the same manner as the free-form coffee cake. With the seam side down, trim the ends straight to make a log about 20 inches long and 1¾ inches thick. On a lightly floured surface fold the log in half, wrapping it around itself twice to form a twisted loaf. Fit the loaf into the prepared pan, brush the top generously with butter and sprinkle with half the topping. Set aside in a warm place to proof until slightly puffy and spongy to the touch, about 2½ hours. Repeat the process with the remaining dough.

Adjust the oven rack to the middle position and preheat the oven to 350 degrees.

Bake the free-form cake for about 1 hour and the loaves for 1 hour and 15 minutes, until nicely browned.

Yield: 2 free-form coffee cakes or 2 loaves

Brioche Pastries

....

BRIOCHE IS A TRADITIONAL FRENCH YEASTED BREAD, MOST COMMONLY baked in loaves or special fluted molds. With plenty of butter and eggs, it yields a fine-textured, rich, and moist crumb. The dough is perfect for both sweet and savory pastries such as Viennese Cream Brioche (page 292), Savory Brioche Pockets (page 84), or Pecan Sticky Buns (page 288).

If you have any substantial pieces of Brioche Dough left over, make a few Sugared Brioche by rolling or stretching the dough into free-form shapes, 1 to 1½ inches thick. Cut some slits in the shape and gently pull apart to widen the slits, or shape the dough into an oval and score a crisscross pattern on the top. Brush with egg yolk, sprinkle with sugar, and allow it to rise until slightly puffy. Bake on parchment-lined baking sheets at 350 degrees for 20 to 30 minutes, until lightly browned.

For a few ABCs of brioche making: Always make sure your butter is very soft (but not greasy) before adding it to the dough. Beware: This dough requires a lengthy mixing time to properly develop, often causing the mixer to jump around on the counter. And: Careful, don't let your mixer overheat, and never place it too close to the edge of the counter.

Brioche Dough

Special Item: INSTA-READ THERMOMETER (OPTIONAL)

³⁄₄ ounce (1 tablespoon) packed fresh cake yeast or 2¹⁄₂ teaspoons active dry yeast
¹⁄₃ cup whole milk, warmed to 100–110 degrees
6 extra-large eggs
3¹⁄₂ cups unbleached all-purpose flour
¹⁄₃ cup granulated sugar
1 teaspoon kosher salt
2 sticks (8 ounces) unsalted butter, very soft, but not greasy

Place the yeast in the bowl of an electric mixer, and pour the milk over to soften for 1–2 minutes. Add 1 of the eggs and 1 cup of the flour and stir to combine. Sprinkle 1 more cup of flour over the mixture, without stirring.

Cover the bowl tightly with plastic wrap and set aside in a warm place until the surface of the flour cracks, about 30 to 40 minutes.

Add the sugar, salt, remaining eggs, and remaining 1¹⁄₂ cups of the flour to the yeast mixture. Using an electric mixer fitted with the dough hook, mix on low for 1–2 minutes, until combined. Turn the mixer up to medium-high and continue to mix for about 15 minutes, until the dough wraps itself around the hook and is smooth, shiny and slightly sticky. It may be necessary to add another tablespoon of flour to encourage the dough to leave the sides of the bowl.

Turn the mixer down to medium-low and add the butter, a few tablespoons at a time. After all of the butter has been added, turn the mixer up to medium-high and beat the dough for about 2–3 more minutes, until the dough wraps itself around the hook. If necessary, add a few pinches of flour to encourage the dough to leave the sides of the bowl. The dough will be smooth and shiny, but not oily.

Remove the dough from the bowl onto a lightly floured work surface and knead a few times to gather into a ball. Clean the mixing bowl and lightly coat it with vegetable oil. Return the dough to the oiled bowl, cover it tightly with plastic wrap and set aside in a warm place until the dough has doubled in size, about 2 to 2¹⁄₂ hours.

Spread the dough out onto a floured parchment-lined baking sheet. Dust the surface of the dough with flour, cover with parchment paper or towels, and refrigerate for 6 to 8 hours or overnight.

Yield: *2¹⁄₄ pounds*

Pecan Sticky Buns

Special Item: 8 DISPOSABLE ALUMINUM POT PIE PANS (1-CUP CAPACITY), LIGHTLY
COATED WITH MELTED BUTTER, OR ¾-CUP-CAPACITY MUFFIN
TIN, LIGHTLY COATED WITH MELTED BUTTER

TO COAT THE BOTTOM OF THE PAN:
¾ cup light brown sugar, lightly packed
½ cup light corn syrup
1¼ cups (4 ounces) pecan halves, about 64

1 recipe (2¼ pounds) Brioche Dough (see page 287), chilled

FOR THE FILLING:
½ cup crème fraîche or sour cream
2 tablespoons (½ ounce) finely chopped pecans
1 extra-large egg, lightly beaten
½ cup light brown sugar, lightly packed

In a small bowl, combine ¾ cup of the brown sugar and the corn syrup, mixing until the sugar is completely absorbed.

Place a heaping tablespoon of the mixture in the bottom of each pan or muffin cup. Arrange 6 pecan halves around the perimeter of each pan and place 2 halves in the middle.

On a lightly floured work surface, roll the dough into an 18 × 12-inch rectangle, about ¼ inch thick, flouring the surface of the dough as necessary and lifting the dough to square off the edges and corners to help maintain a rectangular shape and an even thickness. Trim the edges straight and brush off any excess flour.

Working with the long side parallel to the edge of the surface, spread the crème fraîche over the dough and sprinkle ½ cup brown sugar and chopped pecans over it, leaving a 1-inch border along the bottom. Brush the bottom edge with the beaten egg.

Fold the top edge of dough over about an inch. Using both hands, roll the dough toward yourself, tucking it under with your thumbs to tighten as you work your way across the entire log. As you tuck, gently rock the dough back and forth to keep it taut and even. As you get close to the bottom edge, using two fingers, smear a ½-inch edge of dough into the work surface to thin it out and ensure that the dough seals together. Roll the log onto the smeared edge and rock back and forth to seal. Position it seam side down and trim the ends to make a 20-inch log. Slice the log into eight 2-inch-wide pieces and place each cut side down into prepared tins. Set aside in a warm place to rise, until the dough fills the tin and it's spongy to the touch, about 2 to 2½ hours.

Adjust the oven rack to the middle position and preheat the oven to 400 degrees. Place the tins on a baking sheet and bake for 30 minutes, until nicely browned. Allow to cool slightly and invert.

Yield: 8 buns

Twice-Baked Sour Cherry Brioche

Studded with sour cherries and saturated with orange flower water, these mini brioche loaves are very French with an exotic North African twist. Originally they were invented as a means for bakers to recoup their losses; day-old brioche was collected, moistened, filled with almond cream, and baked again. They are now so popular at the bakery, we can no longer wait for yesterday's stale brioche. They warrant their own fresh batch of dough and their very own shape.

I call for mini loaf pans; it's a great individual-sized pastry. But if you don't have them, bake the brioche in a large loaf pan, slice it, soak it, smear it, and rebake it.

Special Item: TWELVE 4 × 2¹⁄₂ × 1¹⁄₂-INCH OR ³⁄₄-CUP-CAPACITY MINI LOAF PANS, LIGHTLY COATED WITH MELTED BUTTER

1 recipe (2¹⁄₄ pounds) Brioche Dough (see page 287), chilled
¹⁄₃ cup (1¹⁄₂ ounces) dried sour cherries

FOR THE SYRUP:
1 cup water
1¹⁄₂ cups granulated sugar
1 vanilla bean
¹⁄₂ cup orange flower water (see "Sources," page 393)

¹⁄₂ cup (1¹⁄₂ ounces) sliced unblanched almonds
¹⁄₂ recipe Almond Cream (see Almond Log, page 297)

Separate the dough into twelve approximately 3-ounce pieces. On a lightly floured work surface roll the dough into 2-inch balls. Flatten the balls into discs and press 4 to 5 cherries into the center of each. Roll up and fold the dough over, enclosing the cherries and pinching the ends together to form small oval balls. Place the ovals into the prepared pans and set aside in a warm place to rise, until slightly puffy and spongy to the touch, about 2 to 2¹⁄₂ hours.

To prepare the syrup: In a medium saucepan over medium-high heat, combine the water and sugar. Using a small paring knife, split the vanilla bean lengthwise. With the back of the knife, scrape out the pulp and the seeds and add the scrapings and the pod to the sugar mixture. Bring to a boil and cook for another minute. Remove from the heat and stir in the orange flower water.

Adjust the oven rack to the middle position and preheat the oven to 325 degrees.

Spread the almonds on a baking sheet and toast in the oven until lightly browned, about 5 to 7 minutes. Shake the pan halfway through to ensure that the nuts toast evenly.

Turn the oven up to 350 degrees.

Place the loaves on a baking sheet and bake the loaves for about 20 minutes, until lightly browned but not fully cooked.

Remove from the oven and cool for 10 minutes. Remove the loaves from the pans and, using a serrated knife, slice the rounded tops off to make a flat surface. Cut the loaves in half horizontally. Brush each half with about 1½ tablespoons of the syrup. Spread 1 tablespoon of the Almond Cream over the bottom half of each loaf and sandwich the top and bottom halves back together. Spread 1 teaspoon of the Almond Cream over the top surface and 2 teaspoons around the sides of each. Place on a parchment-lined baking sheet and sprinkle with 2 teaspoons of the almonds.

Bake for another 20 minutes, until nicely browned.

Yield: 12 loaves

Viennese Cream Brioche

LIKE A BABY'S HEAD NESTLED ON A FLUFFY PILLOW, THE SOFT CRÈME FRAÎCHE sinks down as the brioche rises and bakes around it. A sublime combination of flavor and texture, this super simple pastry is everyone's favorite. Julia Child was brought to tears the first time she tasted them.

1 recipe Brioche Dough (see page 287), chilled
1 stick plus 1 tablespoon (4½ ounces) unsalted butter, chilled and cut into 12 square pats
1 extra-large egg, lightly beaten
¼ cup large crystallized sugar (see "Sources," page 393) or granulated sugar
2 cups plus 2 tablespoons crème fraîche or sour cream
¼ cup granulated sugar

Separate the dough into twelve 3-ounce pieces. On a lightly floured work surface, roll the dough into 2-inch balls. Flatten the balls into 5-inch discs, about ¼ inch thick. Place on a parchment-lined baking sheet and set aside in a warm place to proof, about 1 hour, until spongy to the touch. Flip the discs over and allow them to finish rising, about 1 more hour.

Adjust the oven rack to the lower position and preheat the oven to 350 degrees.

Press a pat of butter into the center of each disc. Brush around the rim with the beaten egg and sprinkle 1 teaspoon of the crystallized sugar around the edge. Spoon about 3 tablespoons of crème fraîche over the butter in a mound, and sprinkle 1 teaspoon of granulated sugar over it.

Place 2 inches apart on the parchment-lined baking sheet and bake for 20 to 30 minutes, until lightly browned and the center is set.

Yield: 12 brioche

Croissant Pastries

....

Croissants play a starring role in the pastry world. Complete and perfect, a well-made croissant asks for nothing else. As that buttery bite melts in your mouth, you can't wait to pull off the next piece and devour it. One bite is never enough.

The sorcery lies in the dough. Layered with plenty of sweet butter, this yeasted concoction yields the finest, richest pastry. It's not necessary to stop at croissants: This chameleonlike dough, when rolled, twisted, and molded into different shapes and sizes, reinvents itself over and over again. Sprinkled with cinnamon and sugar, it becomes a comforting and satisfying sweet. Though the flavors are basically the same, each unique shape and size creates a whole new pastry, the texture totally transformed. Stretched and twisted dough gives you long and skinny Cinnamon Twists (page 305). Coiled into playful Elephant Ears (page 307) or Palm Leaves (page 310), these flatter shapes make a flakier, more crispy pastry. Larger shapes like the Sugar Buns (page 313) or Princess Ring (page 311) will be softer and squishier in texture. Add an easy walnut filling and shape the dough into triangles for Walnut Bowties (page 316). Slathered and rolled up with almond cream, Almond Snails (page 299) are obscenely rich and decadent.

If you do make plain croissants, don't even think about throwing out the stale leftovers. Turn them into a rich Croissant Bread Pudding (page 306) or Twice-Baked Almond Croissants (page 315).

Croissants

Special Items: SPRAY BOTTLE FILLED WITH WATER, FOR SPRITZING THE OVEN
2 LINEN TOWELS

1½ cups whole milk

*1.3 ounces (1 tablespoon plus 1½ teaspoons packed) fresh cake yeast or 1 tablespoon plus ¼
teaspoon active dry yeast*

1 tablespoon kosher salt

¼ cup light brown sugar, lightly packed

4 to 4½ cups unbleached all-purpose flour

3 sticks (12 ounces) unsalted butter, chilled

In the bowl of an electric mixer fitted with the dough hook, place the milk, yeast, salt, brown sugar, and 4 cups of the flour, and mix on low until the dough is smooth, about 7 minutes. The dough should be soft, but not too sticky.

Turn the dough out onto a lightly floured work surface and knead for a few minutes. Shape the dough into a rectangle, about 1½ inches thick, wrap in plastic, and chill for one hour.

Meanwhile, place the cold butter between 2 linen towels and beat it with a rolling pin to flatten into an approximate 5 × 8-inch rectangle.

On a work surface, using as little flour as possible, roll the dough into a 10 × 16-inch rectangle, ½ inch thick, lifting the dough and stretching the corners to help maintain a rectangular shape and an even thickness. Working with the short side parallel to the edge of the work surface, place the butter in the middle of the dough. Fold the bottom edge up, just beyond the middle, and the top edge down to the bottom edge, as you would a letter.

Enlarge the rectangle by rolling the dough to a 10 × 15-inch rectangle, about ½ inch thick. If any of the butter oozes out, sprinkle with a touch of flour to prevent it from sticking.

Working with the longer side parallel to the edge of the surface, fold the left side over two-thirds across and then fold the right side over to meet the left edge, stretching the corners and squaring off the sides so the edges line up evenly. You have just completed your first fold. Wrap in plastic and refrigerate for 1 hour.

On a lightly floured surface place the open seam to your right and roll the dough out into a 10 × 15-inch rectangle, ½ inch thick. Fold the bottom up to the middle and the top edge down to the bottom edge, to complete your second fold. Wrap the dough in plastic and allow to rest in the refrigerator for 1 hour. Place the open seam to your right and roll and fold the dough in the same manner, squaring off the edges as you roll. Allow to rest in the refrigerator for 1 hour, and repeat the rolling, folding, and resting process once more for a total of 4 times. Wrap the dough tightly in plastic and chill for at least 3 hours, but no longer than overnight.

Note: If you are using the dough for another recipe, either freeze or shape according to directions.

To shape the croissants: Divide the dough in half and return one half to the refrigerator. On a lightly floured work surface, roll it into a 12 × 16-inch rectangle, ¼ inch thick, flouring the surface of the dough as necessary, lifting the dough and stretching the corners to help maintain a rectangular shape and even thickness. Trim the edges straight and brush off any excess flour.

Working with the long side parallel to the edge of the surface, cut the dough down the center vertically and set one half aside. Place the longer side parallel to the edge of the surface and cut the dough vertically into thirds. Cut each third diagonally in half to make 2 triangles. You should have a total of 6 triangles, each with about a 4- to 5-inch base. Holding the base of one triangle in one hand and the top of the triangle in the other, stretch the dough to almost half again its length. Return the enlarged triangle to the work surface, keeping the widest end toward you. With your fingertips, tuck in the wide end of the dough to begin the roll. Continue rolling loosely toward the tip, using the heel of your hand to roll and creating tension by using your other hand to stretch the top of the triangle away from you. The dough should overlap three times with the tip sticking out from underneath.

Place the croissants 2 inches apart on a parchment-lined baking sheet and curve the ends of the croissant inward to form a crescent shape. Set aside in a warm place to rise, until slightly puffy and spongy to the touch, 2 to 2½ hours.

Adjust the oven racks to the lower and upper positions and preheat the oven to 425 degrees.

Open the oven door, spritz the oven heavily with water from a spray bottle, and quickly close the door. Open the oven door again and slide the baking sheets onto the racks. Spritz the oven heavily with water again and quickly close the door.

Reduce the oven temperature to 400 degrees. Refrain from opening the oven door for the next 10 minutes to allow the oven to steam.

After the first 10 minutes, rotate the baking sheets to ensure even baking. Reduce the oven temperature to 375 degrees and continue baking until the croissants are golden brown, about 8 more minutes.

Yield: 24 croissants, or 3 pounds 5 ounces of dough

Almond Log

Made from buttery layers of Croissant dough, this elegant pastry is smeared with almond cream and doused with sliced almonds and powdered sugar. It's the perfect solution for a brunch buffet: large, easy to serve, and pretty to look at. Just before eating, slice it into slender pieces and watch your guests swoon.

FOR THE ALMOND CREAM:

½ cup (2½ ounces) whole unblanched almonds

¼ cup granulated sugar

½ stick plus 1 tablespoon (2½ ounces) unsalted butter, chilled and cut into 1-inch cubes

¼ cup (2 ounces) almond paste (see "Sources," page 393)

1 extra-large egg

1 tablespoon rum

½ teaspoon pure almond extract

½ recipe (1¾ pounds) Croissant dough (page 294), chilled

FOR DECORATING:

1 extra-large egg, lightly beaten

1 cup (3 ounces) sliced unblanched almonds

Powdered sugar, for dusting

To prepare the almond cream: In the bowl of a food processor fitted with the steel blade, combine the almonds and half of the granulated sugar and process until it's the consistency of a fine meal. In the bowl of an electric mixer fitted with the paddle attachment, cream the butter on low, 1 to 2 minutes, until softened. Add the remaining sugar and the ground almond mixture, and mix on medium 2 to 3 more minutes until light and fluffy, scraping down the sides of the bowl as necessary. Crumble in the almond paste one teaspoon at a time, mixing on medium until combined. In a small bowl, whisk together the egg, rum, and almond extract. Turn the mixer to low and slowly add the liquids in a thin steady stream, mixing until incorporated. Chill until set, at least 1 hour.

On a lightly floured work surface roll the dough into a 14 × 11-inch rectangle, ¼ inch thick, flouring the surface of the dough as necessary and lifting the dough to square off the edges and and corners to help maintain a rectangular shape and an even thickness. Trim the edges straight and brush off any excess flour.

Working with the long side parallel to the edge of the surface, spread $\frac{1}{2}$ cup of the almond cream over the dough, leaving a 1-inch border along the bottom. Brush the bottom edge with the beaten egg.

Fold the top edge of dough over about an inch. Using both hands, roll the dough toward yourself, tucking it under with your thumbs to tighten as you work your way across the entire log. As you tuck, gently rock the dough back and forth to keep it taut and even. When you get to the end, rock the log back and forth a few times to seal. Position the log seam side down on a parchment-lined baking sheet. Make a long, $\frac{1}{2}$-inch-deep slit across the top, beginning and ending 2 inches away from each end. Set it aside in a warm place to rise, until slightly puffy and spongy to the touch, about 2 to $2\frac{1}{2}$ hours.

Adjust the oven rack to the middle position and preheat the oven to 325 degrees.

Spread the sliced almonds on a baking sheet and toast in the oven until lightly browned, about 5 to 7 minutes. Shake the pan halfway through to ensure that the nuts toast evenly.

Turn the oven up to 425 degrees.

Bake the log for 30 minutes until it just starts to color. Cool for 10 to 15 minutes and spread the remaining almond cream over the entire surface. Sprinkle the almonds over the top and bake for another 30 minutes until nicely browned.

Allow to cool, and sift a fine layer of powdered sugar over the top.

Yield: 12 slices

Almond Snails

½ recipe (1¾ pounds) Croissant dough (see page 294), chilled
¾ recipe (about 1¼ cups) almond cream (see Almond Log, page 297)
1 extra-large egg, lightly beaten
30 to 36 (about ¼ cup or 1¼ ounces) whole unblanched almonds
Powdered sugar, for dusting

On a lightly floured work surface, roll the dough into a 9 × 13-inch rectangle, just under ¼ inch thick, flouring the surface of the dough as necessary and lifting the dough to square off the edges and corners to help maintain a rectangular shape and an even thickness. Trim the edges straight and brush off any excess flour.

Working with the long side parallel to the edge of the surface, spread ¾ cup of the almond cream over the dough, leaving a 1-inch border along the bottom. Brush the bottom edge with the beaten egg.

Fold the top edge of dough over about 1 inch. Using both hands, roll the dough toward yourself, tucking it under with your thumbs to tighten as you work your way across the entire log. As you tuck, gently rock the dough back and forth to keep it taut and even. As you get close to the bottom edge, using 2 fingers, smear a ½-inch edge of the dough into the work surface to thin it out and ensure that the dough seals together. Roll the log toward the smeared edge and rock it back and forth to seal. Position the log seam side down and trim the ends evenly to make a 12-inch log. Slice it into 1-inch-wide pieces and place them cut side down on a parchment-lined baking sheet, spaced 2 inches apart. Brush with the remaining beaten egg and set aside in a warm place to proof until slightly puffy and spongy to the touch, 2 to 2½ hours.

Adjust the oven rack to the middle position and preheat the oven to 400 degrees.

Spread about 1½ teaspoons of the almond cream over the tops and press 3 whole almonds into the center of each snail.

Bake for 25 minutes, until nicely browned, rotating the baking sheets halfway through to ensure even baking.

Allow to cool, and sift a fine layer of powdered sugar over each.

Yield: 12 snails

Buttercups

ANOTHER VARIATION ON CROISSANT DOUGH, BUTTERCUPS HAVE A LITTLE sugar rolled into the dough and some extra butter brushed on before baking. Sweet and simple, their name says it all: little cups of butter.

Special Items: LARGE MUFFIN TIN, ³/₄-CUP-CAPACITY, HEAVILY
COATED WITH MELTED BUTTER
4¹/₂-INCH ROUND CUTTER

1 recipe (3¹/₂ pounds) Croissant dough (see page 294), chilled
³/₄ stick butter (3 ounces) unsalted butter, melted
1 cup granulated sugar

On a lightly floured work surface, roll the dough into a 21 × 10-inch rectangle, slightly thicker than ¹/₄ inch thick, flouring the surface of the dough as necessary and lifting the dough to square off the edges and corners to help maintain the rectangular shape and an even thickness. Trim the edges straight and brush off any excess flour.

Working with the long side parallel to the edge of the surface, sprinkle ¹/₄ cup of the sugar over the dough and gently roll over with a rolling pin. Fold the dough into thirds, by folding the left side over to the center and the right side over to meet the left edge. Turn the dough so the shorter side is parallel to the edge of the surface. Lightly dust the surface with flour and roll the dough out to a 26 × 7-inch rectangle, ³/₈ inch thick, stretching the corners and squaring off the sides. Brush off the excess flour, sprinkle with ¹/₄ cup of the sugar and gently roll over with a rolling pin. Fold the right side to the center and the left over to the right edge, stretching the dough slightly to square off the sides.

Roll the dough out to a 24 × 12-inch rectangle, about ¹/₄ inch thick. Brush the surface of the dough with melted butter and sprinkle with ¹/₄ cup of the sugar. Cut out twelve 4¹/₂-inch circles and sprinkle each with 1 teaspoon of sugar. Bring 2 opposite sides of the circle together into the center and bring the other 2 sides up to meet in the center. Pinch together firmly in the middle to seal and to form 4 tear-shaped gaps. Place into the prepared tins and set aside in a warm place to rise, for about 1 hour, until slightly puffy and spongy to the touch.

Adjust the oven rack to the middle position and preheat the oven to 400 degrees.

Bake for about 35 minutes, until nicely browned, rotating the baking sheets halfway through to ensure even baking.

Yield: 12 buttercups

Chocolate Croissants

There are special chocolate batons that are shaped with one flat side and one slightly curved side, made to fit perfectly together on the inside of the croissant. You may find them in specialty stores and through mail order; or if not, just chop up some bittersweet chocolate.

½ recipe (3½ pounds) Croissant dough (see page 294), chilled
32 bittersweet chocolate batons or 8 ounces bittersweet chocolate, coarsely chopped

On a lightly floured work surface, roll the dough into a long 10 × 18-inch rectangle, about ¼ inch thick, lifting the dough to square off the edges and corners to help maintain a rectangular shape and an even thickness. Working with the long side parallel to the edge of the surface, cut the rectangle horizontally into 4 strips, each 2½ × 18 inches. Then cut each strip vertically into 4 pieces, each about 2½ × 4½ inches.

Working with one piece at a time, the long side parallel to the edge of the surface, place 2 batons of chocolate, flat sides together, ¾ inch from the left edge, with about ½ inch of the bottom ends of the batons protruding beyond the bottom edge of dough. Fold the left edge of dough over the batons.

Holding on to the ends of the batons with your fingers, roll up the dough, rocking the chocolate back and forth to create a bit of tension. Pinch the seam to seal, and place the croissant seam side down on a parchment-lined baking sheet, pressing down gently to flatten slightly. Continue in the same manner and repeat with the remaining dough.

Using a knife or razor blade, score two diagonal lines across the top of each croissant, about ¾ inch apart. Space the croissants about 2 inches apart on the baking sheet and set aside in a warm place to rise, until slightly puffy and spongy to the touch, about 1½ to 2 hours.

Adjust the oven racks to the upper and lower positions and preheat the oven to 425 degrees.

Bake according to the directions for Croissants on page 294.

Yield: 16 croissants

Cinnamon Buns

N<small>OT TO BE CONFUSED WITH THE DOUGHY,</small> A<small>MERICAN-STYLE</small> "C<small>INN-A-BUN</small>," these are lighter, flakier, and more refined. I like to bake them in small tins (aluminum pot pie tins) for the perfect size bun. If you can't find those, use your ³⁄₄-cup-capacity muffin tin; you'll get twice as many buns, half the size. For a less flaky but still delicious cinnamon bun, use Bobka dough (see page 281) instead.

Special Item: 10 <small>DISPOSABLE ALUMINUM PIE PANS</small> (1-<small>CUP CAPACITY</small>), <small>OR</small> ³⁄₄-<small>CUP-</small>
<small>CAPACITY MUFFIN TIN, LIGHTLY COATED WITH MELTED BUTTER</small>

½ cup light brown sugar, lightly packed
½ cup granulated sugar
½ teaspoon ground cinnamon
1 recipe (3½ pounds) Croissant dough (see page 294), chilled
1 extra-large egg, lightly beaten
1 recipe White Glaze (see Lemon Ginger Muffins, page 207)

In a small bowl, combine the sugars and cinnamon.

On a lightly floured work surface, roll the dough into a 12 × 13-inch rectangle, about ¼ inch thick, flouring the surface as necessary and lifting the dough to square off the edges and corners to help maintain a rectangular shape and an even thickness. (If you're using a ³⁄₄-cup-capacity muffin tin, divide the dough in half, and chill one half while you roll out a 6 × 7-inch rectangle. Repeat with remaining dough.) Trim the edges straight and brush off any excess flour.

Working with the longer side parallel to the edge of the surface, sprinkle the cinnamon-sugar over the dough, leaving a 1-inch border along the bottom. (If making the smaller buns, sprinkle half of the cinnamon-sugar over the surface, reserving the other half for the second half of dough.) Brush the bottom edge with the beaten egg.

Fold the top edge of dough over about an inch. Using both hands, roll the dough toward yourself, tucking it under with your thumbs to tighten as you work your way across the entire log. As you tuck, gently rock the dough back and forth to keep it taut and even. As you get close to the bottom edge, using two fingers, smear a ½-inch edge of dough into the work surface to thin it out and ensure that the dough seals together. Roll the log toward the smeared edge and rock it back and forth to seal. Position it seam side down and trim the ends to make a 16-inch log (or 8-inch log). Slice the log into eight 2-inch-wide pieces. (For smaller buns, repeat with the other half of dough.) Place them in the prepared tins cut side down, and set aside in a warm place to rise, until slightly puffy and spongy to the touch, about 2½ hours, or 1½ to 2 hours for the smaller buns.

Adjust the oven rack to the middle position and preheat the oven to 400 degrees. Place the tins on a baking sheet and bake for 30 minutes, until nicely browned.

Allow to cool for about 10 to 15 minutes and invert the buns onto the work surface. Dip the fingers of your hand into the bowl of White Glaze. Holding your hand just above the bun, quickly move your hand back and forth to drizzle the glaze to make a thin zigzag pattern over the surface, allowing it to run down the sides.

Yield: 10 buns

Cinnamon Twists

1 recipe (3½ pounds) Croissant dough (see page 294), chilled
¾ cup granulated sugar
1¼ teaspoons ground cinnamon
2 tablespoons unsalted butter, melted

Divide the dough in half and return one half to the refrigerator.

In a small bowl, combine the sugar and 1 teaspoon of the cinnamon.

On a lightly floured work surface, roll the dough into a 16 × 20-inch rectangle, slightly thicker than ⅛ inch thick, flouring the surface of the dough as necessary and lifting the dough to square off the edges and corners to help maintain a rectangular shape and an even thickness. Trim the edges straight and brush off any excess flour.

Working with the long side parallel to the edge of the surface, brush the dough with melted butter, sprinkle it with the cinnamon-sugar and gently roll over with a rolling pin. Fold the dough in half, by bringing the left edge over to meet the right edge, patting it down and squaring off the edges. Roll it out to a 10 × 14-inch rectangle, stretching and pulling out the corners as you roll. Sprinkle the remaining ¼ teaspoon of cinnamon over the top and cut twelve ¾-inch-wide strips.

Pick up a strip and, working close to the surface (don't worry if some of the cinnamon-sugar falls out), use your fingers to twist each end in the opposite direction, allowing it to naturally stretch as you twist. Set the strip down on the table if you need to reorient your fingers as you twist. It should become about 18 inches long. Trim the ends if necessary and place on a parchment-lined baking sheet. Continue in this manner with the remaining strips, placing them 1½ inches apart. Scoop up any spilled cinnamon-sugar and sprinkle over the twists. Repeat with the other half of the dough.

Set aside in a warm place to rise for 30 minutes to an hour.

Adjust the oven racks to the upper and lower positions and preheat the oven to 400 degrees.

Bake for about 20 to 25 minutes, until nicely browned, rotating the baking sheets halfway through to ensure even baking.

Yield: 24 twists

Croissant Bread Pudding

Bread pudding came about as a way to use up leftover bread. Our bread pudding came about as a way to use up leftover croissants. Who could bear to throw out all of that butter and all of that hard work? Besides, they make the richest, tastiest bread pudding around.

If you don't have any old croissants hanging around, well, okay, go ahead and buy them, but don't say I said so.

Special Item: 6½-CUP-CAPACITY BAKING DISH

6 extra-large eggs
¾ cup granulated sugar
¼ cup vanilla extract
4 cups half and half

6 large croissants

FOR THE TOPPING:
¼ teaspoon ground cinnamon
2 tablespoons granulated sugar
1 tablespoon unsalted butter

Adjust the oven rack to the middle position and preheat the oven to 350 degrees.

In a large bowl, whisk together the eggs, sugar, vanilla extract, and half and half until combined.

Slice each croissant horizontally in half, and place cut side up in a baking dish. Pour half of the egg mixture over the croissants and place the other croissant halves, cut side up, on top. Pour the remaining egg mixture over the croissants to cover.

In a small bowl combine the cinnamon and sugar. Sprinkle the mixture over the croissants and dot with butter.

Place on a baking sheet and bake for about 1 to 1½ hours until lightly browned and the custard is set.

Yield: 8 servings

Elephant Ears

½ cup granulated sugar
¼ cup light brown sugar, lightly packed
½ teaspoon ground cinnamon
½ recipe (1¾ pounds) Croissant dough (see page 294), chilled
½ cup plus 2 tablespoons (3 ounces) walnuts, finely chopped
1 extra-large egg, lightly beaten

In a small bowl, combine the sugars and cinnamon.

On a lightly floured work surface, roll the dough into a 22 × 11-inch rectangle, slightly thicker than ¼ inch, flouring the surface of the dough as necessary and lifting the dough to square off the edges and corners to help maintain a rectangular shape and an even thickness. Trim the edges straight and brush off any excess flour.

Working with the long side parallel to the edge of the surface, sprinkle the cinnamon-sugar and half of the chopped walnuts over the dough, leaving a 1-inch border along the bottom. Brush the bottom edge with the beaten egg.

Fold the top edge of dough over about an inch. Using both hands, roll the dough toward yourself, tucking it under with your thumbs to tighten as you work your way across the entire log. As you tuck, gently rock the dough back and forth to keep it taut and even. When you get to the end, roll the log back and forth to seal. Position it seam side down and trim the ends evenly to make a 30-inch log.

Cut the log into twelve 2½-inch-wide pieces, keeping the pieces intact and standing upright. Starting ½ inch from the top, make a slice down the middle of each piece, cutting all the way through, leaving them attached at the top. Working with one piece at a time, separate the halves and open them out to form the "elephant ears," being careful not to tear the middle section of dough that holds them together. Place them 1 to 2 inches apart, on two parchment-lined baking sheets. Brush the tops with the beaten egg and sprinkle about ½ teaspoon of the remaining walnuts over each. Set aside in a warm place to rise, until slightly puffy and spongy to the touch, about 2 to 2½ hours.

Adjust the oven rack to the upper and lower positions and preheat the oven to 400 degrees.

Bake for 30 minutes, until nicely browned.

Yield: 12 ears

Espresso Wheels

As you coil the long twisted ropes, you may think you're doing something wrong when you notice that dark liquid filling leaking out onto your counter. Don't worry; just work away from the edge and sop it up later to smear over the wheels. These chocolatey coffee wheels are definitely worth the mess.

¾ cup whole milk
2½ tablespoons ground espresso or coffee
2 extra-large egg yolks
2½ tablespoons granulated sugar
2½ tablespoons light brown sugar, lightly packed
2 tablespoons light corn syrup
1 recipe (3½ pounds) Croissant dough (see page 294), chilled
¼ cup (2 ounces) finely chopped bittersweet chocolate
½ teaspoon ground cinnamon

In a small saucepan over high heat, bring the milk and espresso to a boil. Remove from the heat and allow the grounds to settle at the bottom.

Meanwhile, in the bowl of an electric mixer fitted with the whisk attachment, combine the egg yolks and sugars, and mix on medium until pale and thickened, about 3 to 4 minutes. Add the corn syrup and mix another minute. Turn the mixer to low, and slowly, in a thin, steady stream, pour in the hot milk, leaving the grounds that settled in the bottom of the pan. The mixture will become thin.

On a lightly floured work surface, roll the dough into a 17 × 16-inch rectangle, ¼ inch thick, flouring the surface of the dough as necessary and lifting the dough to square off the edges and corners to help maintain a rectangular shape and an even thickness. Trim the edges straight and brush off any excess flour.

Working with the long side parallel to the edge of the surface, pour ¼ cup of the espresso mixture over the dough, spreading it to about ¼ inch from the edge. Sprinkle over with the chopped chocolate. Quickly fold the right half over to the left side and pinch the open edges together to seal. Sprinkle the cinnamon over the surface.

Cut sixteen ½-inch-wide strips. Pick up 1 strip and, working close to the surface, use both hands to twist each end of the strip in the opposite direction, allowing it to naturally stretch as you twist it into a 20-inch-long strip. Place one end of the strip down on the surface, as you lift the other end up, and begin to coil that end around the other end on the surface, maintaining the twist as you coil. Continue coiling around clockwise and tuck the tail end underneath. Place the coil tail side down on a parchment-lined baking sheet. Repeat with the remaining strips, placing the wheels 2 inches apart on two parchment-lined baking sheets. Brush the remaining espresso mixture over the wheels. Set aside in a warm place to rise for about $1\frac{1}{2}$ hours, until slightly puffy and spongy to the touch.

Adjust the oven racks to the upper and lower positions and preheat the oven to 400 degrees.

Bake for about 30 minutes, until nicely browned, rotating the baking sheets halfway through to ensure even baking.

Yield: 16 wheels

Palm Leaves

³⁄₄ cup plus 2 tablespoons granulated sugar
1 teaspoon ground cinnamon
1 recipe (3¹⁄₂ pounds) Croissant dough (see page 294), chilled

In a small bowl, combine the sugar and cinnamon.

On a lightly floured work surface, roll the dough into a 27 × 12-inch rectangle, ¹⁄₈ inch thick, flouring the surface of the dough as necessary, and lifting the dough to square off the edges and corners to help maintain a rectangular shape and an even thickness. Trim the edges straight and brush off any excess flour.

Working with the long side parallel to the edge of the surface, sprinkle ¹⁄₄ cup of the cinnamon-sugar over the dough and roll over gently with a rolling pin. Fold the left edge of the dough to the center and fold the right edge to the center, leaving a ¹⁄₂-inch gap in the middle. Stretch the dough slightly to square off the corners. Sprinkle ¹⁄₄ cup of the cinnamon-sugar over the dough and gently roll over with a rolling pin. Fold again in the same manner. Sprinkle 2 tablespoons of the cinnamon-sugar onto the left half only. Fold the right side over to meet the left edge and pat down gently with the heel of your hand, to widen and lengthen by 1 inch. Trim the open ends to even. The strip should be about 4 inches wide. Working with the longer side parallel to the edge of the surface, slice the strip into twenty ³⁄₄-inch pieces. Place each piece cut side down on a parchment-lined baking sheet, 1 inch apart, and sprinkle with the remaining cinnamon-sugar. Set aside in a warm place to rise, until slightly puffy and spongy to the touch, about 2 hours.

Adjust the oven racks to the upper and lower positions and preheat the oven to 400 degrees.

Bake for 30 minutes, until nicely browned, rotating the baking sheets halfway through to ensure even baking.

Yield: 20 leaves

Princess Ring

Special Item: 9-INCH SPRINGFORM PAN, LIGHTLY COATED WITH MELTED BUTTER

½ cup granulated sugar
½ cup light brown sugar, lightly packed
½ teaspoon ground cinnamon
⅔ recipe (about 2 pounds) Croissant dough (see page 294), chilled
1 extra-large egg, lightly beaten
½ recipe Streusel Topping (see Chocolate Swirl–Almond Poundcake, page 29)

In a small bowl, combine the sugars and cinnamon.

On a lightly floured work surface roll the dough into a 26 × 10-inch rectangle, about ¼ inch thick, flouring the surface of the dough as necessary and lifting the edges and stretching the dough slightly to square off the corners to help maintain the rectangular shape and an even thickness. Trim the edges straight and brush off any excess flour.

Working with the long side parallel to the edge of the surface, sprinkle the cinnamon-sugar over the dough, leaving a 1-inch border along the bottom. Brush the bottom edge with the beaten egg.

Fold the top edge of the dough over about 1 inch. Using both hands, roll the dough toward yourself, tucking it under with your thumbs to tighten as you work your way along the entire log. As you tuck, gently rock the dough back and forth to keep it taut and even. When you get to the end, roll the log back and forth to seal. Trim the ends to make a log 24 inches long. Position it seam side down and pick up both ends, curving them around and toward each other to form a ring. Along the inside of the ring, about 2 inches from where the 2 ends meet, make a cut 2 inches deep, cutting ¾ of the way through to the outside edge. Make 5 more cuts evenly spaced along the inside of the ring. Place it into the prepared pan, seam side down. Set aside in a warm place to rise, until slightly puffy and spongy to the touch, about 2½ hours.

Adjust the oven rack to the middle position and preheat the oven to 375 degrees.

Brush the surface of the ring with the remainder of the beaten egg and sprinkle the streusel over the top.

Bake for about 40 minutes, until nicely browned.

Yield: 8 to 10 slices

Raisin Swirls

1 recipe (3½ pounds) Croissant dough (see page 294), chilled
½ recipe (1 cup) pastry cream (see Kinder Pies, page 245)
½ teaspoon ground cinnamon
¼ cup plus 2 tablespoons currants or raisins
1 extra-large egg, lightly beaten

FOR DECORATING:
¼ cup apricot jam
¼ cup (1 ounce) finely chopped raw, shelled, unsalted pistachios

On a lightly floured work surface, roll the dough into a 30 × 11-inch rectangle, just under ¼ inch thick, flouring the surface of the dough as necessary and lifting the edges and stretching the dough slightly to square off the corners to help maintain the rectangular shape and an even thickness. Trim the edges straight and brush off any excess flour.

Working with the short side parallel to the edge of the surface, spread the pastry cream over the dough, leaving a 1-inch border along the bottom edge. Sprinkle the cinnamon and currants over the pastry cream. Brush the bottom edge with the beaten egg.

Fold the top edge of dough over about 1 inch. Using both hands, roll the dough toward yourself, tucking it under with your thumbs to tighten as you work your way along the entire log. As you tuck, gently rock it back and forth to keep it taut and even. As you get close to the bottom edge, using 2 fingers, smear a ½-inch edge of dough into the work surface to thin it out and ensure that the dough seals together. Roll the log toward the smeared edge and rock back and forth to seal. Position it seam side down and trim the ends to make a 10-inch log. Slice it into ten 1-inch-wide pieces and place them cut side down on two parchment-lined baking sheets, at least 2 inches apart. Brush the swirls with the remaining beaten egg. Set aside in a warm place to rise, until slightly puffy and spongy to the touch, about 2½ hours.

Adjust the oven rack to the middle position and preheat the oven to 400 degrees.

Bake for 30 minutes, until nicely browned, rotating the baking sheets halfway through to ensure even baking.

In a small saucepan over medium high heat, bring the apricot jam plus a few drops of water to a boil, stirring constantly. Brush the tops of each swirl with apricot jam and sprinkle with 1 teaspoon of the pistachios.

Yield: 10 swirls

Sugar Buns

A FRENCH-AMERICAN HYBRID, MORNING BUNS MADE THEIR FIRST APPEAR-
ance in the mid-1970s at a small French bakery on the northern edge of Oakland.
They instantly became a Bay Area classic, putting La Farine on the map and into the
hearts of many loyal fans. Suffering from withdrawal, enough expats from northern
California persuaded me to come up with a La Brea Bakery version.

Special Item: ³/₄-CUP-CAPACITY MUFFIN TIN, LIGHTLY COATED WITH
                   MELTED BUTTER

1 cup light brown sugar, lightly packed
2 teaspoons ground cinnamon
1 recipe (3½ pounds) Croissant dough (see page 294), chilled
1 extra-large egg, lightly beaten

FOR THE TOPPING:
½ cup granulated sugar
1 teaspoon ground cinnamon

In a small bowl, combine the brown sugar and cinnamon.

On a lightly floured work surface roll the dough into a 12 × 21-inch rectangle, ¼
inch thick, flouring the surface of the dough as necessary and lifting the dough to
square off the edges and corners to help maintain the rectangular shape and an even
thickness. Trim the edges straight and brush off any excess flour.

Working with the long side parallel to the edge of the surface, spread an even layer
of the sugar mixture over the dough, leaving a 1½-inch border along the bottom.
Gently roll over the filling a few times with a rolling pin. Brush the bottom edge with
the beaten egg.

Fold the top edge of the dough over about 1 inch. Using both hands, roll the
dough toward yourself, tucking it under with your thumbs to tighten as you work
your way along the entire log. As you tuck, gently rock the dough back and forth to
keep it taut and even. Roll the log back and forth a few times to seal. Position it seam
side down and trim the ends to make a log 24 inches long. Slice the log into twelve
2-inch-wide pieces. Working with one piece at a time, stretch the tail end (about a
1½-inch piece) of each bun slightly and pull it over to cover the flat side of the coil.

SUGAR BUNS: "EXPATS FROM NORTHERN CALIFORNIA PERSUADED
ME TO COME UP WITH A LA BREA VERSION."

Place each bun tail side down into the prepared muffin tin. Set aside in a warm place to rise, until almost doubled in size and spongy to the touch, about 2 hours.

Adjust the oven rack to the middle position and preheat the oven to 400 degrees. Bake for 25 minutes until lightly browned.

To make the topping: In a small bowl, combine the sugar and cinnamon.

Remove from the oven and cool for about 5 minutes. Roll the buns in the cinnamon-sugar to generously coat them.

Yield: 12 buns

Twice-Baked Almond Croissants

Turn even the most mundane store-bought croissants into a delicious and easy adventure. Drowned in a sweet orange syrup, stuffed with almond cream, and covered with sliced toasted almonds, these croissants are heavenly.

³⁄₄ cup (2 ounces) sliced unblanched almonds

FOR THE SYRUP:
½ cup water
³⁄₄ cup granulated sugar
1 vanilla bean
¼ cup orange juice

8 day-old croissants (see Croissants, page 294)
1 recipe almond cream (see Almond Log, page 297)
Powdered sugar, for dusting

Adjust the oven rack to the middle position and preheat the oven to 325 degrees.

Spread the almonds on a baking sheet and toast in the oven until lightly browned, about 8 to 10 minutes. Shake the pan halfway through to ensure that the nuts toast evenly.

To prepare the syrup: In a small saucepan over medium-high heat, combine the water and sugar. Using a small paring knife, split the vanilla bean lengthwise. With the back of the knife, scrape out the pulp and the seeds and add the scrapings and the pod to the sugar mixture. Bring to a boil and cook for another minute. Remove from the heat and stir in the orange juice.

Turn the oven up to 350 degrees.

Slice the croissants in half horizontally and brush the bottom half of each with about 1 tablespoon of the orange syrup. Spread 2 tablespoons of the almond cream on the bottom half of each, mounding it in the center. Place the two halves together and spread 1 tablespoon of the almond cream over the top. Place them on a parchment-lined baking sheet and sprinkle about 2 tablespoons of almonds over the top of each croissant.

Bake for about 20 to 25 minutes, until nicely browned.

Allow to cool a few minutes, and dust with the powdered sugar.

Yield: 8 croissants

Walnut Bowties

1 recipe (3½ pounds) Croissant dough (see page 294), chilled
1 recipe Nut Filling (see Normandy Apple Tart, page 250)

FOR THE TOPPING:
1 extra-large egg, lightly beaten
3 tablespoons walnuts, finely chopped

Turn the oven up to 375 degrees.

On a lightly floured work surface, roll the dough into a 6 × 27-inch rectangle, ¼ inch thick, flouring the surface of the dough as necessary and lifting the dough to square off the edges and corners to help maintain the rectangular shape and an even thickness. Trim the edges straight to 5 × 25 inches and brush off any excess flour. Cut out ten 5 × 5-inch squares.

Place a heaping tablespoon of the Nut Filling in the palm of your hand and roll it into a 4-inch-long rope. Place it on a diagonal (from top left to bottom right) in the center of the square, approximately ½ inch from the corners. Brush the left and bottom edges of the square with the beaten egg. Fold the right upper corner over to evenly meet the bottom left corner to form a triangle, pressing down gently around the edges to seal. On the left lower corner of the triangle make two 1-inch-long cuts on the sides of the corner, parallel and ½ inch apart from each other. To form the bow-tie shape, lift the lower half of the triangle that you have just cut and flip it over, placing the half triangle on the work surface, stretching it slightly, and leaving the upper half and the middle strip in their original positions. You should now see the bow-tie shape. Separate the top and bottom pieces of dough that form the middle strip (these will be the two "ties"). Wrap the top tie around the middle section once and then wrap the bottom tie around the middle section in the opposite direction, pressing the ends gently to seal. Don't worry if some of the filling peeks through. Place the bowties on a parchment-lined baking sheet, about 2 inches apart, and set aside in a warm place to rise, until slightly puffy and spongy to the touch, about 2 hours.

Brush the ties with the beaten egg and sprinkle each with ½ teaspoon of the chopped walnuts.

Bake for 15 minutes, until nicely browned.

Yield: 10 bowties

DANISH PASTRIES

EVERYONE HAS EATEN A "DANISH," BUT DOES ANYONE REALLY KNOW WHAT a Danish is? Growing up, I called just about any sweet roll with a fruity jam center a Danish. Let the truth be known: A true Danish is made from this yeasted dough, spiked with cardamom and nutmeg and, like Croissant dough, layered with lots of butter. The Danes got their recipe from the Viennese, who also invented the Croissant.

Form this delicious dough into Bear Claws (page 320), spread with almond filling, or Sunshine Buns (page 325), coiled around sweet orange cream, or make some traditional Danish Diamonds (page 324), filled with sweet ricotta cheese and your favorite jam.

"EVERYONE HAS EATEN A 'DANISH,' BUT DOES
ANYONE REALLY KNOW WHAT A DANISH IS?
LET THE TRUTH BE KNOWN!"

Danish Dough

0.6 ounce fresh cake yeast (2 teaspoons) or 1 teaspoon active dry yeast
½ cup plus 2 tablespoons (5 ounces) whole milk
¼ cup granulated sugar
¼ teaspoon cardamom
½ teaspoon freshly grated nutmeg
1 teaspoon kosher salt
2 extra-large eggs
½ stick (2 ounces) unsalted butter, room temperature
2¾ cups unbleached bread flour or unbleached all-purpose flour

FOR LAYERING:
2 sticks (8 ounces) unsalted butter, chilled

Place the yeast in the bowl of an electric mixer and pour the milk over the yeast to soften a few minutes. Sprinkle in the granulated sugar, cardamom, nutmeg, and salt. Add the eggs and room-temperature butter and, using the dough hook, mix on low for a minute until combined. Turn the mixer off, add the flour, and mix on low about 1 minute, until the dough is smooth but sticky.

Turn the dough out onto a lightly floured work surface and roll it into a 12 × 6-inch rectangle, about ½ inch thick, flouring the surface of the dough as necessary and lifting the dough to square off the edges and corners to help maintain a rectangular shape and an even thickness. Wrap the dough in plastic and chill for about 15 minutes.

Meanwhile, thoroughly clean and dry the bowl of an electric mixer. Using the paddle attachment, cream the butter about 2 minutes, until just softened, but still cool and malleable. (The butter should be the same consistency as the dough.)

Working with the longer side parallel to the surface, smear the butter over the right two-thirds of the dough, leaving a ½-inch border around the edges. Fold the dough into thirds by folding the left unbuttered side over to the center and the right side over to meet the left edge, for a letter fold. Gently roll over the dough a few times to widen slightly, keeping the rectangle shape. If the butter peeks through the dough, sprinkle a little flour on the butter to prevent it from sticking. Brush off any excess flour, wrap in plastic and chill for an hour, until slightly firm, but not hard.

On a lightly floured surface, dust the dough with flour and roll into a 16 × 6-inch rectangle, about ½ inch thick. Brush off any excess flour. Working with the longer side parallel to the surface, fold the left half of the dough to the center and fold the right half to the center, leaving a ½-inch gap in the center. Gently roll over the dough a few times to widen the rectangle slightly. Fold the left half over to meet the edge of the right to form a 12 × 8-inch rectangle, just under ¾ inch thick. Roll to widen slightly. Wrap in plastic and chill for 45 minutes to an hour.

On a lightly floured surface, roll to a 24 × 8-inch rectangle and repeat the folds once more. Allow to rest on the table for about 5 to 10 minutes. Roll the dough to widen the rectangle slightly. Wrap in plastic and chill 2 to 3 hours, or overnight or freeze if you want to store longer than 1 day.

Yield: 2 pounds

Bear Claws

Special Item: PASTRY BAG FITTED WITH A WIDE TIP, OPTIONAL

½ cup granulated sugar
1 teaspoon ground cinnamon
1 recipe Almond Cream (see Almond Log, page 297)
½ recipe (1 pound) Danish Dough (see page 318), chilled
1 extra-large egg, lightly beaten
¾ cup (2½ ounces) sliced unblanched almonds

In a small bowl, combine the sugar and cinnamon.

If the Almond Cream is cold and firm, spread it onto a clean work surface with a spatula, moving and spreading it to warm it up and make it malleable. Place the Almond Cream in a pastry bag and set aside.

Turn the dough out onto a lightly floured work surface. Roll the dough into a 21 × 9-inch rectangle, ¼ inch thick, flouring as necessary and lifting the dough to square off the edges and corners to help maintain a rectangular shape and an even thickness. Trim the edges straight and brush off any excess flour.

Working with the long side parallel to the edge of the surface, cut the dough horizontally in half to make two 4-inch-wide strips. Leaving a 1-inch border on the bottom edge, and ½-inch borders on the left and right edges, pipe or spread an even band of the Almond Cream, 1½ inches wide and ¼ inch thick in the center of the strip. Sprinkle over the cinnamon-sugar. Brush the bottom edge with the beaten egg. Fold the top edge over to the center and then fold over one more time to make 3 layers of dough. Dust the surface of the dough lightly with flour and stretch it, by pulling gently on the ends. With the heel of your hand, move along the entire length of the roll, pressing down the 1½-inch bottom edge to flatten it slightly and seal the layers together. The strip should be about 1¾ inches wide. Let the dough rest about 2 to 3 minutes and repeat the process with the other strip of dough. Brush the top and sides of both rolls with the remaining beaten egg and sprinkle on the sliced almonds. Trim the ends evenly and cut into six 5-inch-long pieces.

Cut four ½-inch-deep incisions, about ¼ inch apart along the bottom edge of each piece. Place them on 1–2 parchment-lined baking sheets, and fan out the strip, arching it to form a semicircle. Space the claws 2 inches apart. Set aside in a warm place to rise, about 1 to 2 hours until slightly puffy and spongy to the touch.

Adjust the oven rack to the upper and lower positions and preheat the oven to 400 degrees.

It may be necessary to reopen the "toes" by separating them a bit.

Bake for 25 minutes, until nicely browned, rotating the baking sheets halfway through to ensure even baking.

Yield: About 15 claws

Cat Eyes in the Dark

Jose, our talented night baker, filled these with cinnamon cream and I finished them off with a spoonful of our zesty homemade applesauce. It was the perfect match. Round and glowing like cat eyes at night, these cinnamon Danish are nothing to be afraid of. If you don't have apples for applesauce, use raspberry or apricot jam or try my cheese filling from Cheese Croissants (see page 64).

FOR THE CINNAMON CREAM FILLING:
1 stick (4 ounces) unsalted butter, chilled and cut into 1-inch cubes
2 tablespoons ground cinnamon
2 cups powdered sugar
1 extra-large egg white, lightly beaten

½ recipe (1 pound) Danish Dough (see page 318), chilled
1 extra-large egg, lightly beaten
½ recipe Streusel Topping (see Chocolate Swirl–Almond Poundcake, page 29)
1 recipe Applesauce (see Apple Turnovers, page 332)

To prepare the filling: In the bowl of an electric mixer fitted with the paddle attachment, cream the butter and cinnamon on low, 2 to 3 minutes, until softened. Add the powdered sugar and cinnamon, and turn the mixer up to medium, mixing another 3 to 4 minutes until light and fluffy, scraping down the sides of the bowl as needed. Add the egg white and mix for 1 to 2 minutes until incorporated.

On a lightly floured work surface roll the dough into a 16 × 8-inch rectangle, just under ¼ inch thick, flouring the surface of the dough as necessary, lifting the dough to square off the edges and corners to help maintain a rectangular shape and an even thickness. Trim the edges straight and brush off any excess flour.

Working with the longer side parallel to the edge of the surface, spread the filling over the dough, leaving a 1-inch border along the bottom edge. Brush the bottom edge with the beaten egg.

Fold the top edge of dough over about an inch. Using both hands, roll the dough toward yourself, tucking it under with your thumbs to tighten as you work your way across the entire log. As you tuck, gently rock the dough back and forth to keep it taut and even. Roll the log back and forth to seal. Position it seam side down and trim the ends to make a 15-inch log.

Slice the log into 16 pieces, each just under 1 inch wide. Fold the tail end of the coil underneath and press together with your fingertips to seal. Place the coils, tail side down, 2 inches apart on two parchment-lined baking sheets. Brush the tops with the remaining beaten egg and sprinkle with a generous layer of streusel. Set aside in a warm place to rise until slightly puffy and spongy to the touch, about 1 to 1½ hours.

Adjust the oven racks to the upper and lower positions and preheat the oven to 400 degrees.

Use your fingers to make a ½-inch-deep impression, about the size of a half dollar, in the center of each coil. Place 1 to 2 teaspoons of Applesauce in the well.

Bake for about 30 minutes, until nicely browned, rotating the baking sheets halfway through to ensure even baking.

Yield: 16 cat eyes

Danish Diamonds

FOR THE CHEESE FILLING:

½ cup (six ounces) ricotta cheese

3 tablespoons crème fraîche or sour cream

1 tablespoon finely chopped lemon zest (about 1 lemon)

2 tablespoons granulated sugar

1 recipe (2 pounds) Danish Dough (see page 318), chilled

1 extra-large egg, lightly beaten

¾ cup raspberry jam

⅓ recipe Streusel Topping (see Chocolate Swirl–Almond Poundcake, page 29)

In a small bowl, combine the ricotta, crème fraîche, lemon zest, and sugar, and set aside.

On a lightly floured work surface roll the dough into a 16 × 18-inch rectangle, about ¼ inch thick, flouring the surface of the dough as necessary and lifting the dough to square off the edges and corners to help maintain the rectangular shape and an even thickness. Trim the edges straight to make a 13 × 15-inch rectangle and brush off any excess flour. Cut into twelve 3¾-inch squares. Brush a 1-inch border of the beaten egg around the edges of each square.

Spoon a heaping tablespoon of the cheese filling into the center of each square. Elongate the filling diagonally, from the bottom left corner up to the right corner. Place 1 tablespoon of jam next to the filling, slightly overlapping. Using both hands, pick up the top left corner and bottom right corner with your thumb and forefingers, stretching the dough in the opposite directions, about 1 inch. Bring the top left corner over the filling, pressing to seal, and bring the bottom right corner over, pressing gently to seal them together in the middle. Continue the process with the remaining squares and place on a parchment-lined baking sheet, spaced about 1½ inches apart. Set aside in a warm place to rise until slightly puffy and spongy to the touch, about 2 hours.

Adjust the oven rack to the middle position and preheat the oven to 400 degrees.

Brush the tops of each diamond with the remaining beaten egg and sprinkle generously with the streusel.

Bake for about 25 to 30 minutes, until nicely browned.

Yield: 12 diamonds

Sunshine Buns

I F YOUR FONDEST MEMORIES OF HOME BAKING GO BACK BEFORE THE DAYS OF microwaves and super-convenience foods, then you surely remember those ready-in-minutes rolls found in the deli aisle next to the hot dogs. They came in a cardboard tube that you "popped" against the counter to reveal the smooth raw buns and a tiny can of sugary white glaze. Hot out of the oven (not the microwave), they were soft and squishy and good.

My Sunshine Buns are made with an entire ground orange, no chemicals, and lots of love. They won't be ready in 10 minutes, but if you have your Danish Dough (see page 318) prepared ahead of time, they don't take much longer than the fast-food version. Like their imitation counterpart, these too are best hot—right out of the oven.

FOR THE FILLING:
1 orange or Meyer lemon or tangerine, peeled, cut in quarters, seeds removed
½ cup plus 1 tablespoon water
1 cup granulated sugar
½ teaspoon kosher salt
½ stick plus 1 tablespoon (2½ ounces) unsalted butter
¼ cup plus 1 tablespoon light corn syrup
½ cup unbleached pastry flour or unbleached all-purpose flour
1 extra-large egg

½ recipe (1 pound) Danish Dough (see page 318), chilled

FOR DECORATING:
1 extra-large egg, lightly beaten
½ cup (1½ ounces) unblanched sliced almonds, for sprinkling

FOR THE GLAZE:
2 tablespoons ground orange (reserved from the filling)
2 teaspoons light corn syrup
½ cup powdered sugar

To make the filling: In the bowl of a food processor fitted with the steel blade, pulse until the orange is coarsely ground, about 1 minute. Measure out 2 tablespoons for the glaze and set aside.

In a medium saucepan, over medium-high heat, combine ½ cup of the water, the sugar, salt, butter, corn syrup, and remaining ground orange, and bring to a boil.

In a medium bowl, combine the remaining water and flour and whisk in the egg. Slowly pour the orange mixture over the egg mixture, beating to incorporate. Return the mixture to the saucepan and over medium heat, whisking constantly, bring to a boil. Remove from the heat and transfer to a bowl. Cover with plastic wrap, pressing down on the surface so a skin doesn't form.

On a lightly floured work surface, roll the dough into a 15 × 12-inch rectangle, about ¼ inch thick, flouring the surface of the dough as necessary and lifting the dough to square off the edges and corners to help maintain a rectangular shape and an even thickness. Trim the edges straight and brush off any excess flour.

Working with the longer side parallel to the edge of the surface, spread an even layer of the filling over the dough, leaving a 1-inch border along the bottom edge. Brush the bottom edge with the beaten egg.

Fold the top edge of the dough over about 1 inch. Using both hands, roll the dough toward yourself, tucking it under with your thumbs to tighten as you work your way across the entire log. As you tuck, gently rock the dough back and forth to keep it taut and even. Rock the log back and forth to seal the end. Position the log seam side down and trim the ends to make a 14-inch log.

Slice into 12 pieces and place them cut side down 2 inches apart on 2 parchment-lined baking sheets. Set aside in a warm place to rise until slightly puffy and spongy to the touch, about 1 to 1½ hours.

Adjust the oven rack to the upper and lower positions and preheat the oven to 325 degrees. Spread the sliced almonds on a baking sheet and toast 5 to 7 minutes until lightly toasted. Adjust the oven racks to the upper and lower positions and turn the oven up to 400 degrees.

Brush the buns with the beaten egg.

Bake for 20 to 25 minutes, until nicely browned, rotating the baking sheets halfway through to ensure even baking.

Meanwhile, to prepare the glaze: In a small mixing bowl, combine the 4 tablespoons of ground orange, corn syrup, and powdered sugar. This mixture will be very sticky.

Remove the buns from the oven and cool for a few minutes. Spread about 1 teaspoon of the glaze over the surface of each bun and sprinkle 10 to 12 sliced almonds over each.

Yield: 12 buns

Two-Dough Danish

WHEN YOU'RE CLEANING OUT YOUR FREEZER AND YOU COME ACROSS SOME extra Brioche and Croissant or Danish dough, here's an opportunity to use it. In the end you'll have a pastry with two different layers of dough with two different textures.

¾ recipe (1½ pounds) Danish Dough (see page 318), chilled, or ⅓ recipe (1¼ pounds)
*   Croissant dough (see page 294), chilled*
½ recipe (about 1¼ pounds) Brioche Dough (see page 287), chilled
¾ stick butter (3 ounces) butter, melted
½ cup plus 2 tablespoons granulated sugar
1 extra-large egg, lightly beaten
¼ cup walnuts, finely chopped

On a lightly floured work surface, roll the Danish or Croissant dough into a 22 × 10-inch rectangle, ¼ inch thick, flouring the surface of the dough as necessary and lifting the dough to square off the edges and corners to help maintain the rectangular shape and an even thickness. Trim the edges straight and brush off any excess flour.

Repeat the same process with the Brioche Dough. Place it on top of the Danish or Croissant dough, lining up the edges evenly. Trim to a 21 × 9-inch rectangle. Pour on the melted butter and sprinkle with the sugar.

Fold the top 1-inch edge of dough over. Using both hands, roll the dough toward yourself, tucking it under with your thumbs to tighten as you work your way across the entire log. As you tuck, gently rock the dough back and forth to keep it taut and even. When you reach the halfway point, reverse the roll by placing the rolled-up section on the bottom of the work surface. Fold the top 1-inch edge over and roll in the same manner as above until both logs meet in the middle. Trim the ends evenly to make a 12-inch double log. Cut into twelve 1-inch-wide pieces.

Working on the parchment-lined baking sheet, with one piece at a time, pick up one half of the 2-sided coil and flip it over, so that the 2 coils are facing in opposite directions. Be careful not to tear the dough that connects the two sides. Continue with the remaining pieces and place them 1½ inches apart on 2 parchment-lined baking sheets. Set aside in a warm place to rise until slightly puffy and spongy to the touch, about 2½ hours.

Adjust the oven racks to the upper and lower positions and preheat the oven to 400 degrees.

Brush the top with the beaten egg and sprinkle about a teaspoon of nuts over each.

Bake for 30 minutes, until nicely browned.

Yield: 12 Danish

Puff Pastries

....

You probably have a horror story that involves Puff Pastry and vowed never to make it again. It's not that it's hard to make, honest, it's that you didn't pay attention to the important details. Your first attempt was probably in the middle of a heat wave, way too hot for even expert Puff Pastry makers. And then, you tried to rush and take shortcuts. With Puff Pastry, you just can't do that. The dough has to rest the full amount of time that the recipe calls for, or it will be tough and elastic and difficult to work with. Also, the dough and butter must be the same consistency. If the butter is too cold it will break through the dough; if it's too warm, it will begin to ooze out.

Never waste your Puff Pastry scraps. After you've cut out your shapes, gather the scraps, stack them on top of each other, and freeze. You can roll the thawed Puff Pastry out one more time to make Apple or Lemon Turnovers, Cherry Bundles, or Plum Puffs. Let's be honest, Puff Pastry is time consuming, but once you've mastered it, you can do almost anything in the dessert world. Remember, you must start 2 days ahead. If you're in a hurry, choose another dough.

Puff Pastry

1¼ cups unbleached all-purpose flour or unbleached bread flour
5¼ cups unbleached pastry flour
1 tablespoon kosher salt
1½ sticks (6 ounces) unsalted butter, cut into ½-inch cubes and softened
1¾ cups water

FOR LAYERING:
5 sticks (1 pound, 4 ounces) unsalted butter, cold

In the bowl of an electric mixer fitted with the paddle attachment, combine the flours and salt and mix on low to incorporate. Add the softened butter and mix on low until it's the consistency of a fine meal. Add the water and mix to combine, about 1 minute.

Turn the dough out onto a lightly floured work surface and knead a few times and gather together into a smooth ball. Cut 4 slits into the top of the dough, ¾ inch deep, in a tic-tac-toe pattern. Wrap tightly in plastic and chill overnight.

Remove the dough from the refrigerator and let sit for 1 to 2 hours, depending on the weather, until it is room temperature and soft, but still holds its shape.

Place the cold butter on the work surface and pound it with a rolling pin until it begins to soften. Knead the butter with your fingertips until it's smooth, pliable, and about the same consistency as the dough. As the butter releases excess water, blot it with a towel. Alternately, pound the butter between 2 linen towels until the butter is pliable and the excess moisture is removed. Shape the butter into a 6 × 10-inch rectangle and set aside.

On a lightly floured surface, roll the dough into a 20 × 10-inch rectangle. Lift and reposition the dough frequently while rolling to keep it from sticking and sprinkle more flour underneath, if necessary.

Working with the short side of the dough parallel to the edge of the surface, place the butter in the center of the rectangle and completely enclose it in the dough by folding the bottom up, the top down, and the 2 sides in to meet in the middle. The edges of the dough may overlap slightly where they meet, but it's important that the butter be completely enclosed.

With the rolling pin, press 4 or 5 horizontal ridges down into the dough-butter package, keeping the work surface and rolling pin well dusted with flour. Place the rolling pin into the ridge farthest away from you and begin to roll back and forth, widening the ridge. Place the rolling pin in each successive ridge and move it back and forth until the ridges have doubled in width. Press equally in all the ridges so that the dough maintains an equal thickness. This process helps to anchor the butter and prevents it from oozing out of the dough.

When you reach the last ridge, begin to roll the dough away from you until it makes a rectangle about 8 × 24 inches. As you roll, keep stretching out the corners of the dough so they remain at right angles and don't round out. The dough should at no time be wider than 8 inches. If it starts to widen out as you roll, push in the sides with your hands to keep it in shape.

The dough should be a homogeneous, pale yellow color; you should not be able to see any chunks of butter through it. If the butter does break through, flour it well, and avoid rolling in that spot.

Fold the dough like a letter into thirds, by folding the bottom edge up to the middle and the top edge down to meet the bottom edge. Turn the dough counterclockwise, so the open flap edge is on your right. You have just made the first turn.

Make ridges in the dough again and roll it out to an 8 × 24-inch rectangle, in the same manner as above. Fold in thirds again, brushing off excess flour. Press 2 indentations in the top of the dough to remind yourself that you have made 2 turns. Wrap in plastic and refrigerate for at least $1\frac{1}{2}$ hours, until the dough is thoroughly chilled and relaxed.

Remove the dough from the refrigerator and let it sit at room temperature for 15 to 30 minutes, until it is roughly the same temperature and pliability as it was when you began to incorporate the butter. Give the dough 2 more turns by repeating the rolling and folding process 2 more times. When both turns are finished, mark the dough with 4 indentations to signify 4 turns. Wrap the dough in plastic and chill overnight.

Give the Puff Pastry its fifth and final turn, repeating the folding process once more. Roll into the desired shape and thickness.

Store Puff Pastry no longer than 3 days in the refrigerator or it will spot and turn gray. Freeze for longer storage.

Yield: About 5 pounds

Apple Turnovers

LIGHT AND FLAKY AND FILLED WITH SAUTÉED APPLES AND APPLESAUCE, THESE puff pastry turnovers aren't like any others. The homemade applesauce makes them twice as appley and the Puff Pastry makes them twice as crispy.

Note: To sauté the apples properly, it is important not to overcrowd them in the pan. If your pan is smaller than 12 inches, divide the apples and the other ingredients more or less equally into 3 or 4 batches to sauté.

Special Items: 5½-INCH ROUND CUTTER
12-INCH SKILLET

FOR THE APPLESAUCE:
2 to 3 Granny Smith apples (¾ pound), firm and tart, peeled and cut into
    1-inch cubes, to equal 2 cups
3 tablespoons (1½ ounces) unsalted butter, cut into 1-inch cubes
1 teaspoon fresh lemon juice
2 tablespoons water
2–3 tablespoons granulated sugar, to taste
1 vanilla bean

½ recipe Puff Pastry (about 2 pounds) (see page 330), chilled

FOR THE FILLING:
¾ stick (3 ounces) unsalted butter
1 vanilla bean
4 to 6 (2 pounds) Granny Smith apples, firm and tart, peeled, cut around the core
    and sliced into ⅜-inch-thick slices, to equal 6 cups
¼ cup granulated sugar
¼ teaspoon ground cinnamon
¼ cup brandy or whiskey

FOR THE TOPPING:
1 to 2 extra-large egg whites, lightly beaten
3 tablespoons granulated sugar
¼ teaspoon ground cinnamon

TURNOVERS: "THE BEST TURNOVERS EVER—I PROMISE."

To prepare the applesauce: In a large saucepan, over high heat, combine the apples, butter, lemon juice, water, and 2 tablespoons of the sugar, reserving the other tablespoon of sugar to correct the sweetness after cooking.

Using a small paring knife, split the vanilla bean lengthwise. With the back of the knife, scrape out the pulp and the seeds and add the scrapings and the pod to the apples. Cover the saucepan tightly with aluminum foil, crimping the edges to seal the pan, so the steam can't escape. Bring to a boil, turn down the heat to very low, and cook about 3 to 5 minutes, or until the foil has puffed up. Turn off the heat, and allow to sit, covered, for about 20 to 25 minutes.

Remove the foil. Test the apples for doneness by piercing with a knife. If they're not completely cooked, re-cover and bring back to a boil, turn off the heat, and allow it to sit for 15 to 20 additional minutes.

Remove the vanilla bean and whisk until the apples are pureed. Taste the apple-sauce; if it's not sweet enough, add the remaining sugar and stir to combine. Allow to cool.

Divide the Puff Pastry in half, and return one half to the refrigerator. On a lightly floured work surface roll the Puff Pastry to $\frac{1}{8}$ inch thick, flouring the surface of the dough as necessary. Cutting as closely together as possible, cut out five 5-inch circles and place them on a parchment-lined baking sheet to chill until firm, about 1 hour. Stack the scraps on top of each other, and set aside. Repeat with the other half of dough. Gather the scraps and stack them on top of the other pile and wrap in plastic. Freeze the trimmings for another use.

Meanwhile, to prepare the filling: In a large skillet, over medium heat, melt the butter. Using a small paring knife, split the vanilla bean lengthwise. With the back of the knife, scrape out the pulp and the seeds and add the scrapings and the pod to the butter and heat until bubbly. Add the apples, tossing to coat with the butter. Reduce the heat to medium-low and sauté the apples slowly, without allowing them to color. Cook until they're tender and shiny and begin to release their juices, about 8 to 10 minutes. As they cook, swirl the pan to promote even cooking, keeping the apples in a single even layer. Turn down the heat to low, add the sugar and cinnamon, and toss to combine. Cook until the apples are a golden color, but still slightly firm to the touch, about 5 to 8 minutes. Remove from the heat. Add the brandy (or whiskey) and return it to the heat. Tilting the pan slightly toward the flame, ignite the liquor, letting it burn until the flames die down. Strain the liquid from the apples and transfer them to a baking sheet to cool. Remove the vanilla bean. Allow to cool.

To assemble the turnovers: Spoon 2 tablespoons of applesauce into the center of each circle and place about 6 slices of apple over the sauce. Brush the lower half of the outer edge of each circle with the egg white. Fold the top half over the filling to form a half circle. Press down with your index finger to seal the edges. Transfer to a parchment-lined baking sheet and freeze until firm, at least 1 hour.

Adjust the oven rack to the upper position and preheat the oven to 375 degrees.

In a small bowl, combine the sugar and the cinnamon.

Cut 3 short diagonal lines across the middle of each turnover, cutting all the way through the top of the dough. Place them 1 inch apart on a parchment-lined baking sheet. Brush the tops with the remaining egg white and sprinkle with about ½ teaspoon of the cinnamon-sugar.

Bake for 30 to 40 minutes, until well browned and crispy.

Yield: 10 turnovers

Lemon Turnovers

THESE ARE THE BEST LEMON TURNOVERS EVER—I PROMISE. THE EASY-TO-make cream cheese dough is crisp and flaky. Don't get me wrong, Puff Pastry (see page 330) will always work in a pinch.

Special Item: 5-INCH ROUND CUTTER

FOR THE CREAM CHEESE DOUGH:
4 sticks (1 pound) unsalted butter, chilled and cut into 1-inch cubes
1 teaspoon kosher salt
2 cups (1 pound) cream cheese
4 cups unbleached pastry flour or unbleached all-purpose flour

FOR THE FILLING:
¾ cup lemon juice (about 3 to 4 lemons)
¾ cup granulated sugar
6 extra-large egg yolks
3 tablespoons cornstarch
Zest of 3 lemons, finely chopped
1½ sticks (6 ounces) unsalted butter, softened

FOR THE TOPPING:
1 to 2 extra-large egg whites, lightly beaten
2 tablespoons granulated sugar

To prepare the cream cheese dough: In the bowl of an electric mixer fitted with the paddle attachment, cream the butter, salt, and cream cheese on low, about 1 to 2 minutes, until softened. Turn the mixer off, add the flour, and mix on low about 1 minute, until just incorporated.

Turn the dough out onto a lightly floured work surface and flatten slightly. Roll the dough out to a 14 × 21-inch rectangle, ½ inch thick, flouring the surface of the dough as necessary. Wrap in plastic and chill overnight.

On a lightly floured surface, roll the dough into a 12 × 20-inch rectangle, flouring the surface of the dough as necessary and lifting the dough to square off the edges and corners to help maintain a rectangular shape. Lift and reposition the dough frequently while rolling to keep it from sticking to the work surface. Fold the dough into thirds by bringing the bottom third up to meet the middle and the top edge down to meet the bottom edge, as you would for a letter. Turn the dough counterclockwise so the open flap is on your right. Keeping your rolling pin and work surface well dusted with flour, press 4 to 5 horizontal ridges across the length of the rectangle to help you roll straight. Press equally within the ridges as you roll out a 12 × 20-inch rectangle. Repeat the letter fold in the same manner and turn the dough again so the open flap is on your right. Roll and fold once more in the same manner for a total of 3 turns. Wrap in plastic and chill for at least 2 hours.

To prepare the filling: In a deep, stainless-steel saucepan, over medium-high heat, bring the lemon juice and ¼ cup of the sugar to a boil. Remove from the heat.

In the bowl of an electric mixer fitted with the whisk attachment, beat the egg yolks and remaining sugar on high, until it is very thick, pale yellow, and forms a ribbon when the beater is lifted from the bowl. Add the cornstarch and lemon zest, and mix to combine. Remove the bowl from the mixer and slowly pour ⅓ of the hot lemon juice mixture into the egg mixture, whisking to combine. Pour the egg-lemon mixture into the saucepan, return the saucepan to the stove, and over medium-high heat, bring to a boil, whisking constantly. Remove from the heat and whisk in the butter. Transfer to a bowl and immediately cover the mixture with plastic wrap, pressing down on the surface so a skin doesn't form. Chill until firm and cold.

Divide the dough and return one half to the refrigerator. On a lightly floured surface, roll the dough into a 14 × 18-inch rectangle, ⅛ inch thick. Transfer to a parchment-lined baking sheet and chill for 15 to 20 minutes, to relax the dough. Repeat with the other half of the dough.

To cut and assemble the turnovers: Remove one half of the dough from the refrigerator. Cutting as closely together as possible, cut out 6 to 7 circles. Spoon 1½ to 2 tablespoons of filling in a mound into the center of each circle. Brush the lower half of the outer edge of each circle with the egg white. Fold the top half over the filling to form a half-circle. Press down with your index finger to seal the edges. Transfer to a parchment-lined baking sheet and freeze until firm, about 1 hour. Gather the scraps of dough, stack them on each other, and wrap in plastic to freeze for another use. Repeat with the remaining dough.

Adjust the oven rack to the upper position and preheat the oven to 375 degrees.

Remove the turnovers from the refrigerator and cut 3 short diagonal lines across the middle of each turnover, cutting all the way through the top portion of dough. Sprinkle one tablespoon of sugar onto the parchment-lined baking sheet and place the turnovers on it. Brush the tops with the remaining egg white and sprinkle the remainder of the sugar over each turnover. Space them 1 inch apart on the baking sheet.

Bake for 35 to 40 minutes, until well browned and crispy.

Yield: 12 to 14 turnovers

Armenian Coffee Cake

I'M NOT SURE WHICH I'M MORE GRATEFUL FOR, SUSAN AND STEVE SAHACHIAN'S big, fat juicy raisins, which find their way into many of our breads and pastries, or the incredible Armenian coffee cake they once brought me—soft and buttery, slightly sweet and slightly salty. Obsessed beyond reason, I pestered the Sahachians for the recipe and they in turn pestered their premier Armenian baker in Fresno.

Eat it warm, and if you're like me, you won't be able to stop. Simple, satisfying and comforting, this is the chicken soup of coffee cakes.

Special Item: 9-INCH CAKE RING OR 9-INCH SPRINGFORM PAN WITHOUT THE BOTTOM, OR A 9-INCH ROUND CAKE PAN

FOR THE DOUGH:

2 teaspoons (0.6 ounce) packed fresh yeast or 2¼ teaspoons active dry yeast

⅓ cup warm water

½ cup evaporated milk

1 extra-large egg

⅓ cup vegetable shortening, melted and cooled

¼ cup granulated sugar

¾ teaspoon kosher salt

¼ cup vegetable oil, plus extra for coating the bowl

2¾ cups plus 1 tablespoon unbleached pastry flour or unbleached all-purpose flour

1 stick (4 ounces) unsalted butter, very soft but not greasy

FOR THE FILLING:

½ stick plus 1 tablespoon (2½ ounces) unsalted butter

½ teaspoon kosher salt

1 vanilla bean

1 cup unbleached pastry flour or unbleached all-purpose flour

3 tablespoons granulated sugar

FOR SEALING THE DOUGH:

1 egg yolk, lightly beaten with a few drops of water

Place the yeast in the bowl of an electric mixer and pour the warm water over to soften, about 1 minute. Add the evaporated milk, egg, shortening, sugar, salt, oil, and flour. Using the dough hook mix on low speed for about half a minute, then turn up to medium-high and mix until the dough comes together, about 2 minutes. Add as much as 1 tablespoon of flour if necessary, to prevent the dough from sticking to the sides of the bowl. The dough should be very soft, smooth, and shiny.

Turn the dough out onto a lightly floured work surface, knead a few times, and gather it into a ball. Clean the mixing bowl and lightly coat it with vegetable oil. Return the dough to the oiled bowl, cover it tightly with plastic wrap, and set aside in a warm place until the dough has doubled in size, about 1 to 1½ hours.

Meanwhile, to prepare the filling: In a heavy-duty small saucepan, melt the butter with the salt. Using a small paring knife, split the vanilla bean lengthwise. With the back of the knife, scrape out the pulp and the seeds, and add the scrapings and the pod to the butter. Over medium-high heat, add the flour 2 tablespoons at a time, stirring to incorporate thoroughly between each addition. Once all of the flour has been added, continue to stir and scrape the pan to prevent the mixture from coloring unevenly. Initially, the mixture will be dry, crumbly, and awkward to stir. Flatten and pat it with the back of a wooden spoon, continuing to stir. As it cooks, the mixture will soften and become shiny. Cook about 30 minutes, until pasty and the color of light peanut butter.

Transfer to a bowl. Remove the vanilla bean and stir in the sugar, mixing well to combine. Spread the filling onto a baking sheet and set aside to cool.

Once the dough has doubled in volume, remove to a lightly floured surface. Keeping the shorter end parallel to the edge of the work surface, flatten and gently stretch the dough, pulling out the corners to form a rectangle about 7 × 14 inches, and ½ inch thick. Leaving a 1-inch border around the edges, spread your fingers apart and dimple the dough with your fingertips a few times. Dot the softened butter over the dimpled surface.

Enclose the butter by folding the bottom third of the dough up to the center and pinching the edges to seal. Pull out the corners and carefully stretch the edges to square them off. Fold the top third of the dough down to meet the bottom edge, pulling out the corners and stretching the sides to square them off.

Turn the dough so the open seam is on your right. Gently roll or stretch the dough out to a rectangle 7 × 14 inches, lifting the dough to square off the edges and corners to help maintain a rectangular shape and an even thickness, flouring as necessary and pinching the dough to reseal where the butter pokes through. Fold, turn, and roll the dough two more times in the same manner as above. Brush off any excess flour, cut the dough in half, and pinch the cut edges to seal. Wrap each piece in plastic and chill for at least 15 minutes, but no longer than 30 minutes.

Remove half of the dough from the refrigerator and turn it out onto a lightly floured surface. Pat it into a disc and gently roll and stretch it into a circle about $\frac{1}{4}$ inch thick. Using your ring as a guide, cut out a 9-inch circle, reserving the scraps of dough. Place the ring on a parchment-lined baking sheet and lift the dough into the ring, gently pressing it down and pushing it outward around the edges to fit inside the ring. Dimple the dough and brush a $\frac{1}{2}$-inch border around the edge with egg yolk. Crumble the filling over the surface of the dough, up to the edge of the egg-washed border.

Remove the remaining dough from the refrigerator and turn it out onto a lightly floured work surface. Pat it into a disc and gently roll and stretch the dough, pulling out the corners, to form a circle slightly larger than the 9-inch ring. Cut out a $9\frac{1}{2}$-inch circle, reserving the scraps. Place the circle on top of the filling, pressing down lightly on the edges to seal.

Roll the scraps into long ropes and press them into the gap between the dough and the pan. Dimple the dough about ten times and sift a fine layer of flour over the surface.

Set aside in a warm place to proof for 45 minutes to an hour, until it's slightly puffy and spongy to the touch.

Adjust the oven rack to the middle position and preheat the oven to 375 degrees.

Bake on the baking sheet for 30 to 35 minutes, until nicely browned.

Yield: 8 to 10 servings

Toasted Fruit Wedges

MY FRIEND PAULA OLAND MAKES THE WORLD'S BEST FRUIT FOCACCIA. I LIKE to think I make the world's best hot cross buns. Put two good friends together with two good doughs and you end up with these Toasted Fruit Wedges that are out of this world. Packed full of dried fruit, they're somewhere between a toasted, crusty, holiday bread and a sweet yeasted pastry. This is one of the wettest, stickiest doughs in this book, and you'll need to wash your hands frequently as you work with the dough.

Special Item: 11 × 17-INCH JELLY-ROLL PAN, BRUSHED WITH MELTED BUTTER

3¼ cups (1 pound) yellow raisins
1½ cups (½ pound) dried sour cherries
2 cups (½ pound) dried cranberries
4 teaspoons (1.2 ounces) packed fresh yeast or 4½ teaspoons active dry yeast
1 cup whole milk, lukewarm
2 tablespoons granulated sugar
4½ cups unbleached all-purpose flour
½ cup dark or medium rye flour
2 tablespoons plus 2 teaspoons kosher salt
1 teaspoon ground cinnamon
1 teaspoon ground ginger
¾ stick (3 ounces) unsalted butter, very soft

FOR DECORATING:
1 extra-large egg yolk, lightly beaten with a splash of water
¼ cup large crystallized or granulated sugar
Powdered sugar, for dusting

In a large bowl, cover the raisins, cherries, and cranberries with about 3 cups of water and set aside to soften at least 2 hours or overnight.

Place the yeast in the bowl of an electric mixer and pour the warm milk and sugar over to soften, 1 to 2 minutes.

Place a large strainer over a medium bowl and strain the fruit, pressing out the excess liquid. Measure out 1½ cups of the liquid, pour it into the yeast mixture, and discard the remaining liquid. Add the flours, salt, cinnamon, and ginger to the yeast mixture. Using the dough hook, mix on low to combine for about 1 minute. Turn the mixer up to medium-high and mix for about 8 to 10 minutes, until the dough almost wraps itself around the dough hook and makes a slapping sound against the sides of the bowl. You may need to add a few pinches of flour to encourage it to come together. The dough should be very sticky, soft, and shiny. Turn the mixer down to medium-low and add the butter, a teaspoon at a time. Turn the mixer up to medium-high and mix for 2 to 3 minutes until smooth and shiny. You may need to add another pinch of flour to encourage the dough to almost wrap itself around the hook again.

Flour your hands and turn the dough out onto a floured work surface and stretch the dough into a rough rectangle. Sprinkle one-third of the fruit onto the dough, sprinkle with flour, and fold it over onto itself, to enclose the fruit. Don't worry if some of the fruit spills out. Return the dough to the bowl of the electric mixer and mix on low for about 1 minute, until the fruit is distributed. Turn the dough out onto the floured surface, add half of the remaining fruit, sprinkle with flour, and repeat the folding and mixing 2 more times.

Turn the dough out onto a floured surface and gather into a ball. Clean the mixing bowl, lightly coat it with vegetable oil, and return the dough to the oiled bowl. Cover it tightly with plastic wrap and set aside in a warm place until the dough has risen half its size and feels spongy to the touch, about 3 hours.

Turn the dough out onto a lightly floured work surface and gently roll and stretch the dough out to the size of the jelly-roll pan. Place it on the jelly-roll pan, sprinkle the surface with flour, and dimple the surface. Place a piece of parchment paper or a towel over the pan to cover the dough. Chill for at least 12 hours and up to 24 hours.

Remove the dough from the refrigerator and set aside in a warm place until it comes up to room temperature and is slightly puffy and spongy to the touch, about 2 to 2½ hours. Brush the surface with the egg yolk and sprinkle with crystallized sugar.

Adjust the oven rack to the lower position and preheat the oven to 400 degrees. Open the oven door, spritz the oven heavily with water from a spray bottle, and quickly close the door. Open the oven door again and slide the jelly-roll pan onto the oven rack. Spritz the oven heavily with water again and quickly close the door.

Bake for 45 minutes, until nicely browned and firm to the touch. Allow to cool about 10 minutes. Lift the entire loaf and place it on a work surface. Cut it into 8 large squares and cut each square in half diagonally to form 16 triangular wedges.

Transfer the wedges onto 2 parchment-lined baking sheets, spaced 1 inch apart, and return to the oven for another 25 to 30 minutes, to crisp up the sides.

Allow to cool. Sift a fine layer of powdered sugar over the tops.

Yield: 16 wedges

9. *Doughnuts*

....

Everyone loves doughnuts—anyone who says he doesn't is either lying or has never had a good one. A shiny glazed doughnut—soft, squishy and irresistible; an apple fritter that actually tastes like real apples; a cake doughnut that has the depth and tanginess of buttermilk. A good doughnut may be hard to find, but a good doughnut is *not* hard to make. With a wet and sticky dough and fresh hot oil, you will have a doughnut that is crispy on the outside and moist and tender on the inside.

I've found that people aren't afraid of *making* doughnuts, they're afraid of *frying* them. Frying isn't difficult as long as you have the right equipment, stay organized, and follow a few simple rules. Choose a light, neutral vegetable oil such as canola. The amount of oil depends upon the size of your pan. Normally, the oil should fill the pan halfway. Use a deep, heavy-duty saucepan that holds and maintains heat and a deep-frying thermometer to monitor the temperature of the oil. If the oil isn't hot enough you'll have heavy, greasy doughnuts. If it's too hot, they'll be dark on the outside and raw in the middle. Before you begin frying, have everything you need near the stove: the uncooked doughnuts, tongs or a slotted spoon, and paper towels for draining.

Over medium-high heat, bring the oil up to 375 degrees. One

at a time, drop the doughnuts into the hot oil, leaving enough space between them so they're not crowded. Fry for 1 to 2 minutes on each side, until lightly browned and thoroughly cooked. Remove and drain on paper towels. Always check the temperature between batches and allow the oil to come back up to 375 degrees before frying the next round of doughnuts.

Yeasted doughnuts take a little more time to make because they have to rise. However, Ricotta Fritters (page 365), Carnival Doughnuts (page 351), and Old-Fashioned Buttermilk Cake Doughnuts (page 361) are a cinch and can be made in minutes. Make the yeasted types ahead of time and if you don't plan on frying them all right away, freeze them. First cut your doughnuts out, place them on a parchment-lined baking sheet, and then wrap them well with plastic and freeze. When you're craving a hot, fresh doughnut, allow the doughnuts to defrost and come up to room temperature. Once the doughnuts have risen and are spongy to the touch, you're ready to fry.

Homemade doughnuts are delicious rolled in cinnamon-sugar or dusted with nonmelting icing sugar (see "Sources," page 393) or powdered sugar. As its name implies, nonmelting icing sugar won't melt and won't become pasty on a warm surface. If you use powdered sugar make sure you sift it over the doughnuts when they are cool. But let's admit it, the doughnut gets its naughty reputation from that glossy, sweet, and sticky glaze. You might as well go all the way—brush or dip the doughnuts while still warm, so the glaze melts on the surface and seals that moist, soft center. They're best right out of the pan, so eat your doughnuts when they're fresh and hot.

Apple Fritters

Most recipes for apple fritters call for apple slices dipped in batter and fried. When I think of an apple fritter, I think of chopped apples encased in crispy, light dough. Unfortunately, the doughnut-shop version is always oversized and grease-laden. Fortunately, *this* fritter is delicate, packed with tart, plump pieces of sautéed apples and won't leave you stuffed and full of regrets. Sautéing the apples adds a little extra time and effort, but I think you'll agree it's worth it.

Note: To cook the apples properly it is important not to overcrowd them in the pan. Depending on the size of your pan, you can divide the apples and the other ingredients more or less equally into two or three batches.

Special Items: 10- TO 12-INCH LARGE SKILLET

2½-INCH ROUND CUTTER

HEAVY-DUTY, DEEP SAUCEPAN FILLED HALFWAY WITH VEGETABLE OIL

FOR THE DOUGH:

2 teaspoons (0.6 ounce) packed fresh yeast or 2¼ teaspoons active dry yeast

⅔ cup whole milk

3¼ cups plus 2 tablespoons unbleached pastry flour or unbleached all-purpose flour

4 extra-large egg yolks

½ cup granulated sugar

⅓ cup sparkling apple cider

½ stick (2 ounces) unsalted butter, melted

1 teaspoon kosher salt

½ teaspoon ground cinnamon

1 tablespoon pure vanilla extract

FOR THE APPLES:

½ stick (2 ounces) unsalted butter

1 vanilla bean

7 firm and tart Granny Smith apples (2½ pounds), peeled and cut
    into ½-inch cubes to equal 7 cups

½ teaspoon ground cinnamon

¼ cup granulated sugar

¹⁄₄ cup apple cider vinegar
1 cup sparkling apple cider

FOR THE WHITE GLAZE:
¹⁄₂ cup plus 2 tablespoons powdered sugar, sifted
¹⁄₄ cup heavy cream
¹⁄₂ teaspoon pure vanilla extract
¹⁄₈ teaspoon kosher salt

To prepare the dough: Place the yeast in the bowl of an electric mixer. In a small saucepan, over medium heat, heat the milk until warm to the touch. Pour the milk over the yeast to soften, 1 to 2 minutes. Add 2 cups of the flour to the milk mixture, without stirring. Cover the bowl tightly with plastic wrap and set aside in a warm place until the surface of the flour cracks, about 30 to 40 minutes.

In a small bowl combine the egg yolks and sugar. Add the cider, melted butter, salt, cinnamon, vanilla extract, and 1¹⁄₄ cups of the flour and mix until combined. Add this mixture to the yeast. Using the paddle attachment of an electric mixer, mix on low for half a minute, then turn up to medium for about 1 minute. Add the remaining 2 tablespoons of flour and mix on low for half a minute, then on medium for another half a minute. The dough will be very sticky.

Sift an even layer of flour onto the work surface; scrape the dough out of the bowl, onto the work surface. Clean the mixing bowl and lightly coat it with vegetable oil. Gather the dough and return it to the oiled bowl. Cover it tightly with plastic wrap, and set aside in a warm place until the dough has doubled in size, about 1¹⁄₂ hours.

To prepare the apples: In a large skillet over medium heat, melt the butter. Using a small paring knife, split the vanilla bean lengthwise. With the back of the knife, scrape out the pulp and the seeds of the vanilla bean, and add the scrapings and the pod to the butter. Heat the butter until bubbly. Add the chopped apples, tossing to coat them with butter. Add the cinnamon and sugar, and sauté 3 to 5 minutes until slightly softened and the majority of the apples are deep golden. Add the vinegar and cider, and reduce over medium-high heat. If the apples are becoming too mushy, turn the heat up, so the liquid reduces quickly. If they are still very firm, turn the heat down to reduce slowly. The apples should be cooked, but still slightly firm to the touch. Remove the vanilla bean and place the apples on a baking sheet to cool.

Scrape the dough out onto a floured surface and stretch into a rectangle about 2 inches thick. Spread half of the apples over the dough and fold into thirds by bringing the bottom up and the top down, patting with your hands to flatten slightly. Scatter the remaining apples on top and fold into thirds again. Gather the dough together by tucking under the edges and return it to the oiled bowl. Cover and allow to rise until doubled in size, about 30 minutes.

Heat the oil to 375 degrees.

Scrape the dough out onto a floured surface and gently roll or pat it into a rectangle about ½ inch thick, flouring the surface of the dough as necessary. Dip the cutter in flour and, cutting as closely together as possible, cut out the fritters. Place them on a floured surface and allow to rest for 10 minutes, no longer.

To prepare the glaze: In a small stainless steel bowl set over a pot of gently simmering water, combine the powdered sugar, cream, vanilla extract, and salt. Heat until just warm, stirring frequently. The glaze should be thin and translucent; if necessary, thin it down with more cream.

Dip your hands in flour, and stretch the fritters by pulling them gently, elongating the round shape into a 4-inch oval. Don't worry if you puncture the dough as you stretch it. Drop directly into the hot oil and fry according to instructions (see page 346).

Brush the fritters with glaze while they are warm.

Yield: 16 to 20 fritters

Carnival Doughnuts

EVERY CULTURE HAS A FESTIVAL AND EVERY FESTIVAL HAS ITS RENDITION OF fried dough. The Italians celebrate with frittelle, Mexicans make long, skinny churros, and the French eat beignets. Funnel cakes are the American version of this simple but tasty tradition. Out of that tradition came Carnival Doughnuts—a cross-cultural delight, accented by the aromatic flavors of the Mediterranean, such as orange flower water, readily found at most Indian and Middle Eastern markets.

The loose batter is piped directly into the hot oil, making crispy, delicate snakes of sweet, perfumed dough.

Special Items: PASTRY BAG FITTED WITH A #4 PLAIN TIP
HEAVY-DUTY, DEEP SAUCEPAN FILLED HALFWAY WITH VEGETABLE OIL

4 cups plus 2 tablespoons unbleached pastry flour or unbleached all-purpose flour
1 cup granulated sugar
½ teaspoon baking soda
2 teaspoons baking powder
½ teaspoon kosher salt
2 extra-large eggs
2 cups buttermilk
2 tablespoons mild-flavored honey, such as clover
1½–2 tablespoons pure almond extract, to taste
5–6 tablespoons orange flower water, to taste

FOR DECORATING:
Nonmelting icing sugar or powdered sugar

Heat the oil to 375 degrees.

Over a large mixing bowl, sift to combine the flour, sugar, baking soda, baking powder, and salt. Make a large well in the center and pour in the eggs, buttermilk, honey, almond extract, and orange flower water. Whisk together the liquid ingredients and slowly draw in the dry ingredients. The mixture should be fairly smooth before you draw in more flour.

Fill the pastry bag half full and pipe the batter directly into the hot oil, making random, 3-inch-long squiggles. After you've piped a few, wait until they have risen back to the surface before you pipe more, being careful not to overcrowd the pan.

Pile onto a platter and sift nonmelting icing sugar or powdered sugar over the top.

Yield: 12 servings

Devil's Food Spudnuts

Here, chocolate and potatoes are a surprisingly good combination. The starch in the potatoes holds in moisture and adds an extra lightness to this chocolate-glazed chocolate doughnut. If you're not a chocoholic like me, skip the glaze and simply roll them in granulated sugar.

The darkness of the dough makes it a little tricky to determine when they've finished cooking. Follow your instincts, but you may need to sacrifice one Spudnut as a tester.

Special Items: 2½-INCH DOUGHNUT CUTTER, OR A 2½-INCH ROUND CUTTER
AND A ½-INCH ROUND CUTTER, TO CUT OUT THE HOLES
HEAVY-DUTY DEEP SAUCEPAN, FILLED HALFWAY WITH VEGETABLE OIL

FOR THE DOUGHNUTS:

1 or 2 large russet potatoes (12 ounces), peeled and cut into 1-inch cubes to equal 2 cups

2½ teaspoons (0.8 ounce) packed fresh yeast or 4¼ teaspoons active dry yeast

½ cup granulated sugar

2½ cups unbleached pastry flour or unbleached all-purpose flour

1½ teaspoons baking soda

¼ cup plus 2 tablespoons cocoa powder

4 ounces bittersweet chocolate, melted according to the instructions on page 7

½ cup powdered sugar

1 teaspoon kosher salt

FOR THE GLAZE:

4½ tablespoons water

3 tablespoons unsweetened cocoa powder

2½ ounces bittersweet chocolate, melted according to the instructions on page 7

1½ tablespoons heavy cream

1 tablespoon unsalted butter, melted

½ cup powdered sugar

3 tablespoons brandy

1 tablespoon plus 1 teaspoon light corn syrup

½ cup (2 ounces) chopped pistachio nuts
1¼ cups shredded unsweetened coconut

To prepare the doughnuts: In a large saucepan over high heat, bring the potatoes to a boil in approximately 3¼ cups of water. Cook until tender, about 15 minutes. Drain and reserve the liquid and allow to cool until lukewarm. Return the potatoes to the saucepan and mash with a whisk over medium-high heat until the potatoes are dry, about 1 minute. Measure out 1 cup of the mashed potato and set aside.

Place the yeast in the bowl of an electric mixer and pour ¾ cup of the potato water over the yeast, setting the rest of the potato water aside. Sprinkle over the granulated sugar and allow the yeast to soften, about 2 to 3 minutes. Add 1 cup of the flour and stir to combine. Cover the bowl tightly with plastic wrap and set aside in a warm place until the surface is covered with large, slowly bursting bubbles and is slightly domed, about 30 to 45 minutes.

Meanwhile, in a large saucepan, bring ½ cup plus 1 tablespoon of the potato water to a boil. Stir in the baking soda and the cocoa powder. Add the melted chocolate, the 1 cup of mashed potato, the powdered sugar, and the salt, and stir to combine.

Add the chocolate mixture to the yeast mixture and stir in 1 cup of the flour. Using the paddle attachment, mix on low for about half a minute and then turn up to medium-high for one more minute. Mix in the remaining ½ cup of flour on low and once the flour is incorporated, turn up to medium-high for another half minute. The dough will be shiny and very sticky, similar to a cake batter.

Sift an even layer of flour onto the work surface. Scrape the dough out of the bowl onto the surface. Clean the mixing bowl and lightly coat it with vegetable oil. Gather the dough and return it to the oiled bowl. Cover it tightly with plastic wrap, and set aside in a warm place until the dough has doubled in size, about 1½ hours.

Turn the dough out onto a lightly floured surface. Tuck under the edges to deflate and return the dough to the oiled bowl. Cover with plastic wrap and let rise until doubled in size, about 30 minutes.

To prepare the glaze: In a small saucepan, over high heat, bring the water to a boil. Turn off the heat, add the cocoa powder, and whisk until smooth. Whisk in the remaining ingredients and over medium heat, bring to a boil, stirring constantly for about 2 minutes until bubbly and thick. If the glaze is too thick, thin down with a touch of water and bring to a boil again.

Heat the oil to 375 degrees.

Turn the dough out onto a lightly floured surface and gently roll or pat the dough into a rectangle about ½ inch thick, flouring the surface of the dough as necessary. Dip the cutter in flour and, cutting as closely together as possible, cut out the doughnuts and holes. Place them on a floured surface to rest 15 minutes before frying.

Gather the scraps of dough together, gently roll or pat into ½-inch thickness, and cut out the remaining doughnuts.

Before dropping the doughnuts into the oil, carefully stretch the hole to enlarge it slightly, by pulling gently on the sides of the doughnut. Fry the doughnuts and holes according to the instructions on page 346.

While the doughnuts and holes are still warm, dip half of the doughnut into the glaze, moving side to side as you lift it out of the glaze to evenly coat it. Sprinkle the doughnuts with the nuts or coconut, if desired.

Yield: 20 doughnuts, plus holes

French Doughnuts

THESE DOUGHNUTS GET THEIR FRENCHNESS FROM THE DOUGH THEY'RE MADE from, pâte de choux or éclair dough. A sweet, eggy paste is piped through a decorative star tip and deep-fried to a perfect golden crispness. Dripping with lemon glaze and embellished with candied zest, they're not just French, but fancy too.

Special Items: PASTRY BAG FITTED WITH A #4 STAR TIP
         SEVERAL SHEETS OF PARCHMENT PAPER, CUT INTO THIRTY
             4 × 4-INCH SQUARES
         NONSTICK SPRAY COATING OR VEGETABLE OIL
         HEAVY-DUTY, DEEP SAUCEPAN FILLED HALFWAY WITH VEGETABLE OIL

FOR THE LEMON GLAZE:
2½ cups powdered sugar
¾ cup heavy cream
1 tablespoon plus 2 teaspoons lemon juice

FOR THE DOUGHNUTS:
2 cups unbleached pastry flour or unbleached all-purpose flour
6 to 7 extra-large eggs
1 cup plus 3½ tablespoons whole milk
1¼ cups water
2 teaspoons kosher salt
2 teaspoons granulated sugar
2 sticks (8 ounces) unsalted butter, cut into 1-inch cubes
2½ teaspoons poppy seeds, optional

FOR GARNISHING:
1 recipe Candied Lemon Zest (see page 374), optional
About 1 tablespoon poppy seeds, optional

To prepare the glaze: In a small stainless-steel bowl set over a pot of gently simmering water, combine the powdered sugar, cream, and lemon juice. Heat until just

warm. The glaze should be fairly thin; if necessary, thin down with more cream or lemon juice.

To prepare the doughnuts: Over a small bowl, sift the flour and set aside. In another small bowl whisk the eggs and set aside. In a medium saucepan, over medium-high heat, bring the milk, water, salt, sugar, and butter to a rolling boil. Remove from the heat and add the flour all at once, stirring constantly with a wooden spoon until all of the flour is incorporated.

Return the pan to medium-low heat and cook for about ½ minute, stirring until the dough leaves the sides of the pan. Remove from the heat. While the dough is still warm, begin to incorporate the eggs a few tablespoons at a time, mixing completely between each addition. As soon as the dough breaks as you lift the spoon up and leaves behind a small peak, you have added enough egg. Stir in the poppy seeds.

Heat the oil to 375 degrees.

Working with one at a time, place a square of parchment paper on a flat surface or baking sheet and spray with nonstick coating or lightly coat with oil.

Note: The paper has to be sprayed just before you pipe each circle or the spray begins to melt and the batter will slide as you pipe. To prevent the paper from lifting while you pipe, weigh down two corners or pipe a dot of batter under each corner of the paper to secure it to the surface.

Fill the pastry bag half full with dough and pipe a 2½-inch, double-layered circle in one continuous stroke onto the paper. Continue with the remaining dough.

Note: At this point the doughnuts can be frozen. Bring them back to room temperature before frying.

To fry the doughnuts, flip the paper over the oil to allow the doughnut to slide into the pot and fry according to directions on page 346.

The doughnuts should have an airy, open structure.

While the doughnuts are still warm, dip the top halves into the glaze, moving them side to side as you lift them out of the glaze to evenly coat. While the glaze is still warm and sticky, sprinkle a few strands of Candied Lemon Zest (without the syrup) and a small pinch of poppy seeds, if desired, over the glaze.

Yield: 30 doughnuts

Jelly Doughnuts

Squishy soft dough surrounding a silky jam or lemon center makes these jelly doughnuts irresistible. As elegant as a fancy pastry, this doughnut is a classic in my book.

Special Items: 2-INCH ROUND CUTTER
HEAVY-DUTY DEEP SAUCEPAN, FILLED HALFWAY WITH VEGETABLE OIL
PASTRY BAG FITTED WITH A #1 OR #2 PLAIN TIP

2 teaspoons (0.6 ounces) packed fresh yeast or 2¼ teaspoons active dry yeast
½ cup plus 2 tablespoons buttermilk
¼ cup plus 1 tablespoon dry milk powder
2¼ cups plus 1 tablespoon unbleached pastry flour or unbleached all-purpose flour
¼ cup plus 2 tablespoons granulated sugar
1 teaspoon kosher salt
½ stick plus 1 tablespoon (2½ ounces) unsalted butter, room temperature
2 teaspoons freshly grated nutmeg
¾ teaspoon ground cinnamon
7 extra-large egg yolks

FOR THE FILLING:
About ½ cup raspberry jam or lemon filling (see Lemon Turnovers, page 336)
    or ½ cup Vanilla Pastry Cream (see Kinder Pies, page 245)

FOR DECORATING:
Granulated sugar or nonmelting icing sugar or powdered sugar

Place the yeast in the bowl of an electric mixer and pour ½ cup of the buttermilk over it. Add the milk powder and 1 cup of the flour and allow the yeast to soften for about 2 to 3 minutes without stirring. Using the paddle attachment, mix on low for 30 seconds, then turn up to medium-high and mix until the dough is smooth, shiny, and very sticky, about 1 to 2 minutes.

Sift an even layer of flour onto the work surface. Scrape the dough out of the bowl onto the surface. Clean the mixing bowl and lightly coat it with vegetable oil.

Gather the dough and return it to the oiled bowl. Cover it tightly with plastic wrap, and set aside in a warm place until the dough has doubled in size, about 1 to 1½ hours.

Add the remaining buttermilk, 1 cup plus 3 tablespoons of the flour, the sugar, salt, butter, nutmeg, cinnamon, and 4 of the egg yolks to the dough and mix on low just to combine. Turn the mixer up to medium and continue mixing until incorporated and the dough is shiny, about 1 to 2 minutes. Turn the mixer off and add the remaining flour. Add the remaining egg yolks one at a time, mix on low for half a minute, until incorporated. Turn the mixer up to high and mix for 1 more minute. The dough will be very sticky.

Sift an even layer of flour onto a surface. Scrape the dough out of the bowl onto the surface and sift another layer of flour over the dough. Clean the mixing bowl and lightly coat it with vegetable oil. Gather the dough together and return it to the oiled bowl. Cover the bowl tightly with plastic wrap and set aside in a warm place until the dough has doubled in size, about 1½ hours.

Turn the dough out onto a lightly floured surface. Tuck under the edges to deflate and return the dough to the oiled bowl. Cover the bowl tightly with plastic wrap and allow to rise until doubled in size, about 30 minutes.

Heat the oil to 375 degrees.

Turn the dough out onto a lightly floured surface and gently roll or pat the dough into a rectangle just under ½ inch thick, flouring the surface of the dough as necessary. Dip the cutter in flour and, cutting as closely together as possible, cut out the doughnuts. Place them on a floured surface to rest 15 minutes before frying.

Fry the doughnuts according to directions on page 346.

Allow the doughnuts to cool slightly. On a work surface or baking sheet, turn them upside-down and, using a sharp knife, prick the bottoms in the center of each doughnut. Fill the pastry bag with filling, place the pastry tip about ½ inch into the hole, and squeeze about 1 teaspoon of filling into each doughnut. Turn them right side up and roll the tops in granulated sugar or sift with nonmelting icing sugar or powdered sugar.

Yield: 18 doughnuts

Old-Fashioned Buttermilk Cake Doughnuts

CAKE DOUGHNUTS ARE A CATEGORY ALL THEIR OWN. UNLIKE RAISED DOUGH-nuts, which get their rise from yeast, cake doughnuts traditionally get theirs from baking powder and baking soda (I add a touch of yeast for extra lightness). The fla-vors are rich and zesty and the center soft and moist. For the rushed doughnut maker, these cake doughnuts are a quick fix. Simply mix the batter, roll it to cut out the doughnuts, and drop them into hot oil.

Special Items: 2¹/₂-INCH DOUGHNUT CUTTER, OR A 2¹/₂-INCH ROUND CUTTER
PLUS A ¹/₂-INCH ROUND CUTTER TO MAKE THE HOLES
HEAVY-DUTY, DEEP SAUCEPAN FILLED HALFWAY WITH VEGETABLE OIL

¹/₄ cup crème fraîche or sour cream
3¹/₄ cups unbleached pastry flour or unbleached all-purpose flour
³/₄ cup granulated sugar
¹/₂ teaspoon baking soda
1 teaspoon baking powder
1 teaspoon kosher salt
1¹/₂ teaspoons freshly grated nutmeg
1 teaspoon (0.3 ounce) packed fresh yeast or 1¹/₈ teaspoons active dry yeast
³/₄ cup plus 2 tablespoons buttermilk
1 extra-large egg
2 extra-large egg yolks
1 tablespoon pure vanilla extract

FOR DECORATING:
¹/₂ cup nonmelting icing sugar or powdered sugar

In a small stainless-steel bowl set over a pot of gently simmering water, heat the crème fraîche until just warm.

Heat the oil to 375 degrees.

Over a large mixing bowl, sift to combine the flour, sugar, baking soda, baking powder, salt, and nutmeg, and make a large well in the center. Place the yeast in the well and pour the crème fraîche over it. Allow it to soften, about 1 minute.

Pour the buttermilk, whole egg, egg yolks, and vanilla extract into the well and whisk together the liquid ingredients. Using one hand, gradually draw in the dry ingredients. The mixture should be fairly smooth before you draw in more flour. Mix until it is completely incorporated and forms a very sticky dough. Wash and dry your hands and dust them with flour.

Sift an even layer of flour onto a work surface. Scrape the dough out of the bowl onto the surface and sift another layer of flour over the dough. Working quickly, pat the dough into an even $1/2$-inch thickness. Dip the cutter in flour and, cutting as closely together as possible, cut out the doughnuts and holes. Place the holes and doughnuts on a floured surface. Working quickly, gather the scraps of dough together, pat into $1/2$-inch thickness, and cut out the remaining doughnuts and holes.

Fry the doughnuts and holes immediately according to the directions on page 346.

Sift a layer of nonmelting icing sugar or powdered sugar over the doughnuts and holes.

Yield: 15 doughnuts and holes

Raised Doughnuts: Twists and Holes

THE RAISED DOUGHNUT IS THE QUINTESSENTIAL AMERICAN CLASSIC. A CRISP, glazed outside leads the way to that light and squishy inside we all love so much. I bet you can't eat just one.

Special Items: 2½-INCH DOUGHNUT CUTTER, OR A 2½-INCH ROUND CUTTER
PLUS A ½-INCH ROUND CUTTER TO MAKE THE HOLES
HEAVY-DUTY DEEP SAUCEPAN, FILLED HALFWAY WITH VEGETABLE OIL

2 teaspoons (0.6 ounce) packed fresh yeast or 2¼ teaspoons active dry yeast
¾ cup whole milk
3 cups plus 2 tablespoons unbleached pastry flour or unbleached all-purpose flour
6 extra-large egg yolks
½ cup granulated sugar
¾ teaspoon kosher salt
1 stick (4 ounces) unsalted butter
1 vanilla bean
1 tablespoon pure vanilla extract

FOR GARNISHING:
1 recipe White Glaze, optional (see Apple Fritters, page 348)

Place the yeast in the bowl of an electric mixer. In a small saucepan over medium heat, heat the milk until warm to the touch. Pour the milk over the yeast to soften 1 to 2 minutes. Stir to combine. Add 2¾ cups of the flour to the milk mixture, without stirring. Cover the bowl tightly with plastic wrap and set aside in a warm place until the surface of the flour cracks, about 30 to 40 minutes.

In a large mixing bowl, whisk together the egg yolks, sugar, and salt. Whisk in ¼ cup of the flour and set aside.

In a small saucepan, over medium heat, melt the butter. Using a small paring knife, split the vanilla bean lengthwise. With the back of the knife, scrape out the pulp and the seeds and add the scrapings from the vanilla bean and the pod to the butter. Swirl the pan to ensure the butter cooks evenly and doesn't burn. It will bubble somewhat vigorously as it browns. Continue cooking 3 to 5 more minutes, until the bubbles subside and the liquid is dark brown with a nutty, toasty aroma. Remove the vanilla bean.

Pour the butter and dark flecks over the egg mixture, whisking to combine. Stir in the vanilla extract.

Add the browned butter mixture to the yeast mixture. Using the paddle attachment, mix on low for about 1 minute. Add the remaining 2 tablespoons of flour and mix to combine. Turn the mixer up to medium-high for 1 more minute. The dough will be very sticky.

Remove the dough from the bowl onto a floured work surface and gather it into a ball. Clean the mixing bowl and lightly coat it with vegetable oil. Place the dough in the oiled bowl, cover, and allow to rise for 1½ to 2 hours, until doubled in size.

Turn the dough out onto a lightly floured surface, tuck under the edges to deflate and return the dough back to the oiled bowl. Cover the bowl and allow the dough to rise until doubled in size, about 30 minutes.

Heat the oil to 375 degrees.

Turn the dough out onto a lightly floured surface and gently roll or pat the dough into a rectangle about ½ inch thick, flouring the surface of the dough as necessary. Dip the cutter in flour and, cutting as closely together as possible, cut out the doughnuts and holes. Place them on a floured surface.

To form the twists, flour your hands and pick up one end of the doughnut with your thumb on top and forefinger on the bottom. Using the other hand, pick up the other end of the doughnut, reversing the finger placement. Turn each side away from the other, in opposite directions, stretching slightly to form a doughnut with 2 twists. (When you fry the twists they will untwist once.) Place on a floured surface to rest for 15 minutes before frying.

Gather the scraps of dough together, gently roll or pat into ½-inch thickness and cut out the remaining doughnuts.

Fry the doughnuts and the holes according to the directions on page 346.

While still warm, dip the top half of the doughnut into the White Glaze, moving side to side as you lift the doughnut out of the glaze to evenly coat it. Dip the holes in the glaze to coat.

Yield: 18 doughnuts and holes

Ricotta Fritters

Simple to make, these soft, cheesy pillows require little time and effort. Use the best-quality ricotta available and add a little extra salt if the cheese isn't salted.

Special Item: HEAVY-DUTY, DEEP SAUCEPAN, FILLED HALFWAY WITH
VEGETABLE OIL

1 cup (8 ounces) ricotta cheese or large-curd cottage cheese
¾ cup unbleached pastry flour or unbleached all-purpose flour
2½ tablespoons granulated sugar
1½ teaspoons baking powder
½ teaspoon freshly grated nutmeg
2 extra-large eggs
2 tablespoons mild-flavored honey, such as clover
1 tablespoon pure vanilla extract

FOR DECORATING:
Nonmelting icing sugar or powdered sugar

Heat the oil to 375 degrees.

Place the ricotta in a mixing bowl and break it up a little, just to loosen.

In a large mixing bowl, sift together the flour, sugar, baking powder, and nutmeg. Make a well in the center and pour in the eggs, honey, and vanilla extract. Whisk the liquid ingredients until combined and then slowly begin to draw in the dry ingredients. The mixture should be fairly smooth before you draw in more of the dry ingredients.

Add the ricotta to the batter and barely combine. Do not overmix; there should still be visible chunks of ricotta.

Scoop about 1 tablespoon of the mixture at a time and drop into the oil. Fry until the outside is a light golden brown and the center is still a bit runny, about 20 to 30 seconds on each side.

Pile on a platter and sift a fine layer of nonmelting icing sugar over them, or allow to cool and sift powdered sugar over the top. Serve with jam or preserves.

Yield: 28 fritters

10. *Confections*

....

In the world of sweets, there's nothing more frustrating than trying to make fancy filled chocolates at home. By the time you're
done, you're usually covered head to toe in chocolate and won-
dering why you didn't just buy them from your favorite candy
store for what now seems a very affordable price. Filled ganaches,
cream-centered bonbons, and molded chocolates require a lot of
time and skilled technique. The confections in this chapter will
give you the same satisfaction as their fancier cousins, but won't
leave you wishing you'd chosen a different dessert. Sesame–
Pumpkin Seed Brittle (page 391) is just what it says it is: seeds and
sugar, so easy, and ready in minutes. Both young and old will love
the Salted Peanut Treats (page 389) made with Rice Krispies and
homemade Marshmallow (page 382). The elegant Chocolate-
Dipped Candied Nuts (page 377) are first candied, dipped in
melted chocolate, and finally covered in cocoa powder. Caramel
Candy Kisses (page 375), wrapped individually in wax paper, are
buttery and delicious.

The most complicated are those few confections that require
the chocolate to be tempered—a process of melting chocolate,
cooling it down, and warming it back up again. Almond Bark

(page 372)—dark, rich, and nutty—is a delicate sheet of tempered bittersweet chocolate broken into jagged irregular-size pieces. Both English Toffee (page 379) and Kim's Honeycomb (page 380) have a perfect coating of shiny chocolate. If you dipped your candy into ordinary melted chocolate, when it cooled the surface would be streaked and blotchy and would easily melt. The key to that hard, shiny, candy-store coating of chocolate is tempering. Without changing the flavor of the chocolate, this process alters its character by melting down the "bad" cocoa crystals that cause the chocolate to look dull and streaked, but leaving intact the "good" cocoa crystals that give the chocolate a shiny, smooth glow. Like anything else, with a little practice, a few deep breaths, and some good instructions, tempering will no longer seem like a mysterious process.

For tempering use a high-quality chocolate known in the candy world as *couverture,* not packaged chocolate chips. Couverture has a higher percentage of cocoa butter, causing it to melt easily and flow smoothly and making the coating and dipping process possible. Couverture chocolates do vary in flavor and sweetness depending upon the types and amount of cocoa beans. Where the beans were grown, how they were fermented and roasted, and the variety of beans will influence the quality and final outcome of the chocolate. My favorite type of chocolate is bittersweet and my favorite manufacturers are Valrhona, Sharffen Berger, and Chocolates El Rey.

To Temper Chocolate: Before you begin to temper, have your candy made, cooled, and ready to dip. Choose a flat, clean, and dry surface. A marble slab, Formica countertop, plastic cutting board, or Plexiglas board will all work fine. Make sure you also have an accurate insta-read thermometer with a range from 70 degrees to 120 degrees.

To start, bring a large pot of water to boil and turn it down to a gentle simmer. Chop ¾ pound of chocolate into 2-inch pieces. Place the chocolate pieces into a clean, dry stainless-steel bowl several inches larger than the pot so the steam doesn't rise and contaminate the chocolate, which will cause it to lump. Cover the bowl tightly with plastic wrap and set over the pot of simmering water. You'll need to melt more chocolate than you actually use. The more chocolate in the bowl, the more slowly it will cool off, and the easier it is to dip into. (Leftover tempered chocolate can be stored at room temperature and retempered or remelted and used for recipes that call for melted chocolate.) Keep the flame very low and be sure the bowl isn't touching the water, or it will burn and ruin the chocolate.

When bittersweet chocolate reaches 118 degrees, it's ready. When milk chocolate reaches 116 degrees, it's ready. Remove the bowl from the pot of water and use a towel to wipe any moisture from the bottom of the bowl. Pour about two-thirds of the melted chocolate onto your flat work surface, leaving the remaining third in the bowl placed nearby. Using a bench scraper, or large offset spatula, work the chocolate back and forth, by scooping underneath and turning it back over onto itself. Keeping it in a contained area, continue to work the chocolate, constantly moving it. Both dark and milk chocolate must cool down to 80 degrees, until it's thickened and begins to stick to the work surface, about 5–8 minutes. Pour or scrape it back into the bowl of remaining chocolate and stir together to combine. Check the temperature; it should be at 91 degrees for dark and 85 to 87 degrees for milk chocolate. If the chocolate is not warm enough, return it briefly to the simmering water, stirring constantly. When it reaches the proper temperature, your chocolate is tempered. To test it, dip the edge of a plate into the chocolate and freeze for half a minute or so, until set. If properly tempered, the chocolate coating should be flawless and have a smooth, glossy sheen.

To Dip the Candy: Working with one piece of candy at a time, drop it into the tempered chocolate, making sure the entire piece is immersed. Using a clean fork, lift the candy out. Knock the bottom of the handle of the fork against the edge of the bowl to remove excess chocolate and place the candy on a parchment-lined surface to set, without disturbance. Stir the chocolate occasionally between dips, to help regulate and maintain the temperature. If the temperature drops and the chocolate begins to thicken, you can rewarm it over the water bath, without retempering, as long as the temperature hasn't dropped significantly. Allow the chocolate to set completely. Store in the refrigerator in an airtight container.

If your first try at tempering isn't successful, don't give up—your mistakes can be camouflaged. There's nothing a little cocoa powder, chopped nuts, or powdered sugar won't hide. The satisfaction of making these confections will certainly sway you away from your expensive candy counter and into your own kitchen.

Almond Bark

Toasted almonds set into a crisp, snappy piece of bittersweet dark chocolate is a marriage made in heaven. And toasted macadamias and bittersweet chocolate make for a very serious relationship. Pour the tempered chocolate onto a cellophane-covered board (cellophane can be found at paper supply stores as well as floral shops), which will help give you a shiny surface and can easily be transferred to the refrigerator so the chocolate can set. Size and shape are up to you; however, the proportion of chocolate and nuts in this recipe is for an 11 × 17 surface, so your board should be no smaller than that.

Special Items: 11 × 17-INCH BAKING SHEETS OR ONE THIN CUTTING BOARD,
OR A THICK PIECE OF CARDBOARD
SHEET OF CELLOPHANE, ENOUGH TO COVER WORK SURFACE
LARGE OFFSET SPATULA OR BENCH SCRAPER

½ cup (2½ ounces) whole unblanched almonds or macadamia nuts
¾ cup melted chocolate, tempered and 82 degrees (see page 369)

Adjust the oven rack to the middle position and preheat the oven to 325 degrees.

Spread the nuts on a baking sheet and toast in the oven until lightly browned, about 15 to 20 minutes. Shake the pan halfway through to ensure that the nuts toast evenly. Cool and coarsely chop into uneven-size pieces.

Meanwhile, wrap the bottom, flat side of another baking sheet or your cutting board tightly in cellophane. Tape it down underneath, making sure there are no wrinkles in it. Set aside.

Pour the chocolate onto the upper portion of the baking sheet or board. Working quickly, using an offset spatula, sweep the chocolate in broad strokes in the same direction, to evenly coat the work surface. It should be no thicker than ¹/₁₆ inch. If it's too thick, move your board to the edge of the counter and spread the chocolate, sweeping the excess into a bowl for another use.

Immediately sprinkle the chopped almonds over the surface of the chocolate. Using a spatula, gently press on the nuts to ensure that they stick.

Place the board in the refrigerator until set and hardened, about half an hour.

If you have leftover chocolate, store in a covered bowl at room temperature for another use.

Break up the bark into large, uneven shards. Store in an airtight container, refrigerated, 3 to 5 days, or until the nuts lose their crispness.

Yield: About twenty irregularly sized shards

ALMOND BARK: "TOASTED ALMONDS AND BITTERSWEET
DARK CHOCOLATE: A MARRIAGE MADE IN HEAVEN."

Candied Lemon Zest

3 lemons
1¼ cups granulated sugar
1½ cups water
¼ cup light corn syrup

Using a zester, zest the peel of the lemons into 2-inch-long strips. In a small stainless-steel saucepan, bring the lemon zest to a boil in just enough water to cover. Boil for 1 minute and drain.

In the same saucepan, bring the sugar, water, corn syrup, and zest to a boil. Using a pastry brush dipped in water, wash down the sides of the pan to dissolve the sugar. Continue to simmer, without stirring, over low heat for about 20 to 30 minutes, until the zest is translucent, shiny and tender. Transfer to a container and store in the syrup at room temperature for up to several weeks.

Caramel Candy Kisses

When Teri Gelber worked at Campanile, occasionally she'd sneak a See's Scotch Kiss into my mailbox, knowing I had a weakness for those caramel-wrapped marshmallows. She tried to convince me to make up a recipe for them to put in this book, but for some reason I was resistant. Many unsubtle hints, constant reminders, and threats that she would make them herself still couldn't motivate me. The weekend her laptop computer was stolen, I finally got motivated. To cheer her up, I surprised her with a big basket of wax-paper-wrapped Caramel Candy Kisses.

To retain the melted caramel while you sandwich it with the marshmallow, you'll need thin steel bars or a cake pan. Have your hardware store cut the bars into two 7-inch pieces and two 9-inch pieces so when placed together they form a rectangular border. Set the bars up on a flat work surface or directly on a baking sheet so that when you remove the bars, the kisses readily lift off the surface.

Note: Though you don't need the entire recipe of marshmallows, make them all anyhow. You can wrap the marshmallows and refrigerate to use for Salted Peanut Treats and hot chocolate.

Special Items: CANDY THERMOMETER (CHECK YOUR THERMOMETER'S ACCURACY
IN BOILING WATER; IT SHOULD READ 212 DEGREES)
BOWL OF ICE SET OVER A CONTAINER OR SINK OF ICE
METAL BARS LIGHTLY COATED WITH MELTED BUTTER OR ONE
9-INCH SQUARE PAN, LINED WITH WAX PAPER
SEVERAL PIECES OF WAX PAPER, CUT INTO RECTANGLES LARGE
ENOUGH TO WRAP THE CANDIES IN

1 cup heavy cream
1 stick (4 ounces) unsalted butter
1 vanilla bean
1/4 cup light corn syrup
1 1/2 cups granulated sugar
1 recipe Marshmallow (see page 382), 1/4 of the recipe spread to approximately
 1/4 inch thick, cut to fit the size of the mold or pan you are using

In a small saucepan over medium heat, warm the cream and butter. Using a small paring knife, split the vanilla bean lengthwise. Using the back of the knife, scrape out the pulp and the seeds and add the scrapings and the pod to the butter. Cook until the butter is melted and the mixture is hot. Remove from the heat and set aside. Remove the vanilla bean.

In a heavy-duty, medium-size saucepan, over medium heat, cook the corn syrup until bubbly. Add a few tablespoons of sugar, stirring constantly, without allowing the mixture to color. When the sugar has melted and the mixture is bubbling around the edges, add a few more tablespoons of sugar. Continue in this manner until all of the sugar has been added. The mixture will become opaque, grainy, and slightly thickened. Cook 3 to 4 more minutes, stirring and swirling the pan until the caramel is thin, runny, and has turned a pale straw color—310 degrees on a candy thermometer.

Remove from the heat and add the warm cream mixture in 3 batches. The mixture will spatter, so be careful as you pour. Return the saucepan to medium heat and cook for about 2 to 3 minutes, stirring until any undissolved sugar remelts and the mixture turns the color of light commercial caramels—330 degrees on a candy thermometer. Remove from the heat and pour the caramel into the bowl set over ice to stop the caramel from coloring further and to cool a bit. Do not allow it to solidify.

Pour half of the warm caramel into the pan or mold. Using an offset spatula or the back of a spoon, smooth over the surface of the caramel. It should be between ⅛ and ¼ inch thick. Allow it to cool completely.

Place the marshmallow over the caramel layer. As soon as the remaining caramel is cool enough not to melt the marshmallow, pour it over. (If it's too thick at this point, return it to the heat to thin out and recool again.) Use your fingers to smooth and even. Allow to set.

Remove the bars or turn the caramel out of the pan and, using a buttered knife, cut the candy into 1 × 1½-inch pieces. Wrap individually in wax paper, twisting the ends to seal. Store at room temperature for up to 1 week, or in the refrigerator for several weeks.

Yield: 36 pieces

Chocolate-Dipped Candied Nuts

You may think nuts dipped in chocolate are a treat, but if you haven't had them candied then you're in for a real surprise. Taking the extra step of dunking the nuts in hot caramel before coating them in chocolate is worth every bit of time and effort.

Special Item: SILPAT MAT (SEE "SOURCES," PAGE 393), OPTIONAL

35 nuts: whole raw unsalted macadamia, whole unblanched almonds,
*   raw hazelnuts, or a combination of all three*
½ cup water
2 cups granulated sugar
2 cups unsweetened imported cocoa powder
1 pound dark, bittersweet chocolate, melted according to directions on page 369
*   and kept warm, about 88 degrees*

Adjust the oven rack to the middle position and preheat the oven to 325 degrees.

Spread the nuts on a baking sheet and toast in the oven until lightly browned, about 10 to 15 minutes. Shake the pan halfway through to ensure that the nuts toast evenly. For hazelnuts, allow to cool and gather them into a kitchen towel and rub together to remove the skins. Set aside to cool.

In a heavy-duty, deep saucepan, stir together the water and sugar. Over medium-high heat, bring the mixture to a boil without stirring. Using a pastry brush dipped in water, brush down the sides of the pan to remove any undissolved sugar granules. When the sugar begins to color, after about 3 to 4 minutes, tilt and swirl the pan to cook evenly. When the mixture reaches a deep amber color, immediately remove from the heat and set the pan in a bowl of ice water for about 20 seconds to keep it from coloring any further. Remove from the ice water and prop the pan on top of a folded towel, allowing the liquid to accumulate on one side of the pan.

Drop 1 nut at a time into the deeper part of the caramel. Using a fork, lift it out and tap the handle of the fork against the edge of the pan, shaking off any excess caramel. Drop the nut onto a Silpat or a parchment-lined baking sheet. Continue with the remaining nuts, not allowing them to touch as they cool. If the caramel begins to cool and thicken, return it to the stove to remelt. As you remelt, watch to make sure it doesn't get too dark or begin to smoke. If it does, you should make another batch.

Sift a 1-inch-deep layer of cocoa powder into a wide, shallow container.

Prop the bowl of melted chocolate on top of a folded towel, allowing the chocolate to run to one side of the bowl. Working one at a time, drop a nut into the chocolate to coat completely. Remove the nut from the chocolate with a fork, knocking the handle against the edge of the bowl to remove any excess chocolate.

Immediately drop the nut into the cocoa powder, not allowing it to touch other nuts, and not shaking the container. When you have one layer of nuts in the cocoa powder, place the container in the freezer for about 15 minutes, allowing the melted chocolate to set.

Cover the tops of the nuts with the surrounding cocoa powder.

Remove the nuts with a fork and shake off the excess cocoa powder. Transfer the nuts to another container and continue the dipping process with the remaining nuts. If your melted chocolate cools and thickens, return it to the heat for a few minutes to bring the temperature back up.

Store in an airtight container in the freezer indefinitely.

Use the remaining cocoa powder for more nuts, or reserve for another use.

Yield: 35 dipped nuts

English Toffee

I'M SURE YOU'VE HAD ENGLISH TOFFEE—THE CLASSIC BUTTER-AND-CREAM-based candy. We dip ours in milk chocolate and sprinkle it with chopped nuts for a confection that's rich, luxurious, and surprisingly easy to make.

Special Item: ONE SILPAT (SEE "SOURCES," PAGE 393) OR AN II × 17-INCH BAKING SHEET, LIGHTLY COATED WITH VEGETABLE OIL

1 cup granulated sugar
½ cup heavy cream
½ cup light corn syrup
2 sticks (8 ounces) unsalted butter, cut into 1-inch cubes
1 recipe tempered milk chocolate (see page 369)
1 cup (4 ounces) walnuts, finely chopped

In a medium, heavy-duty saucepan, stir together the sugar, cream, and corn syrup. Over medium heat, bring the mixture to a boil without stirring. Using a pastry brush dipped in water, brush down the sides of the pan to remove any undissolved sugar granules. Add the butter and, without stirring, cook for about 12 minutes, occasionally tilting and swirling the pan to encourage even coloring. When the mixture reaches a light caramel color, begin to stir with a wooden spoon, cooking until the caramel turns the color of peanut butter.

Pour immediately onto the prepared mat or baking sheet. Using an oiled offset spatula, spread the toffee to about ¼ inch thick. The surface will be glassy and smooth, and will begin to sweat as it cools. Allow to harden.

Using a knife, tap the surface of the toffee to break it into irregular chunks, about 2 inches long.

Store in an airtight container at room temperature until ready to dip.

For chocolate dipping instructions, see page 371.

Place the dipped toffee on the Silpat or parchment-lined sheet and sprinkle with the chopped walnuts before the chocolate hardens. Allow to set completely.

Store in an airtight container in the refrigerator; the toffee will keep for several weeks.

Yield: Approximately twenty-five 2-inch pieces

Kim's Honeycomb

HONEYCOMB IS A SWEET, HONEY-COLORED CANDY RESEMBLING THE PER-forated texture of a bee's honeycomb. It's a favorite of my pastry chef, Kim, who was driven to discover its secret. A little research and lots of experimenting finally led her to this perfect honeycomb. To achieve the porous interior, baking soda is added to lightly caramelized sugar, causing it to bubble and fill with air pockets, and finally to harden into a golden, crunchy candy. When dipped in dark chocolate, the caramel flavors are further intensified by the bitterness of the chocolate.

There are a few important things to remember. Sugar and water are cheap, but chocolate isn't. When you pour out the caramel mixture, allow it to spread and harden without touching it. It will puff up slightly, and solidify into a smooth and glossy mass. If it deflates too much, the texture will be dense, and too hard. Before you dip the honeycomb in chocolate, taste it to ensure that it's not too dark and bitter and the texture is light and airy. If not, you're better off making a new batch of honeycomb, rather than wasting your good chocolate.

Special Items: SILPAT (SEE "SOURCES," PAGE 393) OR BAKING SHEET LIGHTLY
COATED WITH VEGETABLE OIL
CANDY THERMOMETER (CHECK YOUR THERMOMETER'S ACCURACY IN
BOILING WATER; IT SHOULD READ 212 DEGREES)

¼ cup water
1½ cup granulated sugar
¼ cup light corn syrup
1 tablespoon baking soda, sifted
1 recipe tempered dark chocolate (see page 369)

In a deep, heavy-duty, medium saucepan, stir together the water, sugar, and corn syrup. Clip the thermometer onto the side of the pan. Over medium-high heat, bring the mixture to a boil without stirring. Using a pastry brush dipped in water, brush down the sides of the pan to remove any undissolved sugar granules. Continue cooking until the sugar reaches 300 degrees on a candy thermometer (hard crack stage) and immediately remove from the heat. The mixture should be a very pale straw color.

Working quickly, add the baking soda to the mixture and whisk for a few seconds, until the baking soda is incorporated. The liquid will bubble up and become foamy. In one even movement, pour it onto the Silpat or baking sheet. It will spread out, puff up slightly and have a slightly porous, shiny surface.

Allow to harden and cool completely for about 20 minutes, without touching. If you're not dipping immediately after it hardens, cover the surface with plastic wrap.

Using the point of a knife, break the honeycomb into uneven chunks, about 1½ inches long.

Store in an airtight container at room temperature until ready to dip. The refrigerator will cause the undipped candy to soften. Dip in chocolate according to instructions on page 371. Once dipped, store in an airtight container in the refrigerator for up to several weeks.

Yield: Approximately 20 unevenly sized pieces

Marshmallow with the World's Best Hot Chocolate

Wᴴɪʟᴇ ʏᴏᴜ ᴍᴀʏ ɴᴏᴛ ᴛʜɪɴᴋ ɪᴛ'ꜱ ʀɪᴅɪᴄᴜʟᴏᴜꜱ ᴛᴏ ᴍᴀᴋᴇ ʏᴏᴜʀ ᴏᴡɴ ʜᴏᴛ ᴄʜᴏᴄ-olate, you may think it's ridiculous to make your own marshmallow. Haven't you ever wondered what's wrong with those perfectly packaged fluffy ones we all grew up eating? Once you try this homemade version, you'll understand. The flavor is far better, there are no preservatives or stabilizers, and the size and shape is up to you, depending on what you plan to do with them.

I've included a few recipes to use your homemade marshmallows in. For floating on top of your hot chocolate, you'll want to cut the marshmallow out with a round cutter slightly smaller than the size of your cup. Sweet and sticky Salted Peanut Treats (page 389) need marshmallow to help everything bind together and balance the salt. Caramel Candy Kisses (page 375) sandwich the soft marshmallow with a satiny and super buttery vanilla caramel. And of course you all know the recipe to that Girl Scout favorite: Sandwich together some marshmallows between homemade Graham Crackers (page 124) and a slab of good chocolate, and your S'mores will be the envy of every campsite in the vicinity.

Special Items: ᴄᴀɴᴅʏ ᴛʜᴇʀᴍᴏᴍᴇᴛᴇʀ (ᴄʜᴇᴄᴋ ʏᴏᴜʀ ᴛʜᴇʀᴍᴏᴍᴇᴛᴇʀ'ꜱ ᴀᴄᴄᴜʀᴀᴄʏ
ɪɴ ʙᴏɪʟɪɴɢ ᴡᴀᴛᴇʀ; ɪᴛ ꜱʜᴏᴜʟᴅ ʀᴇᴀᴅ 212 ᴅᴇɢʀᴇᴇꜱ)
ʀᴏᴜɴᴅ ᴄᴜᴛᴛᴇʀ

½ cup powdered sugar
1 heaping tablespoon gelatin
¼ cup plus 2 tablespoons water
1 cup plus 1 tablespoon granulated sugar
1 cup light corn syrup
2 extra-large egg whites
1 tablespoon pure vanilla extract

ꜰᴏʀ ᴛʜᴇ ʜᴏᴛ ᴄʜᴏᴄᴏʟᴀᴛᴇ:
6 cups whole milk
2 cups heavy cream

¹⁄₂ cup granulated sugar
¹⁄₂ cup unsweetened cocoa powder
1¹⁄₂ teaspoons cardamom
2 cinnamon sticks
1 vanilla bean
5 ounces bittersweet chocolate, coarsely chopped

Sift half the powdered sugar in a heavy layer onto a parchment-lined baking sheet and set the rest aside.

Place the gelatin in a small bowl and pour 2 tablespoons of the water over to cover, making sure the gelatin is completely saturated. You may need to add a few more drops of water. Set aside.

In a small saucepan, stir together the remaining water, 1 cup of the granulated sugar, and the corn syrup. Over medium heat, bring the mixture to a boil, without stirring. Using a pastry brush dipped in water, brush down the sides of the pan to remove any undissolved sugar granules. As soon as the surface of the syrup is covered with bursting bubbles, begin to beat the egg whites.

In an electric mixer fitted with the whisk attachment, beat the egg whites on low until frothy, about 2 to 3 minutes. Turn the mixer up to medium-high, sprinkle in the remaining tablespoon of the granulated sugar and beat the egg whites until stiff, glossy peaks form.

Continue cooking the sugar mixture without stirring for about 4 to 5 minutes, until it reaches the soft ball stage—234 to 240 degrees on a candy thermometer. Remove the sugar and pinch it together with your fingers; it should form a soft ball. Remove from the heat and stir in the gelatin mixture and vanilla extract.

Mixing on high, very gradually add the syrup to the egg whites, pouring in a thin, steady stream. You may have to stop pouring to allow the whites to firm up again. If some of the mixture sticks to the sides of the bowl, leave it. Keep beating, for another 3 to 4 minutes, until shiny and glossy, but still warm.

Pour the marshmallow onto the powdered parchment paper and sift a generous layer of the remaining powdered sugar and cornstarch over the surface. Using your hands, press the marshmallow into a ¹⁄₂-inch-thick rectangle or circle (if you're making Caramel Candy Kisses, it should be about ¹⁄₄ inch thick). Allow to set at room temperature for about 1 hour.

To serve with hot chocolate: Cutting closely together, cut out as many circles as possible, slightly smaller than the diameter of your serving cup. If you're not using for hot chocolate, cut into other desired shapes.

Store in an airtight container at room temperature.

To prepare the hot chocolate: In a large, heavy-duty saucepan, combine the milk, cream, sugar, cocoa powder, cardamom, and cinnamon sticks. Using a small paring knife, split the vanilla bean lengthwise. Using the back of the knife, scrape out the pulp and the seeds and add the scrapings and the pod to the cream mixture. Over medium-high heat, bring to a boil. Reduce the heat to low and simmer for about 30 minutes, until slightly thickened.

Stir in the chocolate, and cook a few more minutes until melted and incorporated. Remove the vanilla bean.

Serve hot or refrigerate and reheat when ready to use. If too thick, or too chocolatey, thin down with milk.

Yield: 16 ounces marshmallow; ten $^3/_4$-cup servings hot chocolate

Lollipops

WHEN THE PEOPLE AT *MARTHA STEWART LIVING* MAGAZINE FIRST SAW MY LOL-lipops, not only did they ask for the recipe, they made an entire kit for their mail-order catalog (see "Sources," page 393).

There are two types of lollipop molds out there. One is a plastic tray mold with multiple sections that comes in a variety of shapes (see "Sources," page 393). It's easy to use: Simply lay the stick in the mold and pour in the warm syrup. Unfortunately, in order for the stick to be enclosed, you have to fill the mold completely, resulting in a thicker, chunkier-style lollipop. I prefer what I call the metal strip and clip ver-sion, which allows you to pour a thinner layer of syrup for a more delicate lollipop. This version is included in the Martha by Mail lollipop kit or is just as easily con-structed at home from flexible ½-inch nonperforated metal strapping and metal clips available at hardware stores or air-conditioning supplies stores.

Color or flavor your Lollipops with vibrant-colored powders (see "Sources") and concentrated natural flavorings such as fruit-flavored oils, extracts, or coffee. (When flavoring, use only a few drops per batch of syrup so it doesn't interfere with the hardening process of the candy.) Accent the Lollipops with decorations that are compatible with your flavorings. If you like, add Candied Lemon Zest (see page 374) to a lemon Lollipop or coffee beans to a coffee-flavored sucker or embellish a plain Lollipop with a simple lavender flower. For that really special occasion, make them into party favors—wrap the Lollipops in cellophane and tie them with a fancy French ribbon.

Special Items: LOLLIPOP MOLDS (SEE "SOURCES," PAGE 393)
LOLLIPOP STICKS (SEE "SOURCES," PAGE 393)
SILPAT MAT SET ON A FLAT SURFACE OR A LIGHTLY OILED FLAT
   COUNTER (SEE "SOURCES," PAGE 393)
CANDY THERMOMETER (CHECK YOUR THERMOMETER'S ACCURACY IN
   BOILING WATER; IT SHOULD READ 212 DEGREES)

FOR THE SYRUP:
¾ cup water
2 cups granulated sugar
1 cup mild-flavored honey, such as clover
A few drops of flavoring or coloring or both, optional

Lavender flowers, Candied Lemon Zest (see page 374), or coffee beans, optional

For the plastic tray molds: Place the sticks in the slot, making sure they reach about ½ inch into the mold, and sprinkle in the decorative accents if you're using them. Set aside.

For the strip-and-clip version: Cut the metal strip to size and bend into the desired shape. Place the stick halfway into the "shape," close to the counter but not touching, to allow the syrup to flow underneath the stick. Fasten the two ends of the strip with the metal clip to hold the stick in place, making sure your form is flush against the flat oiled surface. Sprinkle in the decorative accents if you're using them, and set aside. Make sure the stick is not resting directly on the mat or counter, or it will not get covered by the syrup.

In a heavy-duty, small saucepan, stir together the water, sugar, and honey. Over medium-high heat, cook the mixture until it comes to a boil. Using a pastry brush dipped in water, brush down the sides of the pan to remove any undissolved sugar granules. It may be necessary to tilt and swirl the pan to ensure that the mixture cooks evenly. Continue to cook without stirring, until it reaches 300 degrees (hard crack stage) on a candy thermometer. Remove from the heat and allow to sit for I minute, until the bubbles subside. If you're using flavoring or coloring, add it and swirl or stir to combine.

Pour just enough sugar syrup into the mold to cover the stick. Allow to cool for about 15 to 20 minutes, until hardened.

Yield: About 2 dozen 1½-inch round lollipops

Pan Forte

At our farmers' market, there's a stand that's about 15 feet long selling more dried fruits than I ever thought existed. Every time I walk by, I get the urge to make my pan forte. I was happy with the recipe from my other cookbook until I went to Siena, where the pan forte is more peppery and spicy, apropos of the translation: "strong bread." More candylike than breadlike, this chewy, intense confection makes the perfect gift for holidays. Follow the Italian tradition by making the pan forte in small 4-inch discs. Wrap it in wax paper and then a sheet of brown butcher paper, tied with string and sealed with embossed sealing wax.

My favorite combination has a balance of pale, orange, and dark-fleshed fruits. White figs and raisins make a good contrast to the darker fruits such as prunes, raisins, and apricots. Always use soft and supple fruit. Hard fruit will give you a beautiful pan forte that's too hard to chew.

Special Items: CANDY THERMOMETER (CHECK YOUR THERMOMETER'S ACCURACY
        IN BOILING WATER; IT SHOULD READ 212 DEGREES) OR SMALL
        BOWL OF ICE WATER
    9-INCH CAKE RING OR FLAN RING OR SEVERAL 4-INCH FLAN RINGS
        PLACED ON A PARCHMENT-LINED BAKING SHEET, GENEROUSLY
        COATED WITH MELTED BUTTER AND DUSTED WITH UNSWEETENED
        COCOA POWDER
    SHEET OF RICE PAPER (SEE "SOURCES," PAGE 393)

1¼ cups (6 ounces) whole unblanched almonds
1½ cups (6 ounces) whole unblanched hazelnuts
1 teaspoon ground cinnamon
¾ teaspoon ground ginger
¼ teaspoon ground cloves
¼ teaspoon freshly grated nutmeg
1 teaspoon freshly ground black pepper
1 cup plus 2 tablespoons unbleached all-purpose flour
1 tablespoon unsweetened cocoa powder, plus extra for dusting

1¼ pounds dried fruits, preferably organic—any combination of black currants,
  white or black raisins, black mission figs, white figs, sour cherries, plums, prunes,
  pears, peaches, nectarines, or cranberries and apricots and candied ginger
⅔ cup mild-flavored honey, such as clover
1 cup granulated sugar

Place the ring or mold over the sheet of rice paper on a parchment-lined baking sheet. Adjust the oven rack to the middle position and preheat the oven to 325 degrees.

Spread the nuts on a baking sheet in two separate piles, and toast in the oven until lightly browned, about 10 to 15 minutes. Shake the pans halfway through to ensure that the nuts toast evenly. Allow to cool a few minutes. Gather the hazelnuts into a kitchen towel and rub them together to remove the skins.

Turn the oven down to 300 degrees.

In a large bowl combine the nuts with the cinnamon, ginger, cloves, nutmeg, pepper, flour, and cocoa powder.

Cut the fruit into ½-inch pieces and toss with the nut mixture.

In a small saucepan, stir together the honey and sugar. Over high heat, bring to a boil without stirring. Using a pastry brush dipped in water, brush the sides of the pan to remove any undissolved sugar granules. Cook until the sugar reaches 224 to 240 degrees (soft ball stage) on a candy thermometer. Remove from the heat and pour into the fruit mixture. Stir to combine as well as possible. The mixture will be very thick and sticky.

Dip your hands in water and press the fruit mixture evenly into the pan. Bake for 1 hour, until the top is slightly puffed and the surface is matte. Remove from the oven and cool completely in the pan. Trim the rice paper around the edge of the mold.

Store at room temperature, wrapped tightly in plastic wrap, for several weeks.

Yield: 12 to 20 slices

Salted Peanut Treats

I NEVER REALLY UNDERSTOOD THE FASCINATION WITH RICE KRISPIES TREATS. My mother never made them, and even when I did have them, I never liked them. If something has only three ingredients, they'd better all be perfect. Commercial marshmallows, margarine, and boxed cereal are not my idea of perfection. But just mention Rice Krispies Treats and people start to swoon—so much so that I felt the pressure to come up with a better version.

Every once in the while, by tweaking a standard recipe—adding some real butter, some homemade marshmallows, and salted peanuts—you can actually turn it into something better. Now, even I can appreciate this 1950s childhood classic.

Since you won't need the entire batch of Marshmallow for Salted Peanut Treats, save the leftovers for that late-night cup of Hot Chocolate (see page 382).

Special Item: CANDY THERMOMETER (CHECK YOUR THERMOMETER'S ACCURACY IN BOILING WATER; IT SHOULD READ 212 DEGREES)

1 cup (4 ounces) raw unsalted peanuts
1 teaspoon peanut or vegetable oil
1½ teaspoons kosher salt
½ stick (2 ounces) unsalted butter, plus a little extra for coating your hands
¾ cup plus 2 tablespoons heavy cream
1 vanilla bean
1½ teaspoons gelatin
1 tablespoon cold water
5 ½ cups crisped rice cereal
¼ cup light corn syrup
¾ cup granulated sugar
¼ recipe Marshmallow (see page 382), powered sugar dusted off, and cut into 1–inch pieces

Adjust the oven rack to the middle position and preheat the oven to 325 degrees.

In a medium bowl, toss together the peanuts, oil, and salt. Spread the peanuts on a baking sheet and toast in the oven until lightly browned, about 8 to 10 minutes. Shake the pan halfway through to ensure that the nuts toast evenly.

In a small saucepan over medium heat, begin to melt the butter with the cream. Using a small paring knife, split the vanilla bean lengthwise. With the back of the knife, scrape out the pulp and the seeds and add the scrapings and the pod to the butter mixture. Cook until the butter is melted and the mixture begins to bubble. Remove from the heat and set aside. Remove the vanilla bean.

Place the gelatin in a small bowl and pour the cold water over to cover, making sure the gelatin is completely saturated. You may need to add a few more drops of water.

In a large bowl, combine the crisped rice cereal with the peanuts.

In a heavy-duty, medium-size saucepan, over medium heat, cook the corn syrup until bubbly. Add a few tablespoons of sugar, stirring constantly, without allowing the mixture to color. When the sugar has melted, and the mixture is bubbling around the edges, add a few more tablespoons of sugar. Continue in this manner until all of the sugar has been added. The mixture will become opaque and grainy and slightly thickened. Cook 3 to 4 more minutes, stirring and swirling the pan until the caramel is thin, runny, and has turned a pale straw color—310 degrees on a candy thermometer.

Remove from the heat and add the warm cream mixture in 3 batches. The mixture may spatter, and seize and harden. Return the saucepan to medium heat, and cook for about 2 to 3 minutes, stirring until any undissolved sugar remelts and the mixture turns the color of light commercial caramels—330 degrees on a candy thermometer.

Remove from the heat and stir in the Marshmallow and the gelatin mixture. Return to low heat and cook another 4 to 5 minutes, stirring until the Marshmallow melts and the mixture returns to a commercial caramel color.

Add the caramel to the cereal mixture, mixing thoroughly. Transfer to a flat work surface or parchment-lined baking sheet.

Generously coat your hands with butter. As soon as the mixture is cool enough to handle, pat, mold, and shape it, pushing the sides in to compress it into a dense rectangle, approximately 1 inch thick and about 12 inches long.

Allow to set and cut into bars. Store at room temperature.

Yield: Approximately 12 pieces, 1 inch wide

Sesame—Pumpkin Seed Brittle

Found in the open markets of Mexico City, this lovely translucent brittle is packed with toasted seeds for a nutty, crunchy candy. This candy is so good, you'll probably want to make more. My suggestion is to make it in 2 batches, because the candy hardens very quickly, making it too difficult to cut out.

Special Items: SILPAT (SEE "SOURCES," PAGE 393) OR BAKING SHEET
LIGHTLY COATED WITH VEGETABLE OIL
1- OR 2-INCH ROUND CUTTERS OR OTHER SHAPES SUCH
AS STARS OR MOONS

¼ cup water
1 cup granulated sugar
½ cup (2 ounces) hulled pumpkin seeds
⅓ cup white sesame seeds

In a heavy-duty, small saucepan, stir together the water and sugar. Over medium-high heat, bring the mixture to a boil without stirring. Using a pastry brush dipped in water, brush down the sides of the pan to remove any undissolved sugar granules. When the sugar begins to color, after about 3 to 4 minutes, tilt and swirl the pan to cook evenly. When the caramel reaches a light amber color, stir in the pumpkin and sesame seeds. Continue to cook, stirring constantly, about 1 to 2 more minutes, until the sesame seeds begin to color, the pumpkin seeds begin to pop, and the caramel turns a mahogany color.

Immediately pour the mixture onto the Silpat or oiled baking sheet, scraping the pan with a wooden spoon lightly coated with vegetable oil. Using a lightly oiled offset spatula or the back of a spoon, spread the caramel in a thin even layer, about ⅛ inch thick. Allow to set for about 1 minute.

Working quickly, cut out the circles or shapes, cutting as close together as possible and pressing down hard to cut through the caramel and seeds.

Break up the leftover scraps into small odd shapes.

Store in an airtight container, separated by wax paper or foil, for up to 1 week.

Yield: 15 to 20 pieces, depending on size of cutter

SOURCES

ALL SPICE
507 N. Fairfax
Los Angeles, California 90036
323-782-1893
As the name implies, they stock all types of fresh spices.

AMORETTI
818-718-1239
A good source for fresh almond paste and extracts.

BRIDGE KITCHENWARE
214 East 52nd Street
New York, New York 10022
212-688-4220
www.bridgekitchenware.com
They have both a store and a mail-order catalog with everything for the kitchen: knives,
tartlet or decorative molds, Canellé molds, Venison molds, tart rings, Teflon tart molds,
all types of cutters, whisks, strainers, pastry bags, and other specialty baking needs.

CHOCOLATES EL REY
P.O. Box 853
Fredericksburg, Texas 78624
800-ELREY-99
High-quality couverture chocolate needed for baking. They don't mail direct, but will tell
you where their chocolate is available in your area.

A COOK'S WARES
800-915-9788
www.cookswares.com
A mail-order catalog for gourmet cooking equipment. They also carry the chocolate batons for Chocolate Croissants. They don't ship chocolate in the summer (June 1–September 15), so plan accordingly.

DEAN & DELUCA
800-221-7714
www.deandeluca.com
Retail stores and mail-order catalogs. Natural food colorings and flavorings for lollipops as well as a huge supply of baking and cooking ingredients, plus a good selection of tools and utensils, including Silpats.

THE-HOUSE-ON-THE-HILL
P.O. Box 7003
Villa Park, Illinois 60181
www.houseonthehill.net
For a catalog, send two dollars to the above address or visit their website. Best known for their Swedish-style rolling pins and cookie molds, they are a good source for baker's ammonia, Linzer punch cutters, pastry tools, natural flavorings for lollipops, pure extracts, and orange flower water.

JB PRINCE
36 East 31st Street, 11th Floor
New York, New York 10016
212-683-3553
A mail-order catalog and retail outlet that sells kitchen equipment, decorative molds, cutters, tart rings, utensils, and specialty bakeware and cookware.

KING ARTHUR FLOUR
P.O. Box 876
Norwich, Vermont 05055-0876
800-827-6836
www.kingarthurflour.com
A mail-order source that sells several types of flours, including unbleached pastry and unbleached all-purpose flour. Other hard-to-find ingredients, such as baker's ammonia, *pain au chocolat* sticks for Chocolate Croissants, maple sugar, and nonmelting icing sugar, also called glazing sugar, are available.

MARTHA BY MAIL
800-950-7130
They carry several specialty items for baking and candy making, such as cookie cutters, decorative molds, lollipop molds, natural colorings, and crystallized sugars.

MADE IN FRANCE
800-266-9611
A specialty food distributor that carries a wide variety of high-quality ingredients, including frozen fruit purees.

MATFER
800-766-0333
A mail-order catalog that offers virtually every baking utensil available, including my favorite utensil for stirring—the flat wooden spoon called a boxwood spatula. They also carry bottomless meat-pie molds used for Cheese Bars and Nut Slices.

NEW YORK CAKE AND BAKING
56 West 22nd Street
New York, New York 10010
800-942-2539
A shop in New York as well as a mail-order catalog, they offer specialized bakeware and utensils. They also have a wide range of decorating necessities, such as crystallized sugars and natural colorings. You can also order rice paper from them.

PENZEYS, LTD.
P.O. Box 933
Muskego, Wisconsin 53150
414-679-7207
A spice catalog that carries hundreds of spices, all very fresh and high quality. A good source for Tahitian and Madagascar vanilla beans as well as extracts and natural flavorings.

PREVIN CATALOGUE
215-985-1996
They sell mostly commercial kitchenware and lots of imported French baking utensils, such as copper Canellé molds and other decorative molds.

Sur La Table
800-243-0852
There are retail stores now located in the western United States, as well as an excellent mail-order catalog. A huge and excellent assortment of cookware, bakeware, and utensils plus a vast selection of baking molds and tins, both imported and domestic.

Sweet Celebrations
800-328-6722
www.sweetc.com
A mail-order catalog for both baking and candy making. They carry the edible rice paper for Pan Forte as well as a variety of lollipop molds.

White Lily Foods
Knoxville, Tennessee
800-264-5459
www.whitelily.com
Popular in the southeastern United States, White Lily baking flour is made from 100 percent soft winter wheat. I use it to make biscuits and the tender crust of the White Lily Savory Tart.

Williams Sonoma
800-541-2233
Stores located all over the United States, and a mail-order catalog. They also sell some finer ingredients, such as White Lily flour, salts, chocolate, and so on. A big selection of baking and cookware.

INDEX

NANCY SILVERTON owns and operates, with her husband,
Mark Peel, Campanile restaurant and the La Brea Bakery in
Los Angeles. She is the author of *Desserts* and *Nancy Silverton's
Breads from the La Brea Bakery* and the coauthor, with Mark Peel,
of *Mark Peel and Nancy Silverton at Home: Two Chefs Cook for Family
and Friends* and *The Food of Campanile*. She lives in Los Angeles
with her husband and their three children.

TERI GELBER is a food writer and public radio
producer living and eating well in Los Angeles.

STEVEN ROTHFELD created the images for *Nancy Silverton's
Breads from the La Brea Bakery* and *The Food of Campanile* and has
contributed to many other books, including *French Dreams,
Italian Dreams, Irish Dreams, Patricia Wells's Trattoria,* and *The New Italy
the Beautiful Cookbook*. His photographs have appeared in
*European Travel & Life, Departures, Travel & Leisure, Bon Appetit,
Gourmet,* and *Food & Wine*. He travels throughout the world
but loves to return to his home in the Napa Valley.